Brenda Chapman

LINCOLNSHIRE
MOODS

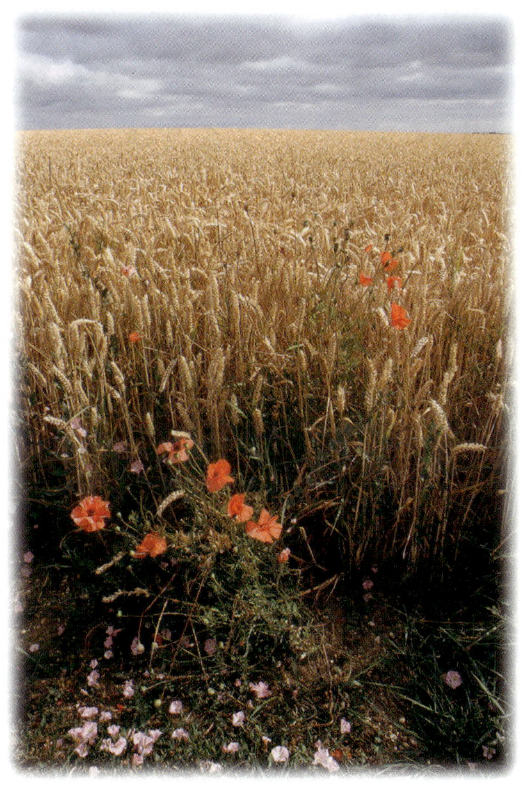

JANET AND PETER ROWORTH

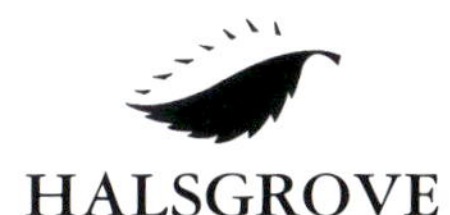

HALSGROVE

First published in Great Britain in 2006

Title page photograph: Field bindweed and poppy.

British Library Cataloguing-in-Publication Data
A CIP record for this title is available from the British Library

ISBN 1 84114 471 1
ISBN 978 1 84114 471 9

HALSGROVE
Halsgrove House
Lower Moor Way
Tiverton, Devon EX16 6SS
Tel: 01884 243242
Fax: 01884 243325
email: sales@halsgrove.com
website: www.halsgrove.com

Printed and bound by D'Auria Industrie Grafiche Spa, Italy

INTRODUCTION

Lincolnshire used to be the second largest in the country. Although the northern boundaries have changed as a result of local government reorganisation, we have chosen to regard the county in its original, historic form.

Lincolnshire is a county of endlessly varied landscapes. In the far north-west is the Isle of Axholme, so named because the higher ground with its associated settlements rises above the level of the surrounding, frequently-flooded marsh and peat bog of the Humberhead Levels. The county's western boundary with Nottinghamshire runs through the broad expanse of the Trent Valley. This is edged by the steep scarp slope of the limestone cliff and heath, a line of high ground which stretches from north to south, cut in two by the River Witham flowing through the Lincoln Gap.

In the northern half of the county, the limestone dips gently to the east and it gives way to the clays and sands of the central vale. A second line of hills, this time capped by chalk, forms the rolling Lincolnshire Wolds, until they also dip to the east under the coastal marshes. In the southern half of the county, the limestone heath gives way to the Fens, fertile flatlands of peat and silt encircling the Wash.

We hope our view of Lincolnshire, dismissed by many as being flat and therefore uninteresting, will show you that this is untrue on both counts. You only have to drive along Caistor High Street, the ancient road which runs the length of the western edge of the Wolds, or walk from Lincoln city centre up to the cathedral, to know that the county has some amazing hills.

And where it is flat across the Fens and marshes, the scenery is still stunning, with a patchwork of fields and dykes beneath wide-open skies. The combined effects of drainage and land reclamation mean that the county now has some of the finest agricultural land in the country.

We have travelled the length and breadth of the county, capturing the landscape in all its moods. Our seasonal journey begins in the clear cold light of January, taking you into spring as flowers begin to appear, trees and hedges come into leaf, and the countryside turns every shade of green.

Through May and June the scenery changes rapidly as farm crops grow, and soon we reach the golden days of summer. Harvest merges into autumn, and as the leaves fall and temperatures drop, we endure days of fog and frost which finally give way to the snows of winter.

Our portrait of a year in the life of Lincolnshire has come full circle.

Janet and Peter Roworth

DEDICATION

To George and Henry

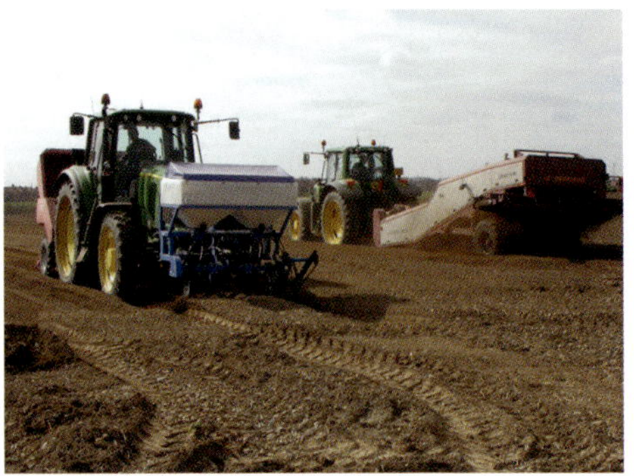

ACKNOWLEDGEMENTS

We would like to acknowledge the farmers and growers of Lincolnshire whose machinery and crops feature in many of our photographs.

We also wish to thank Roly Smith, editorial manager for Halsgrove, for his help and encouragement. Thanks are also due to Eric and Audrey Wright for their support and friendship since Moor Farm days, and to Pete and Glen Singleton for their hospitality when we travelled to the south of the county.

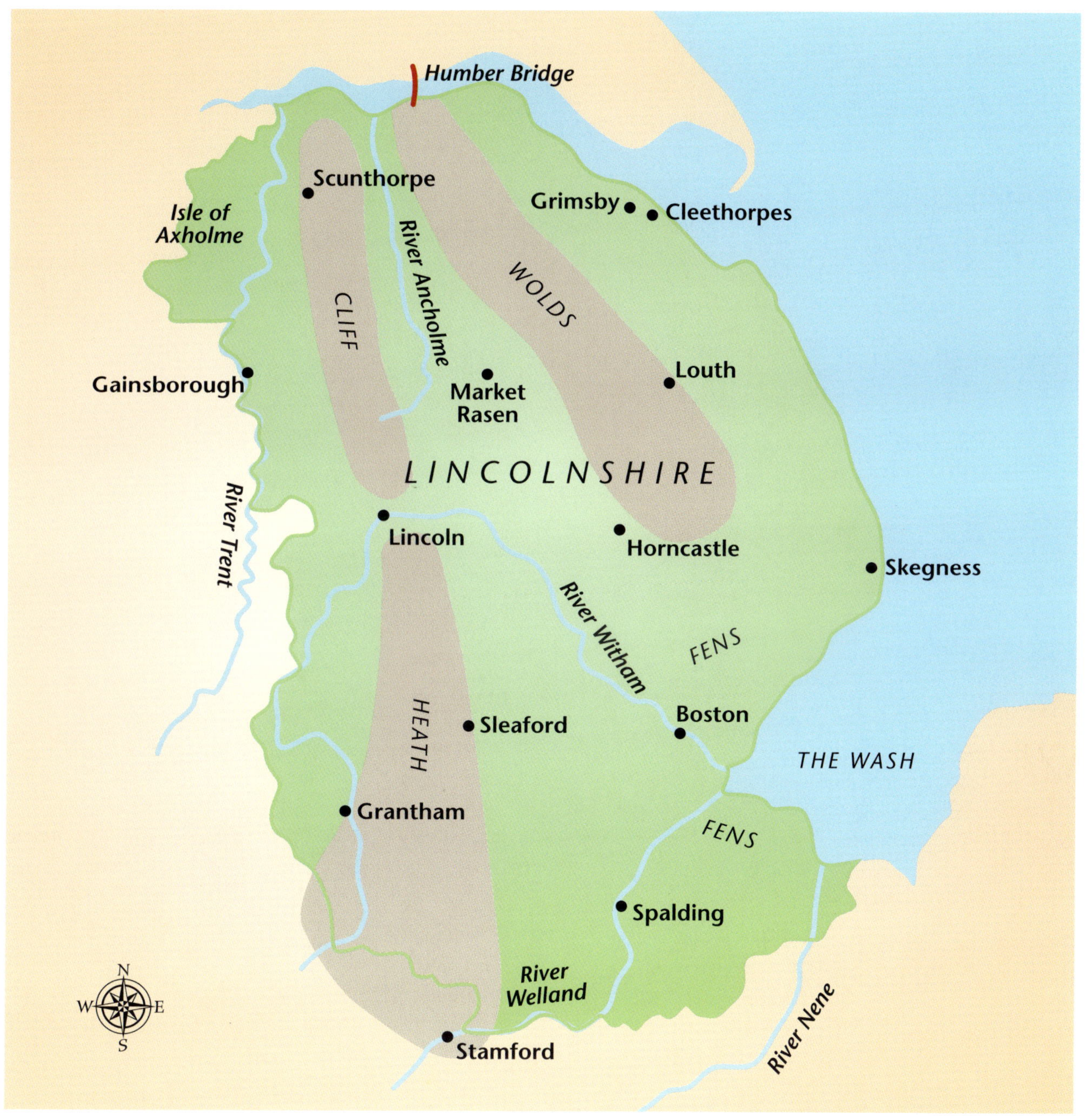
Humber Bridge
Scunthorpe
Isle of Axholme
Grimsby
Cleethorpes
River Ancholme
WOLDS
CLIFF
Gainsborough
Louth
Market Rasen
LINCOLNSHIRE
River Trent
Lincoln
Horncastle
Skegness
River Witham
FENS
HEATH
Sleaford
Boston
THE WASH
Grantham
FENS
Spalding
River Welland
Stamford
River Nene
N
W E
S

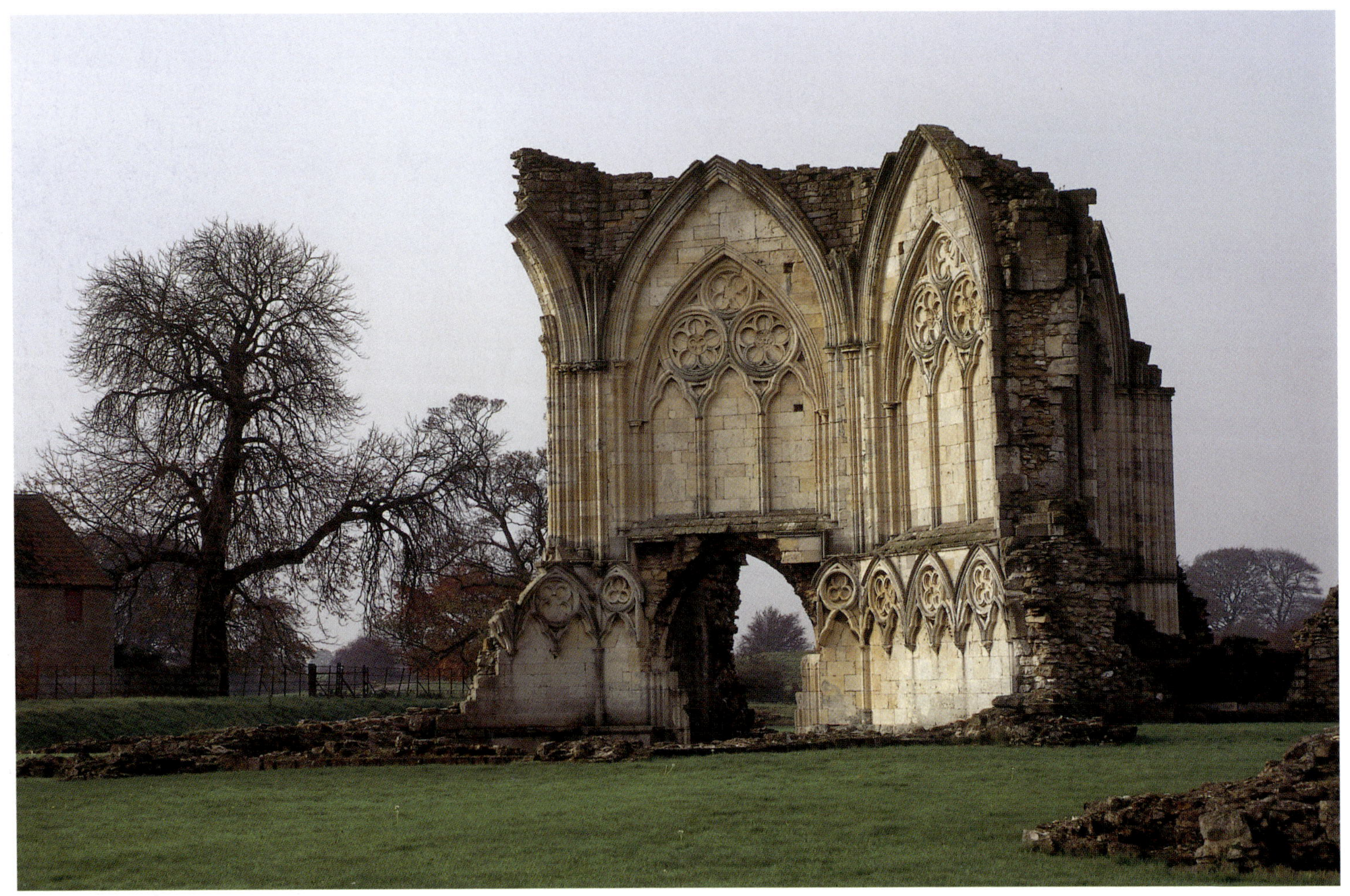

Thornton Abbey
Weak winter sunlight highlights the Gothic carving on the remains of the chapter house of Thornton Abbey.

Opposite: **Walesby church**
Known as the 'Ramblers' Church', the old church of All Saints at Walesby stands alone on the hilltop overlooking the village.

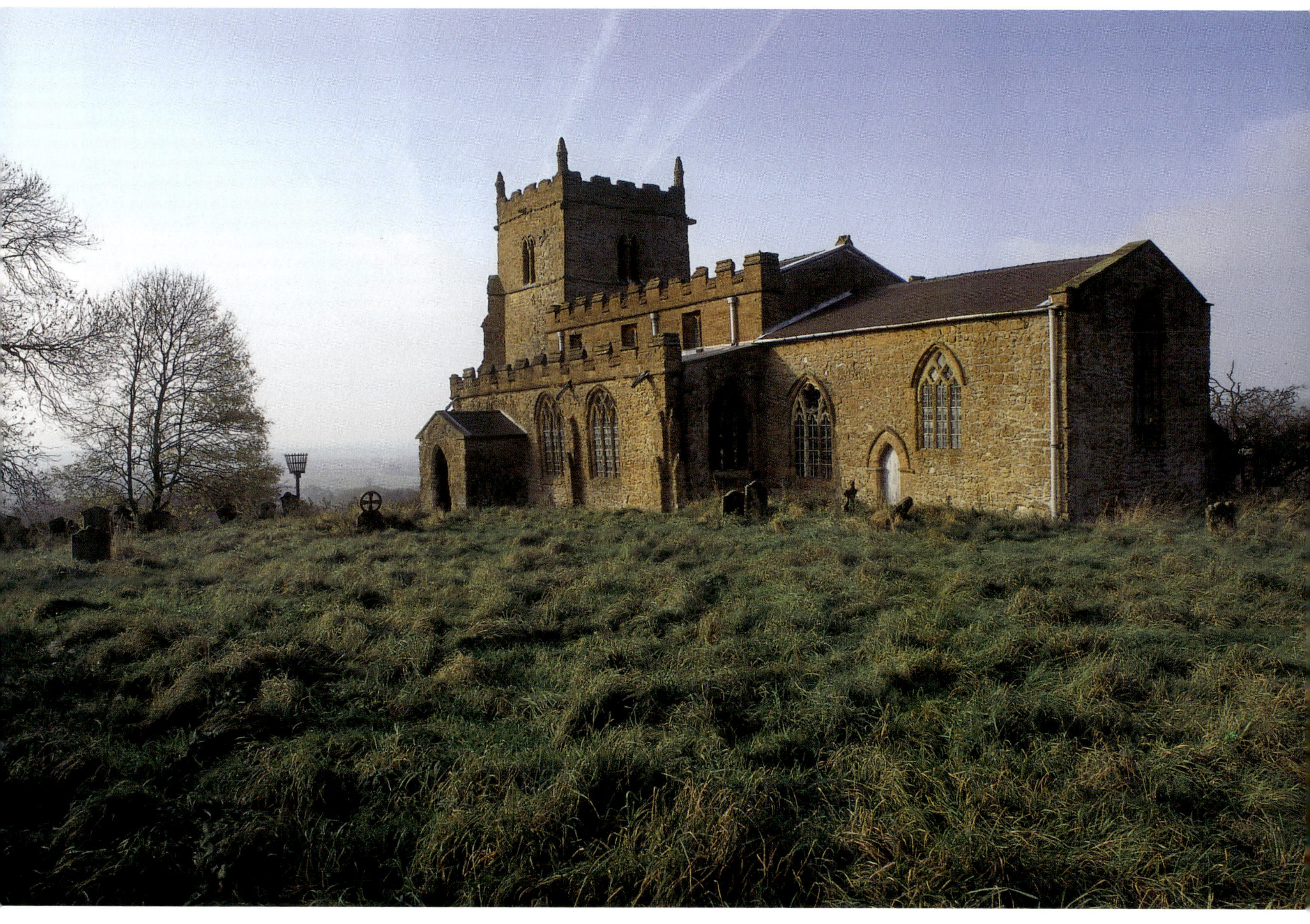

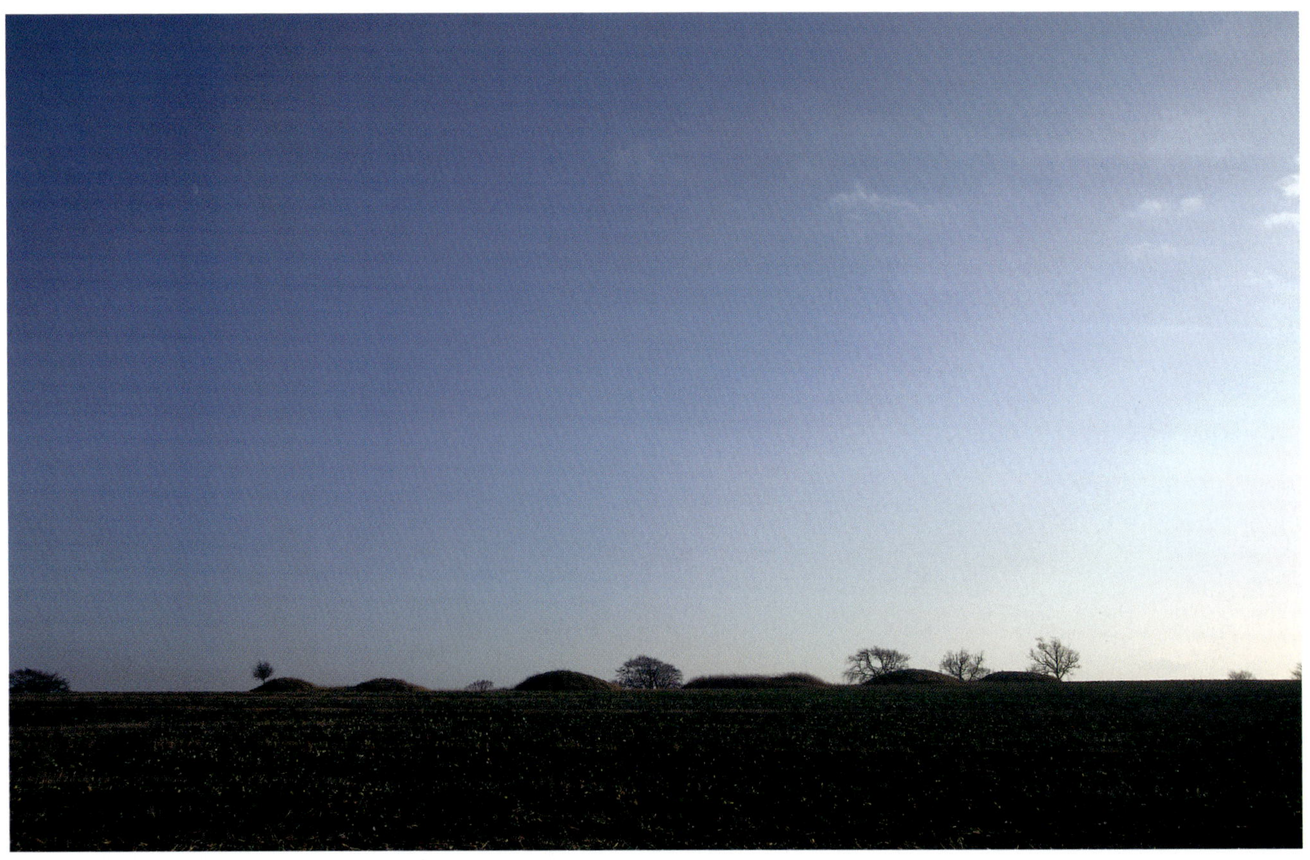

Barrows on Bully Hill, near Tathwell
The distant outline of six Bronze Age barrows can be seen on the horizon in clear winter light.

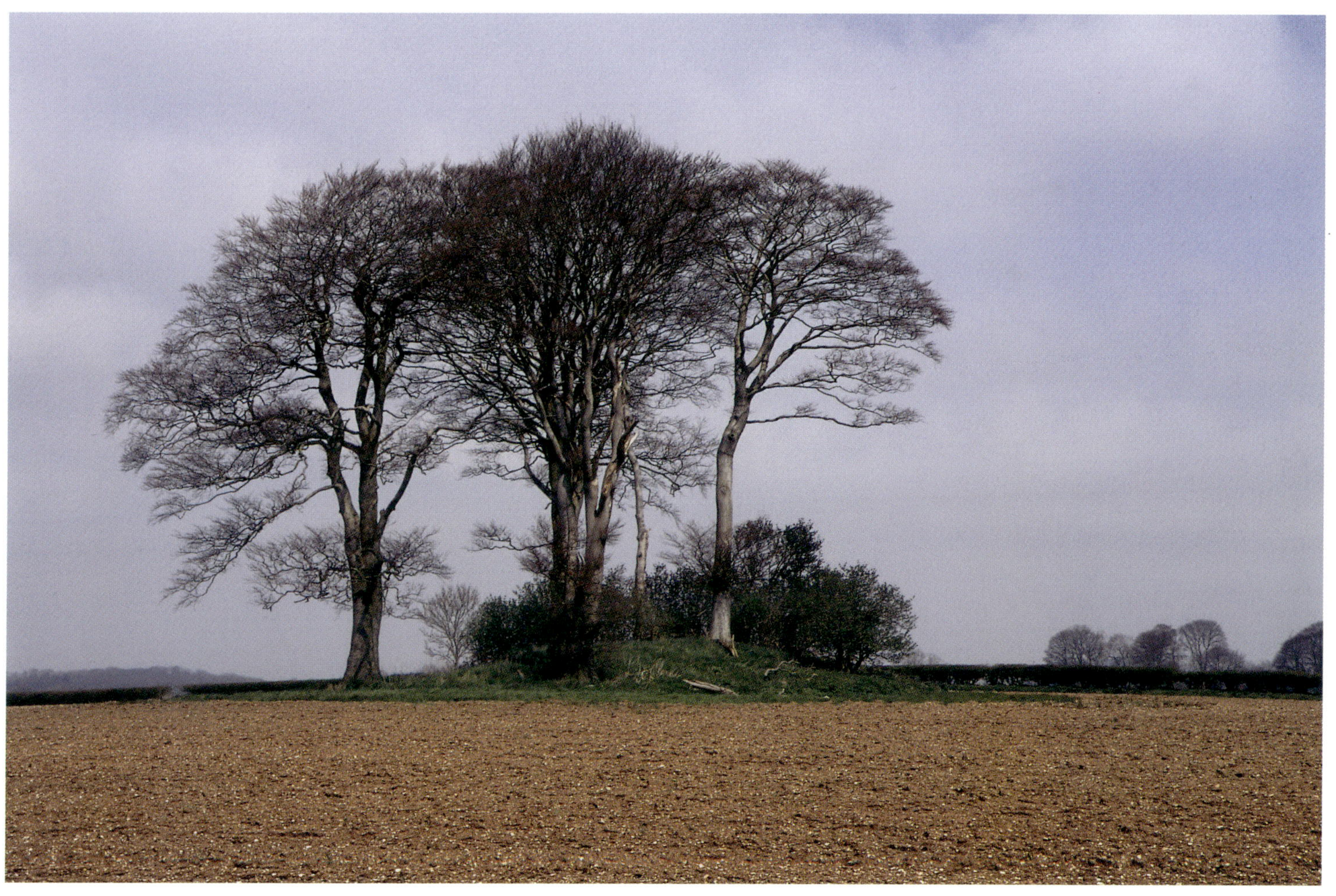

Barrow at Burgh Top, near Biscathorpe
An isolated clump of beech trees tops the barrow at Burgh Top. Barrows were built in prominent places and several
can be seen along Caistor High Street, the ancient road which runs along the western edge of the Wolds.

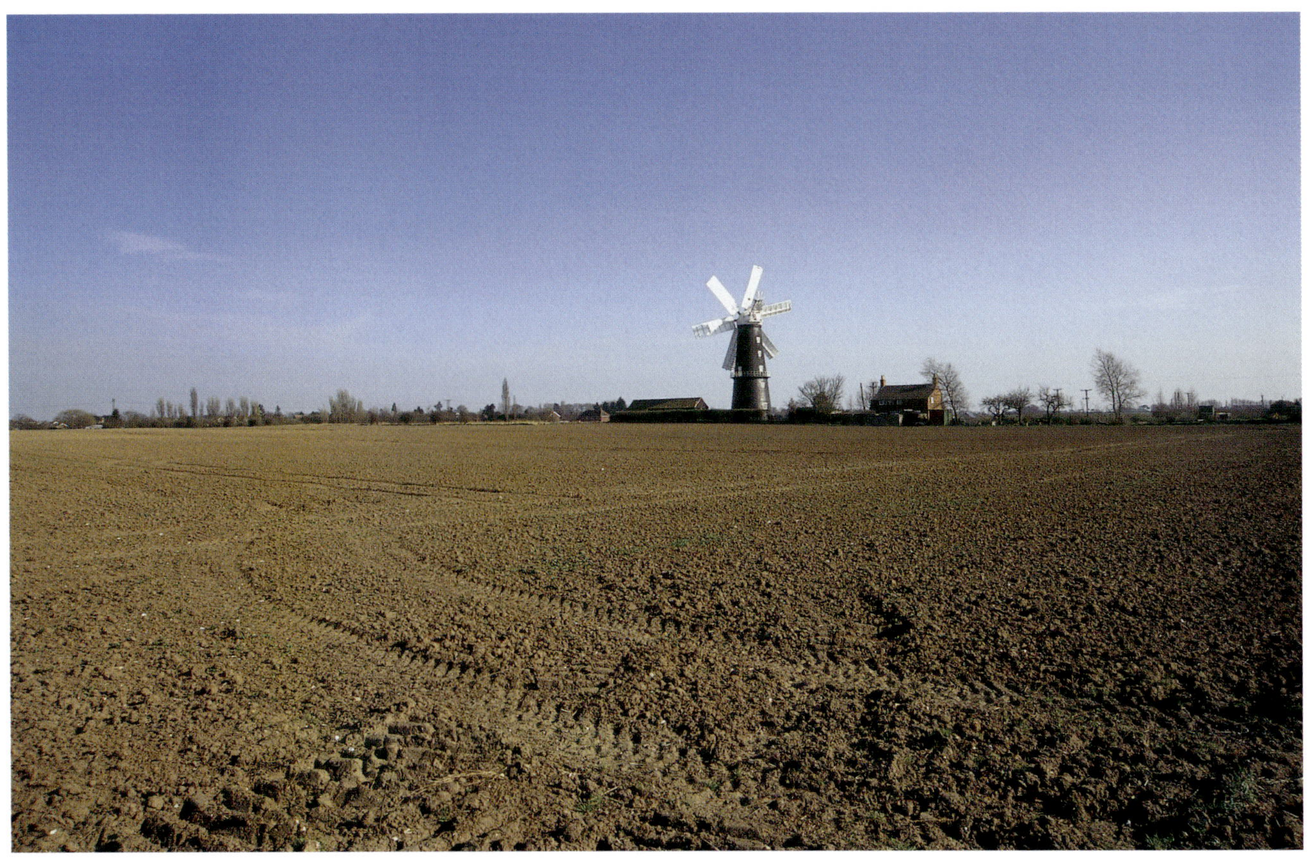

Sibsey Trader Mill
The six sails of the trader mill at Sibsey stand tall above the fenland, north of Boston.

Opposite: **Ellis's Mill at Lincoln**
Bright sunshine lights up the white-painted sails, cap and fantail of this tower windmill at Lincoln.

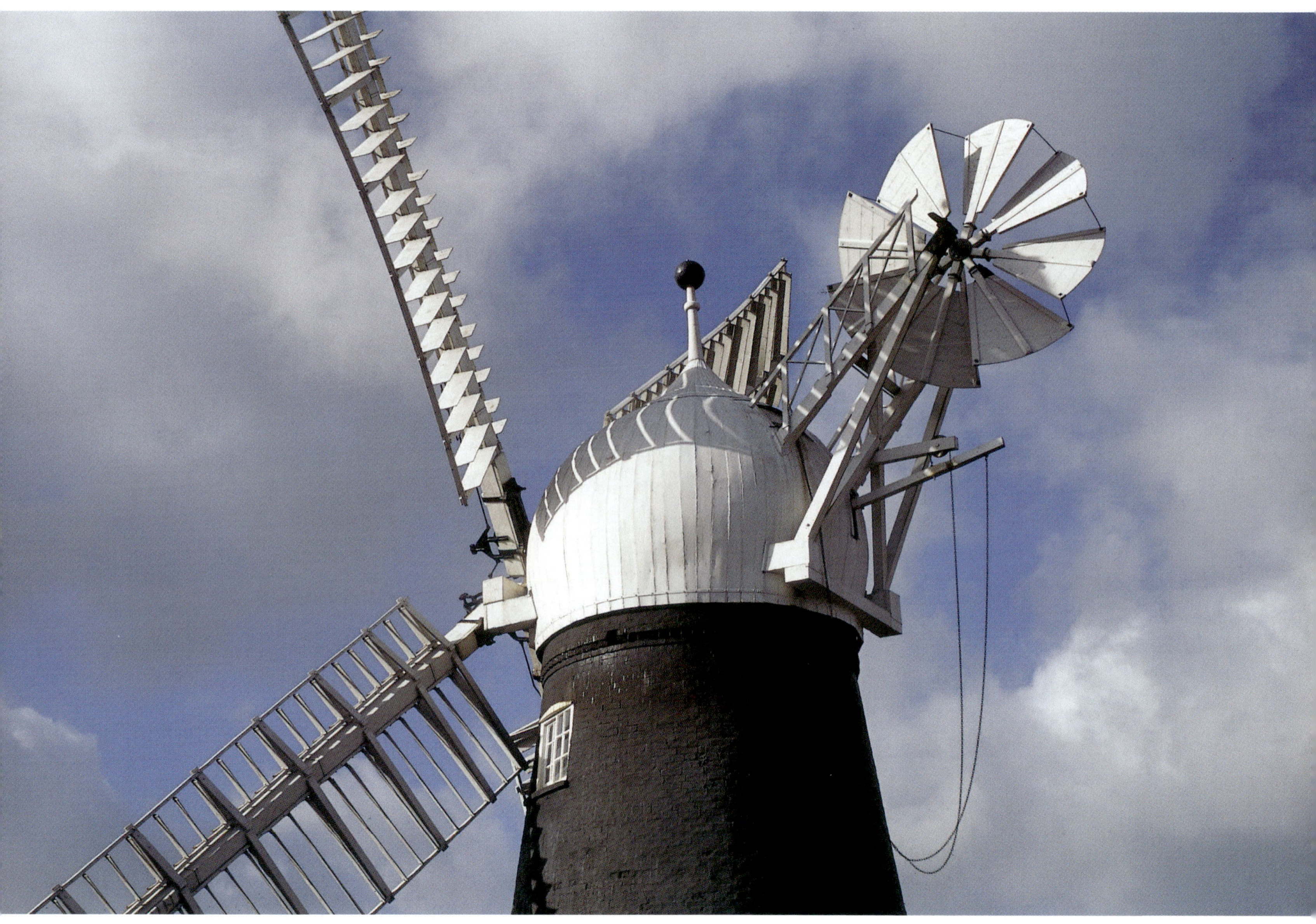

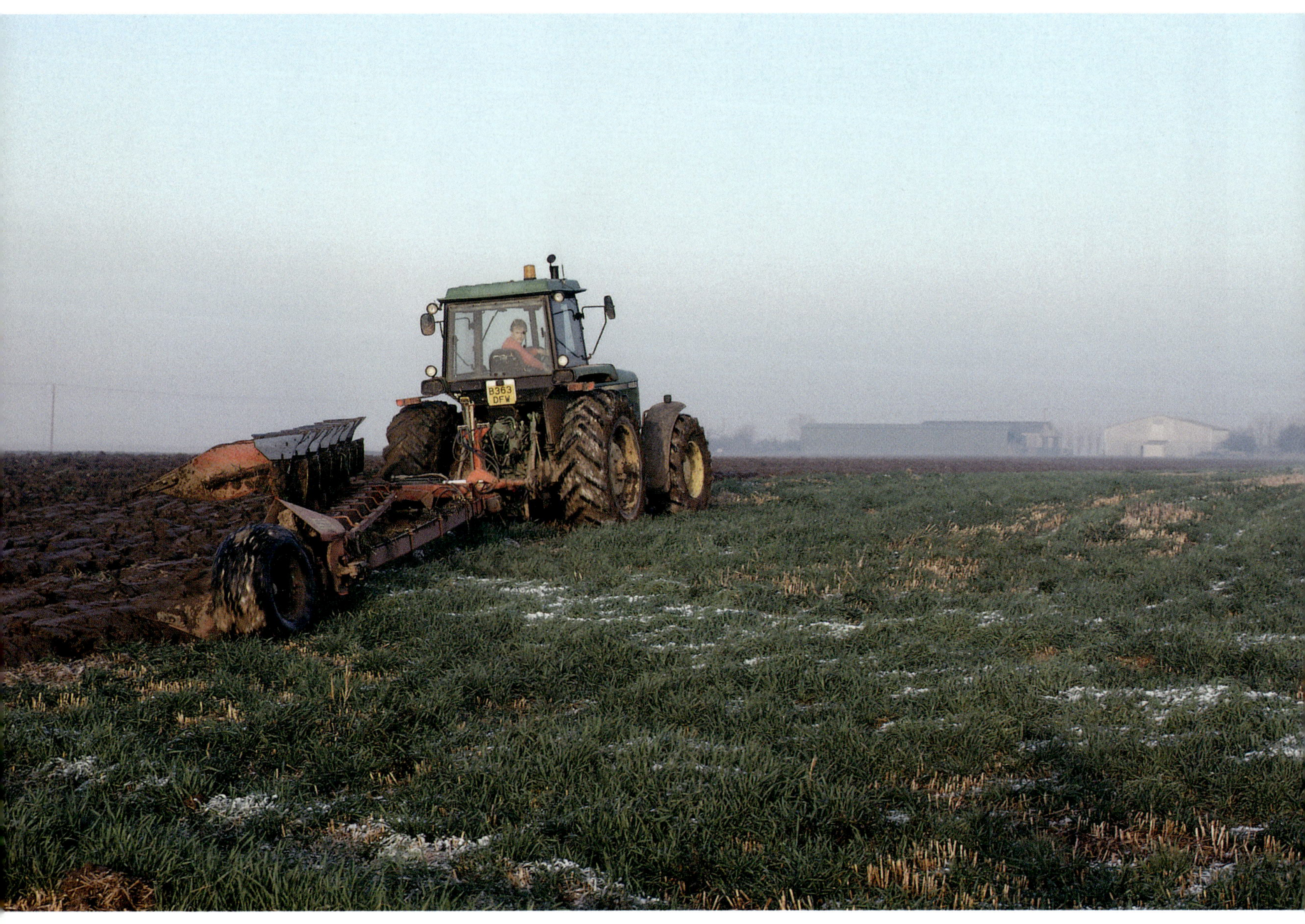

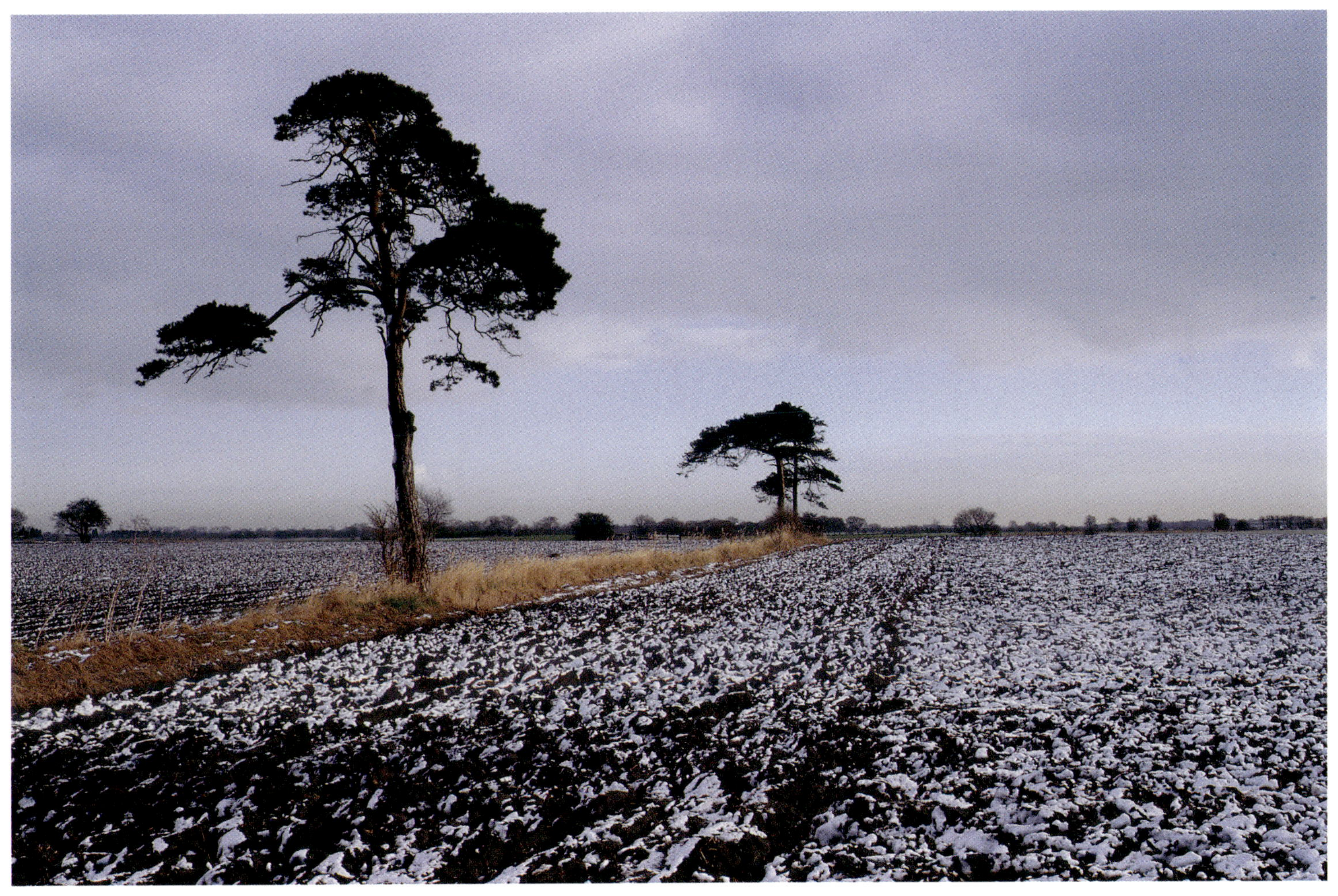

Pine trees in snow
A light snowfall covers the dark peaty soils of the Levels near Sandtoft, in the Isle of Axholme,
where Scots pine trees mark the field boundary.

Opposite: **Winter ploughing**
Ploughing heavy land in the northern part of the county on a cold January day, with frost still on the ground.

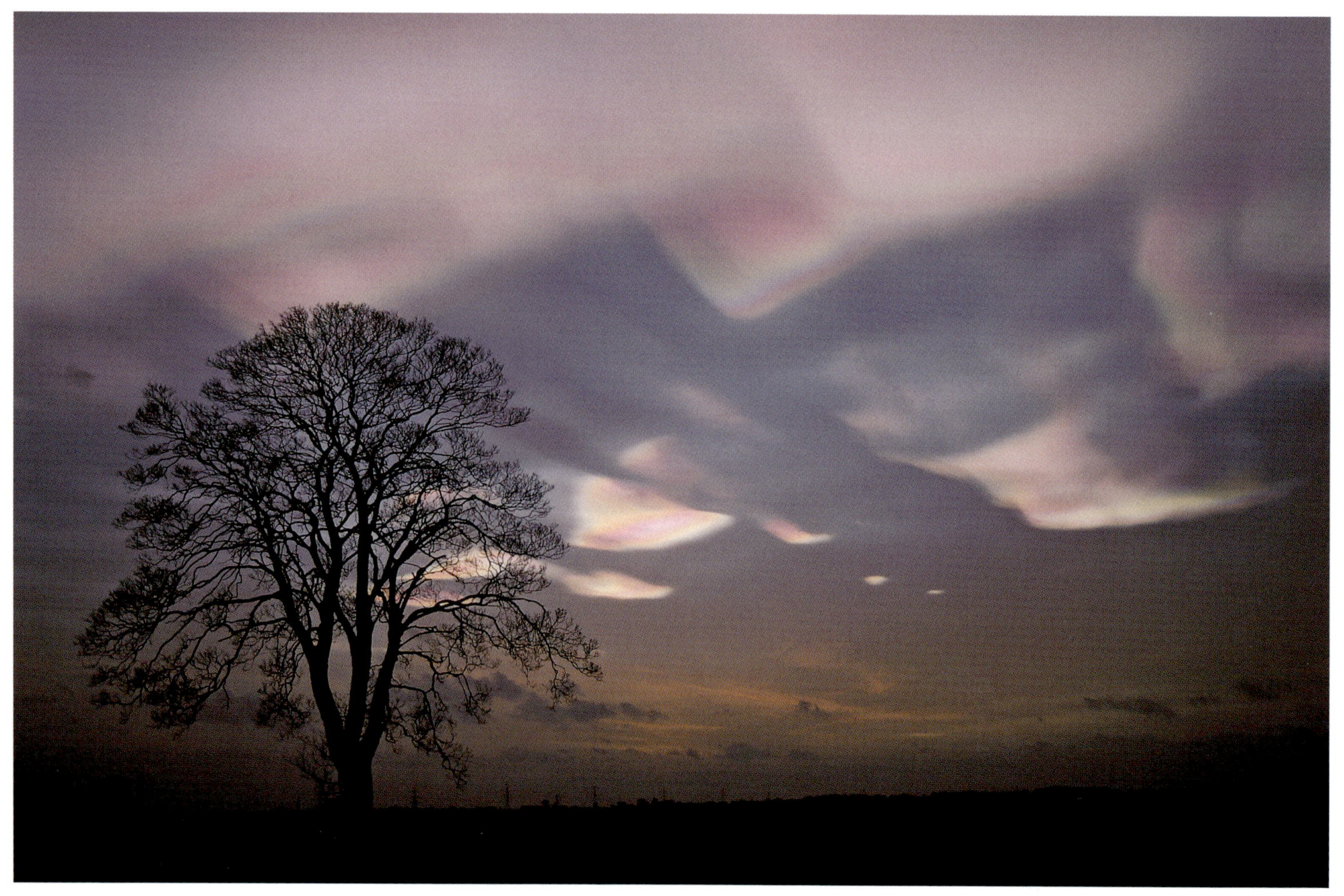

Mother-of-pearl sky
The delicate pastel colours of 'mother-of-pearl', or nacreous, clouds were photographed at sunset near Crowle.
This is a rare phenomenon occurring when ice crystals in high clouds are refracted by the fading sun.

Opposite: **Sunset over Hatfield Waste Drain**
Hatfield Waste Drain in the Isle of Axholme reflects the glowing colours of the winter sunset.

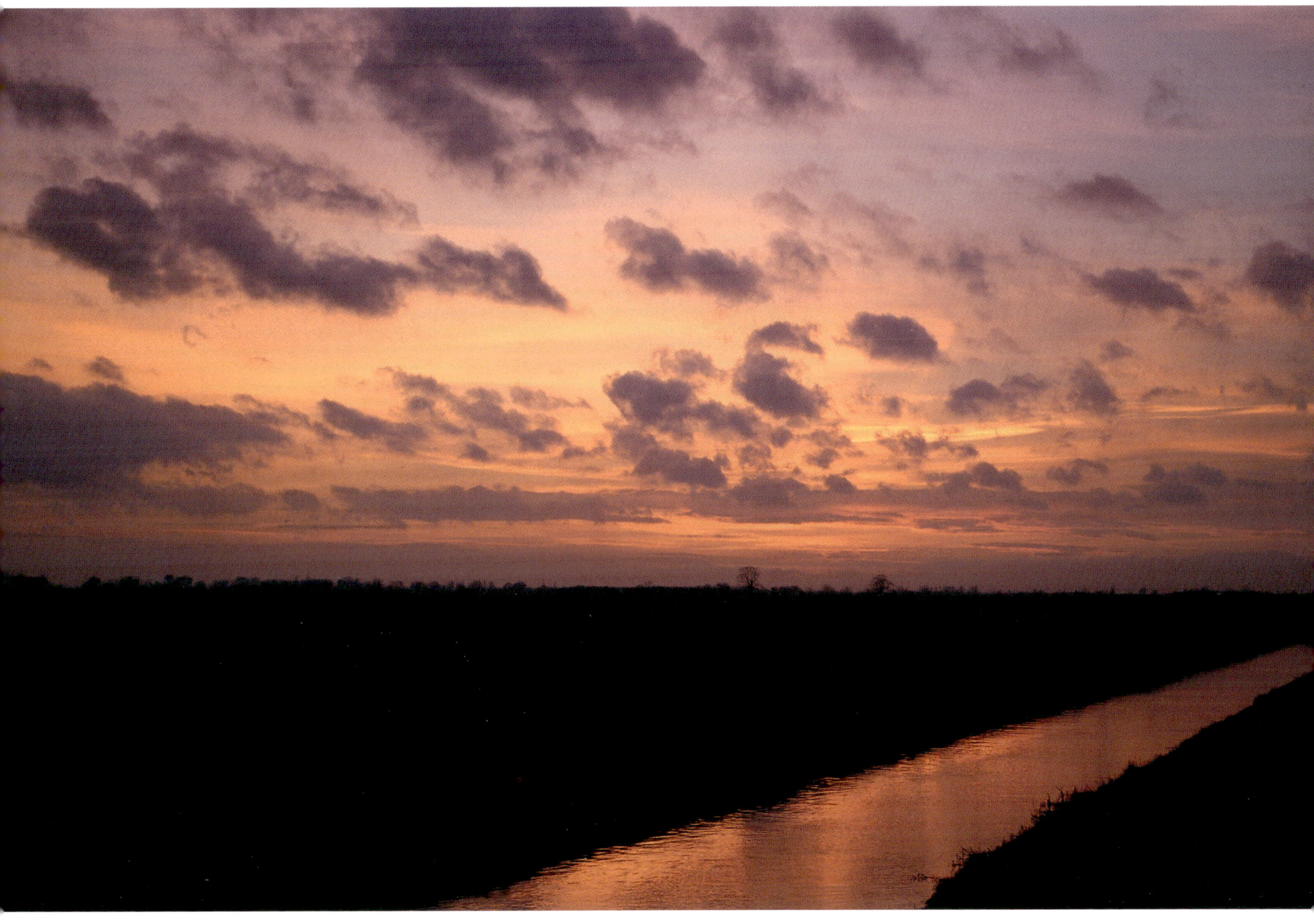

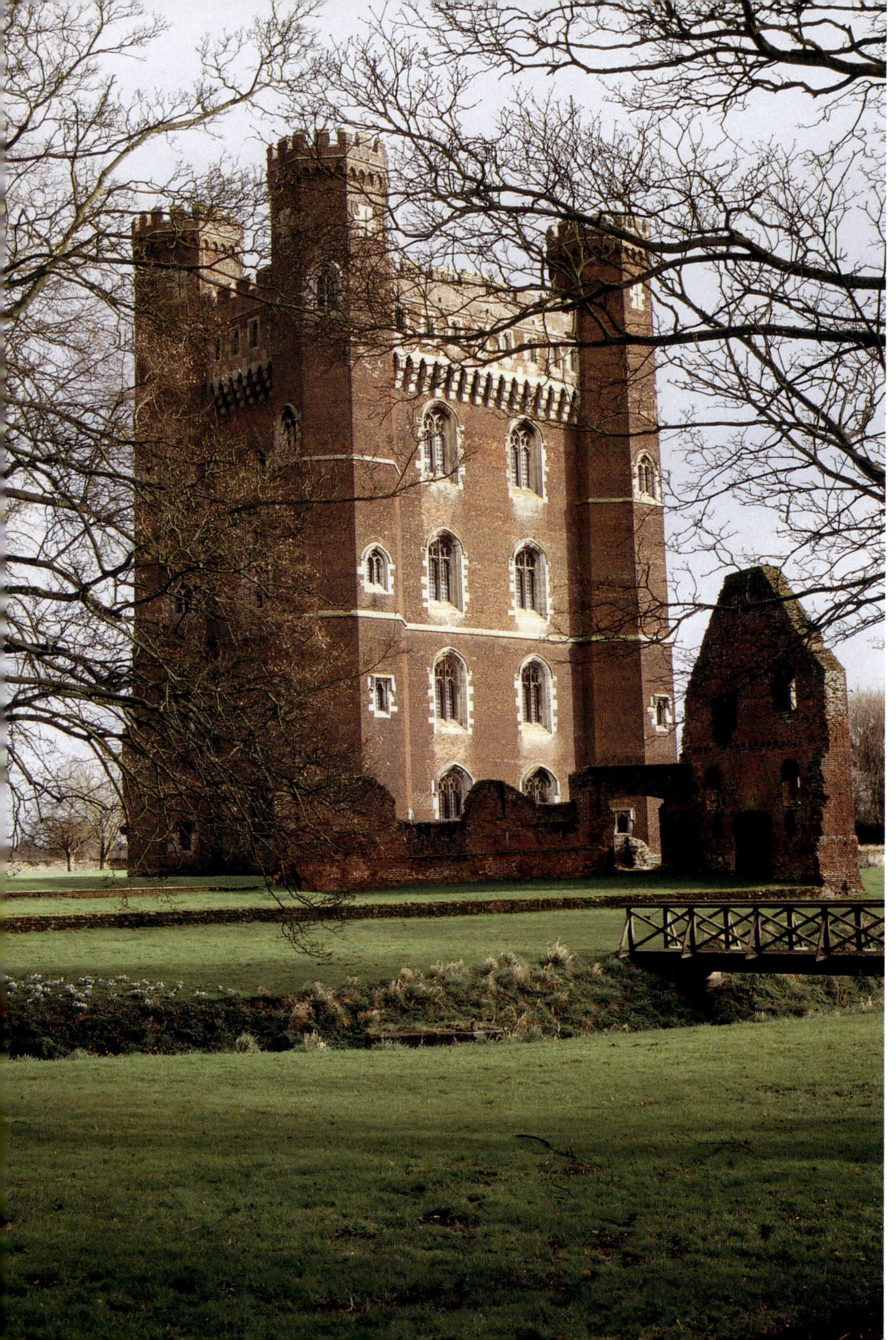

Tattershall Castle
The castle keep, dating from the fifteenth century, can be seen through a tracery of bare branches. It was built by Lord Cromwell, treasurer to Henry VI, and is unusual in its brick construction.

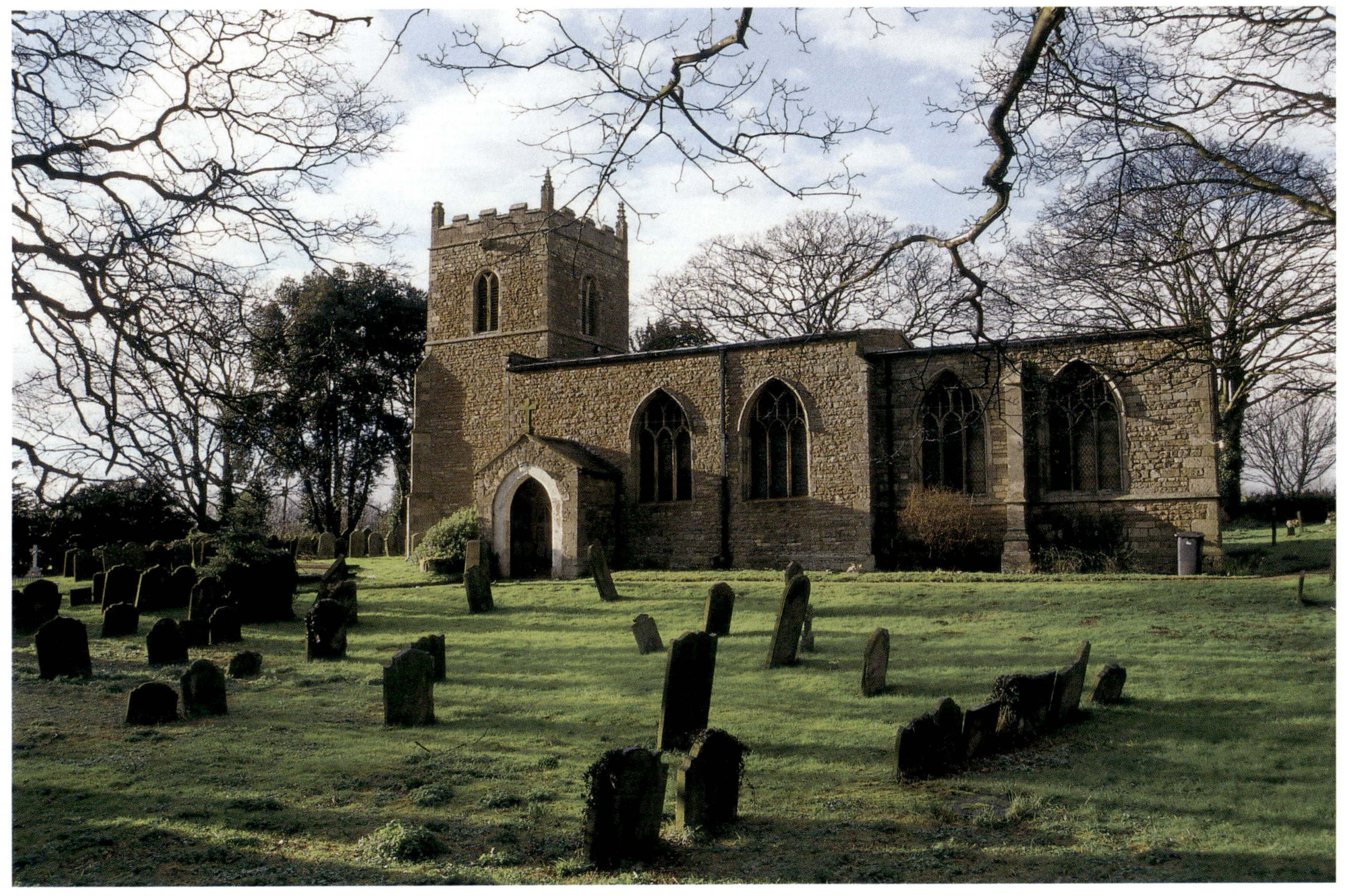

West Halton church
Bright winter sunshine lights up the parish church at West Halton and sends long shadows across the churchyard.

Overleaf: **Snow and daffodils**
A February snowfall lies between the rows of young daffodils growing near Gedney Dyke.

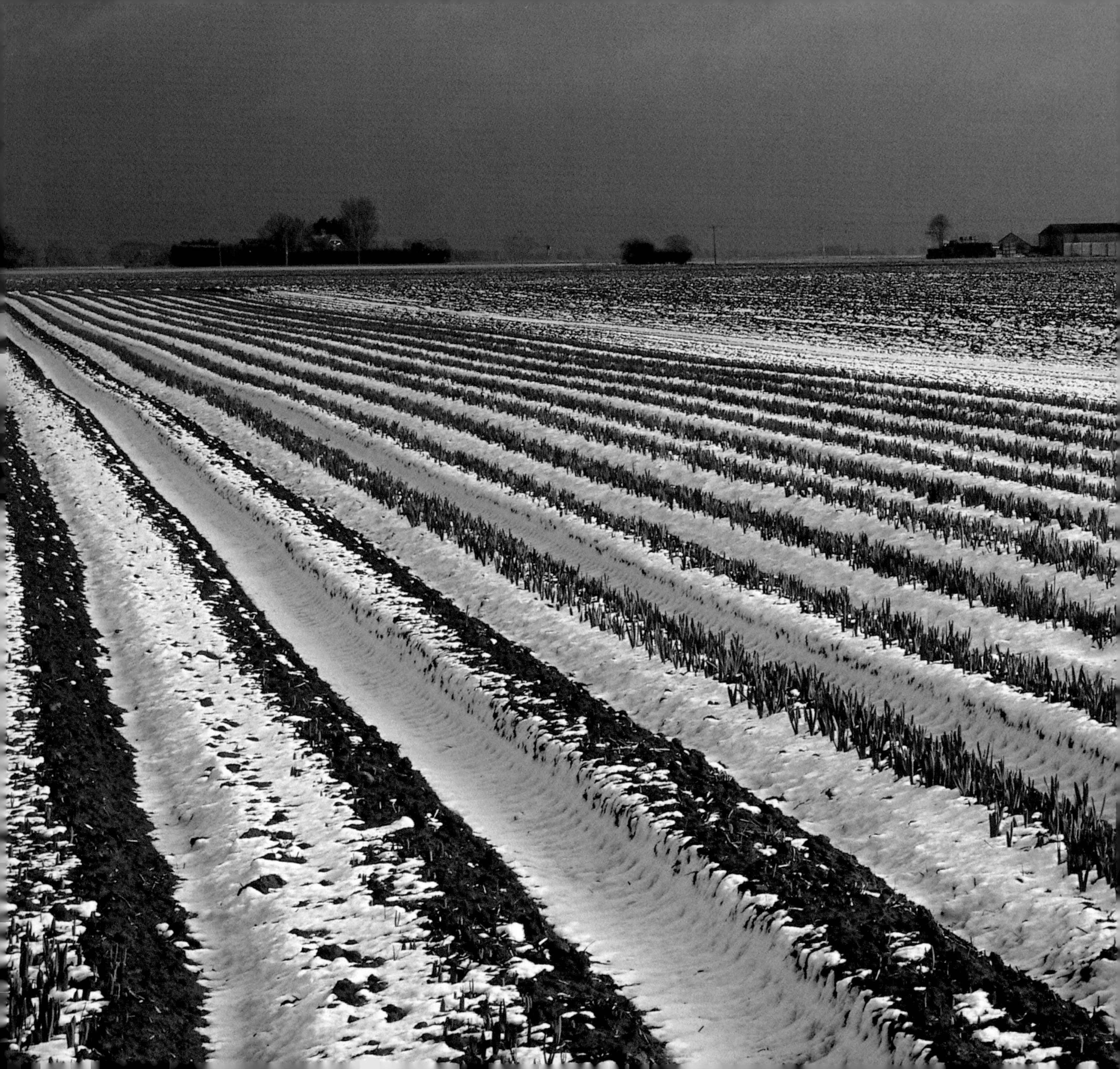

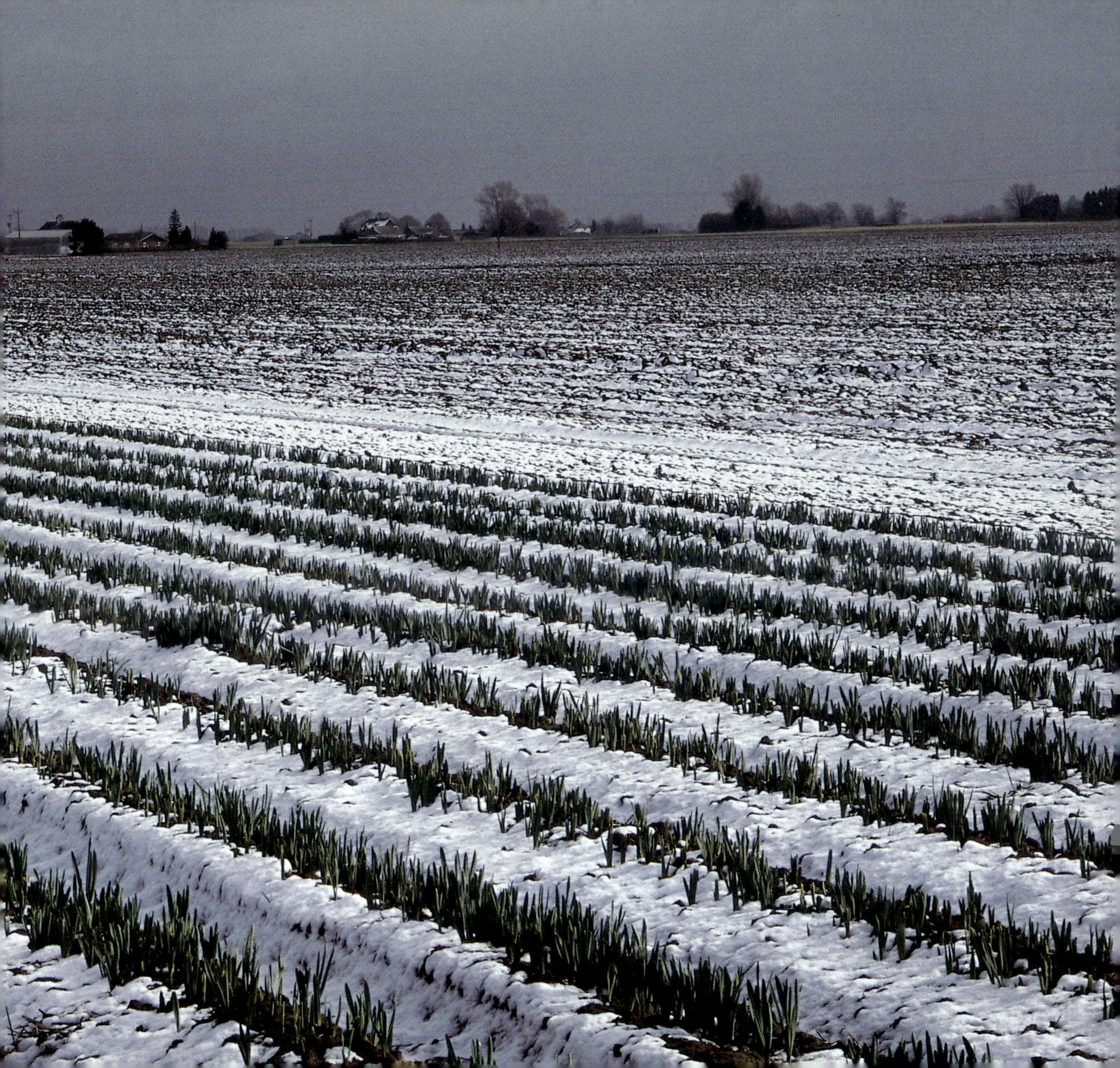

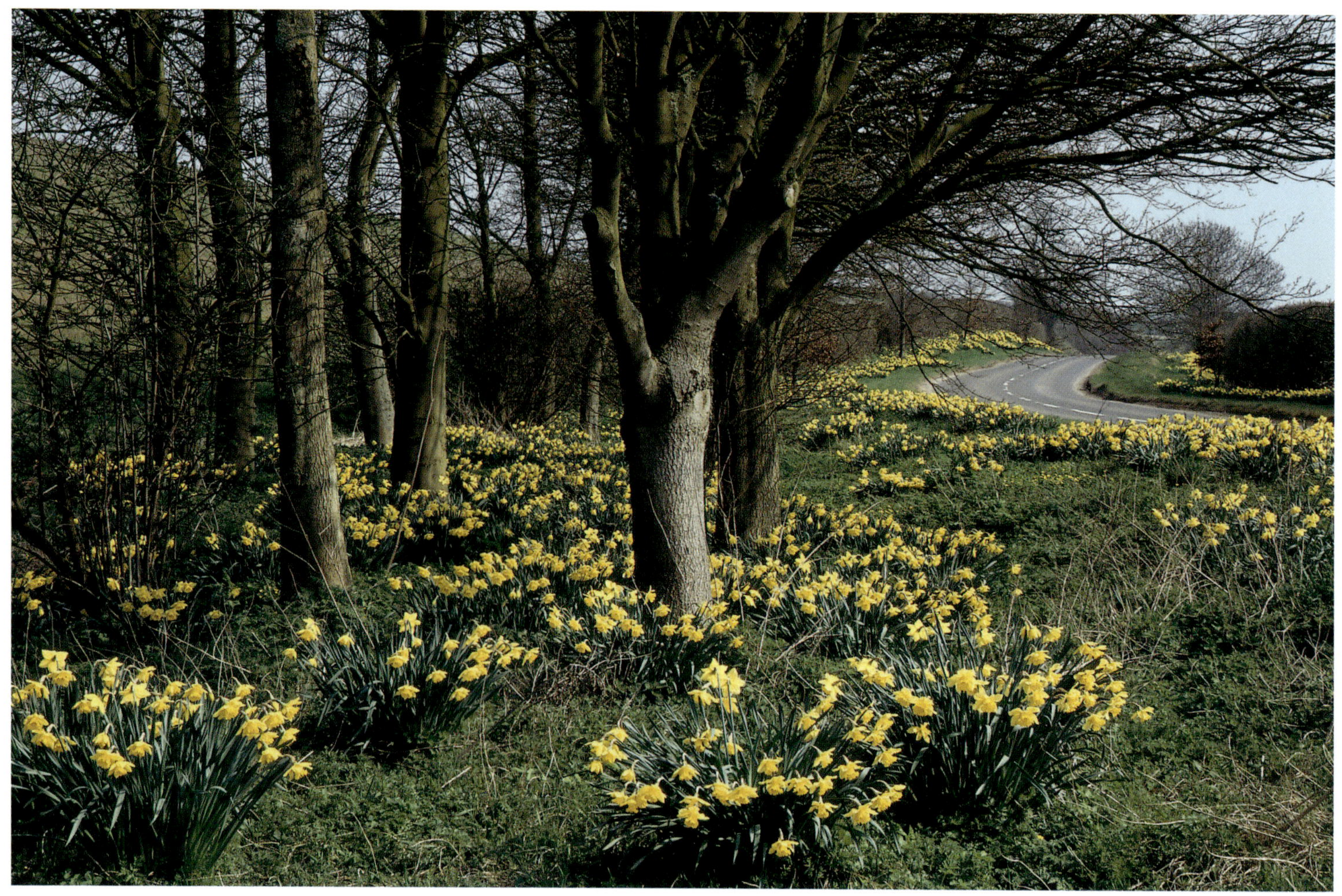

Roadside daffodils
Daffodils line the roadside verges providing a spring spectacle around the village of Rothwell.

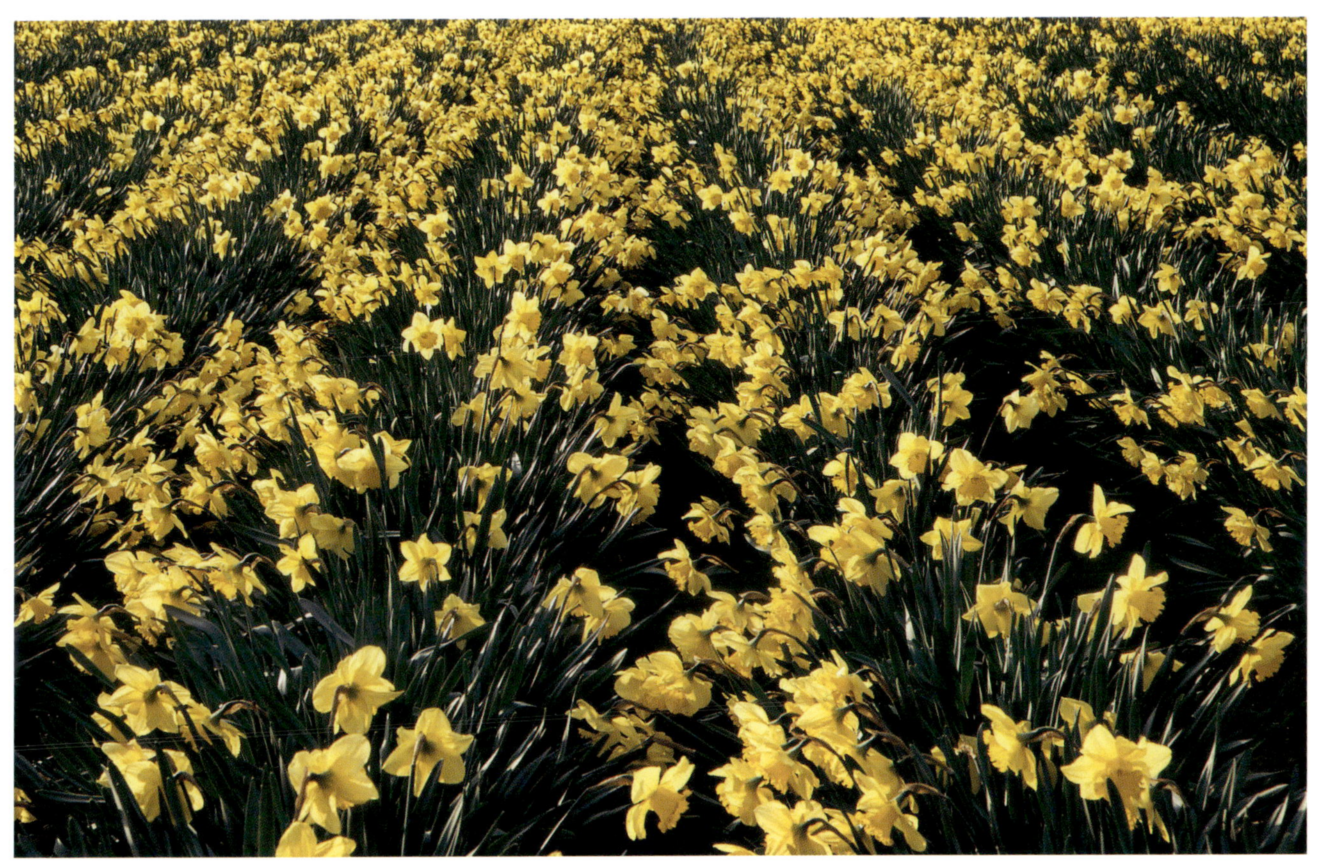

Field daffodils
Commercially-grown daffodils paint a mass of rich yellow colour throughout the Fens in March.

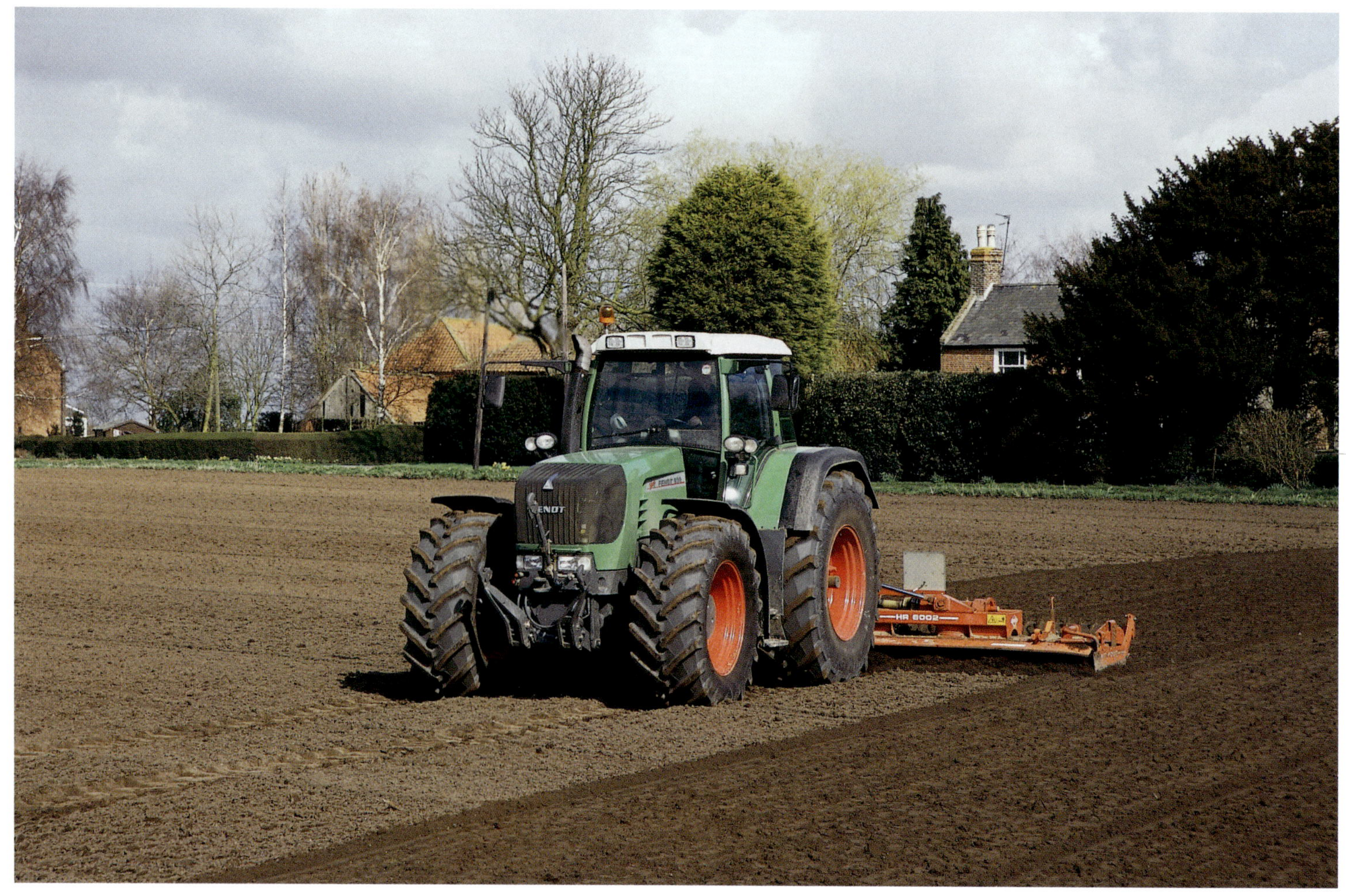

Tractor power-harrowing
A high-powered four-wheel drive tractor prepares the seedbed on fertile arable land near Quadring Eaudike.

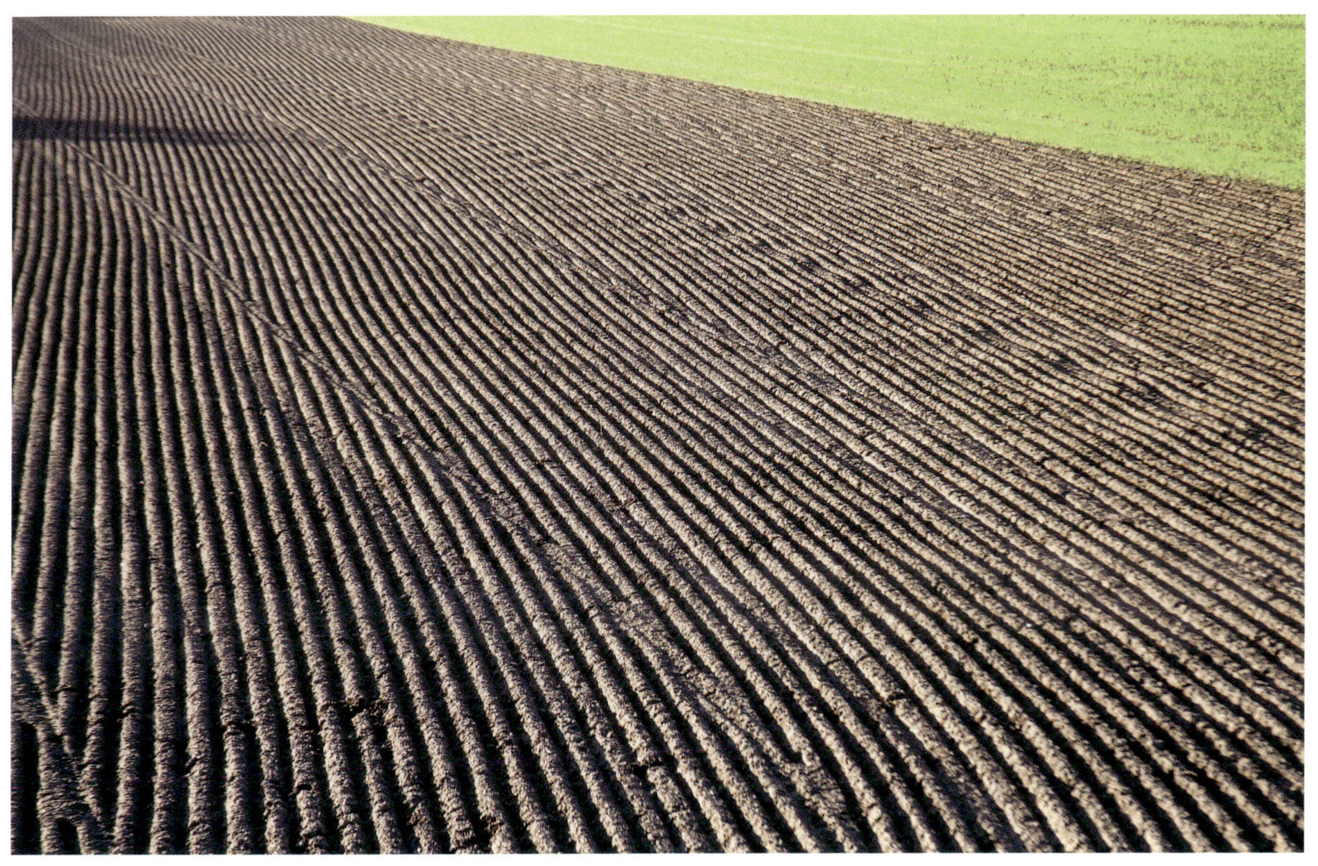

Land pattern
Early morning sunshine highlights the distinctive pattern left by a soil press.

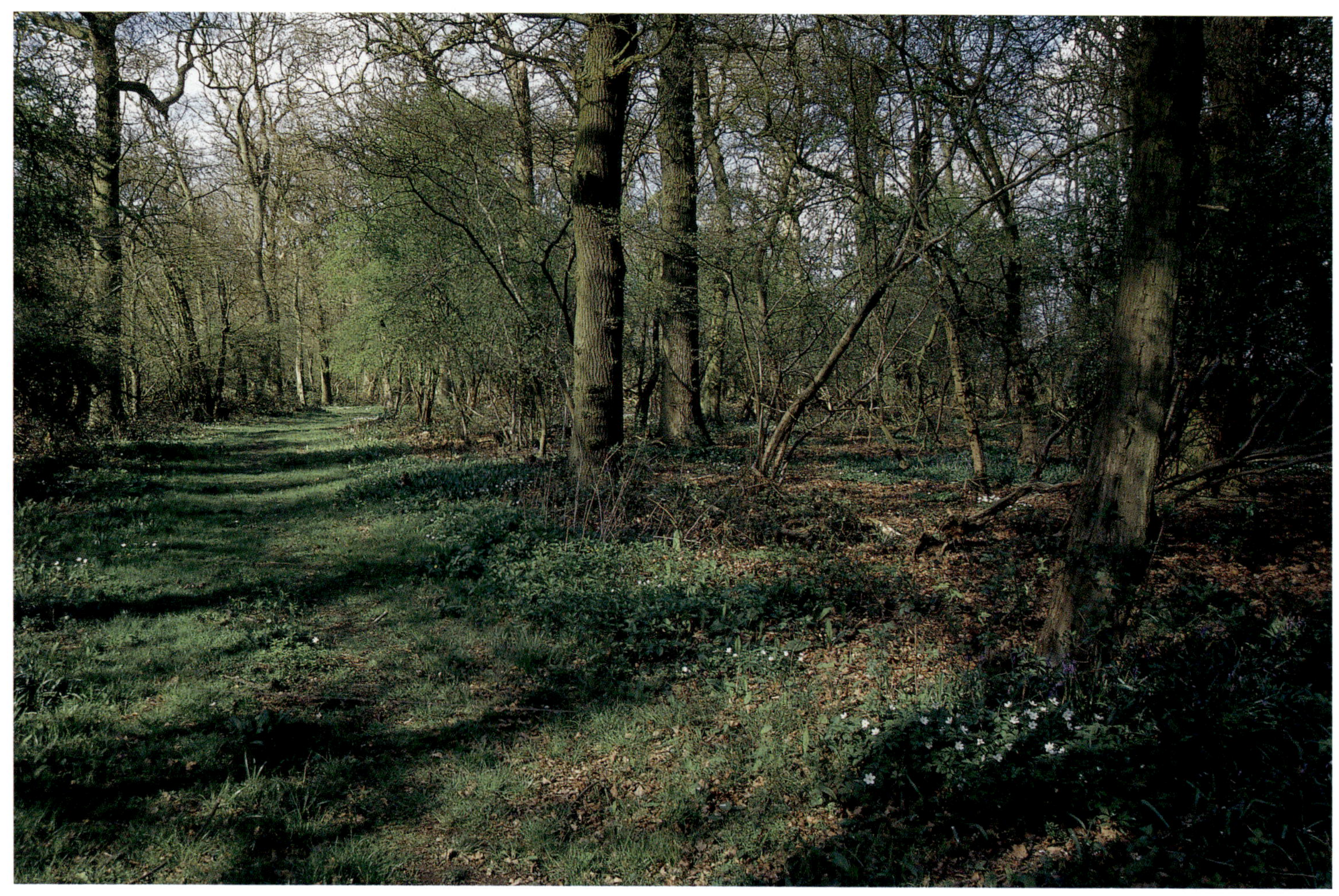

Tortoiseshell Wood Nature Reserve
In early spring, sunlight filters through to the woodland floor encouraging
primroses, violets, wood anemones and bluebells to flower.

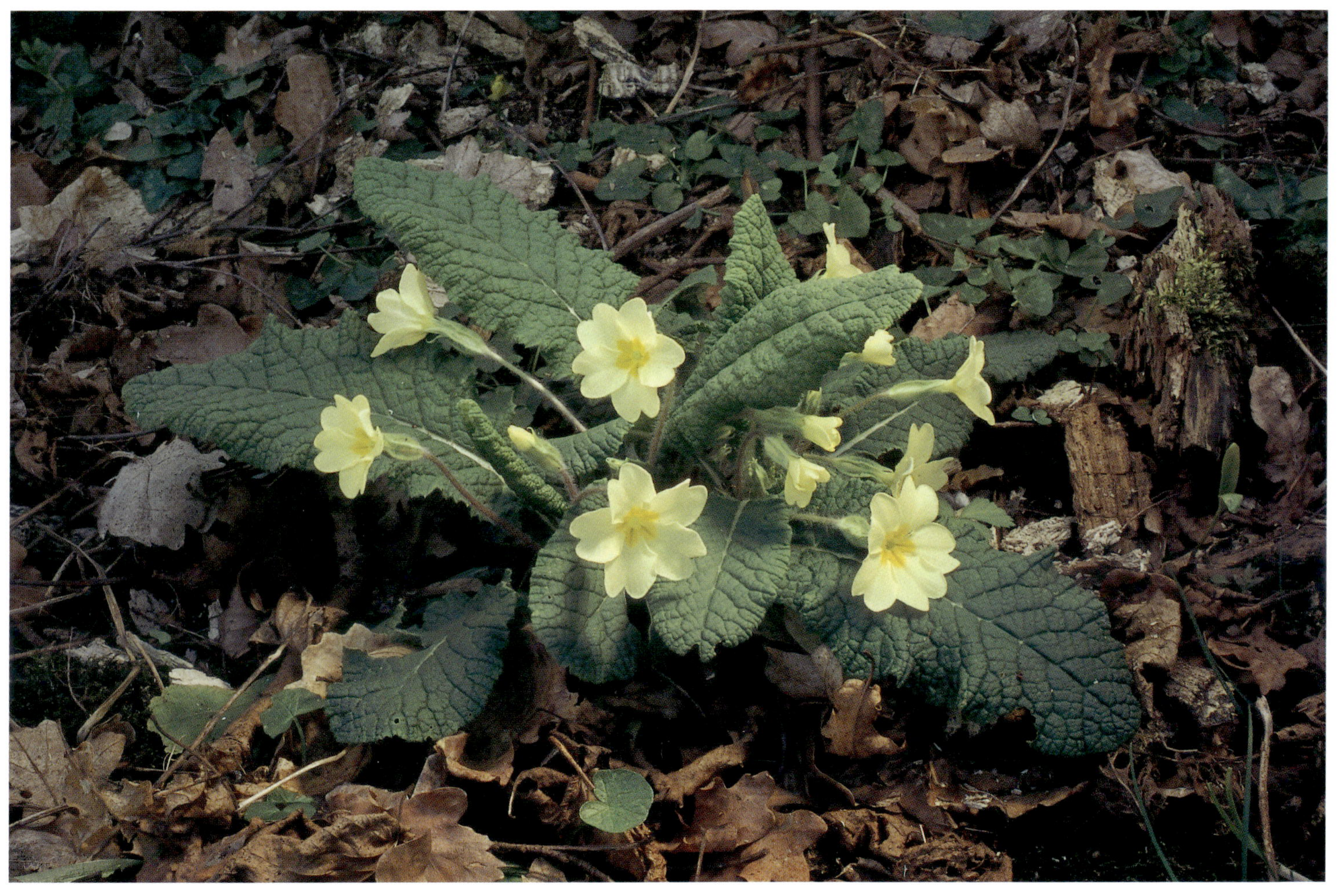

Primroses
A clump of primroses, one of the most eagerly-awaited spring flowers, photographed in
Goslings Corner Wood Nature Reserve, near Wragby.

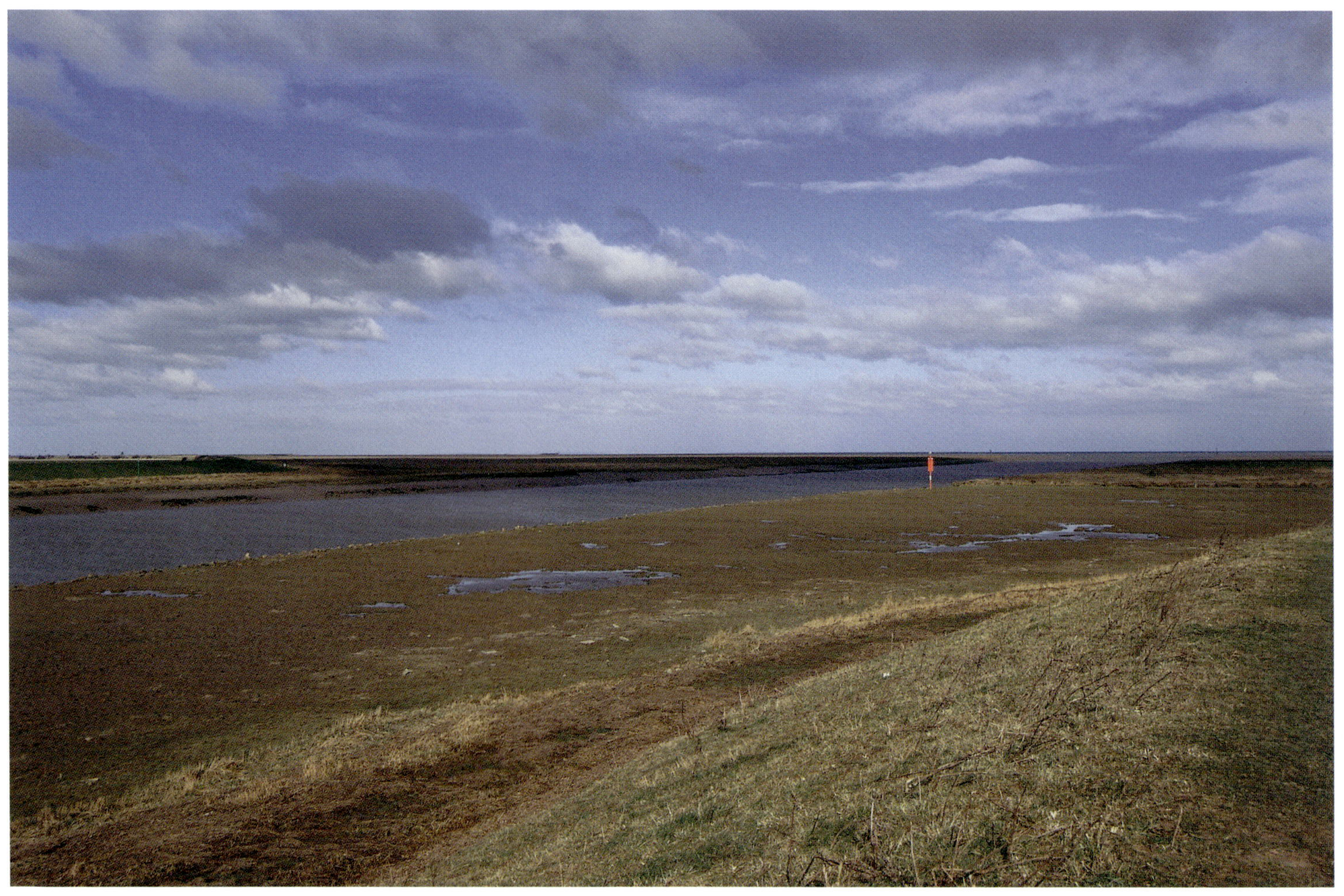

Nene Outfall Cut
Flanked by mudflats, the River Nene flows into the vast expanse of the Wash.

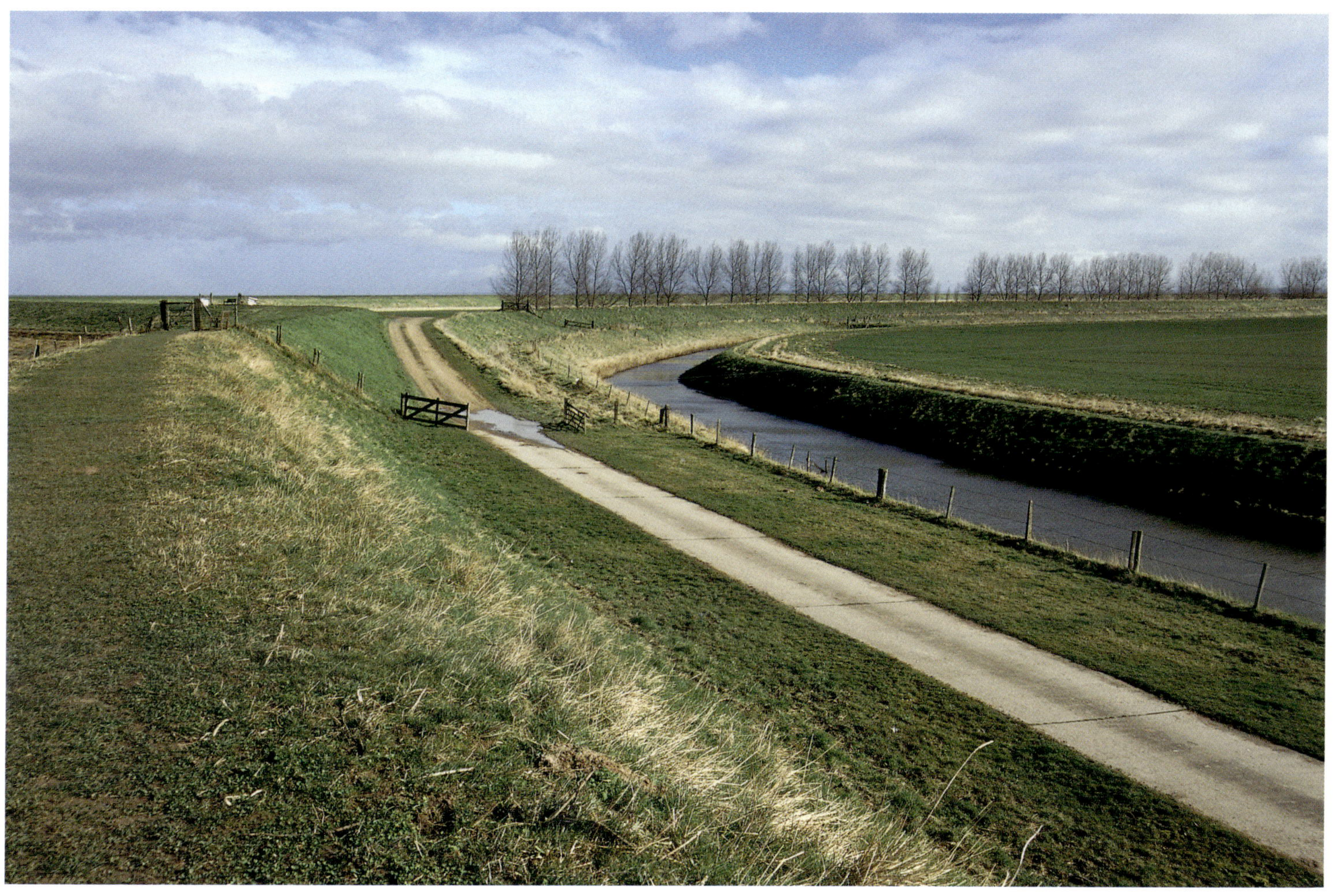

Sea bank at the Nene Outfall
High banks at the mouth of the River Nene protect the reclaimed and low-lying farmland from the sea.

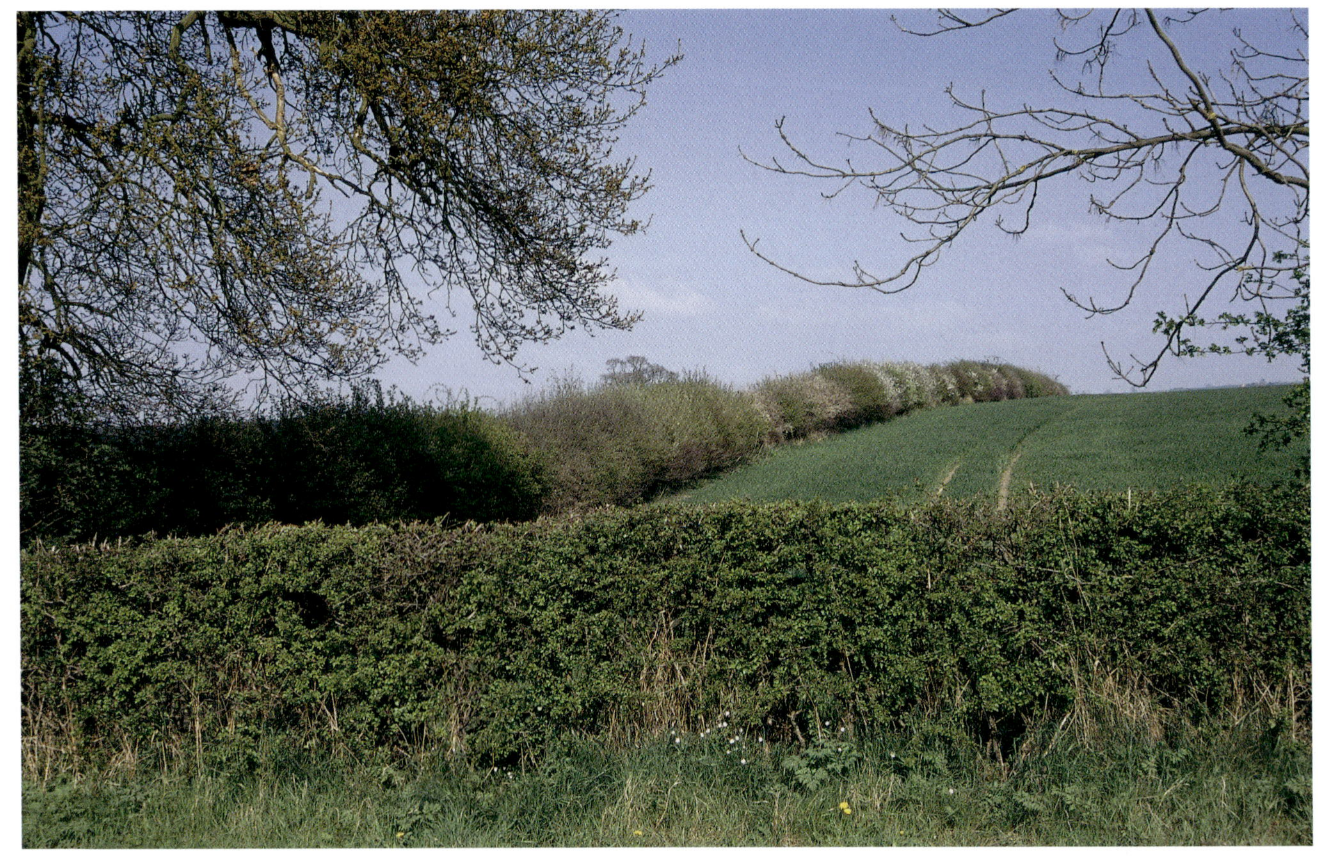

Hedgerow at Sixhills
By mid-April, hawthorns are coming into leaf but the blackthorn is already flowering.
With its blossom appearing so early in the spring, often when the weather is still
very cold, it has given rise to the expression: a 'blackthorn winter'.

Opposite: **Blackthorn blossom**
The attractive white flowers of blackthorn appear before the leaves.
Later in the season these thorny bushes will carry bitter sloe berries.

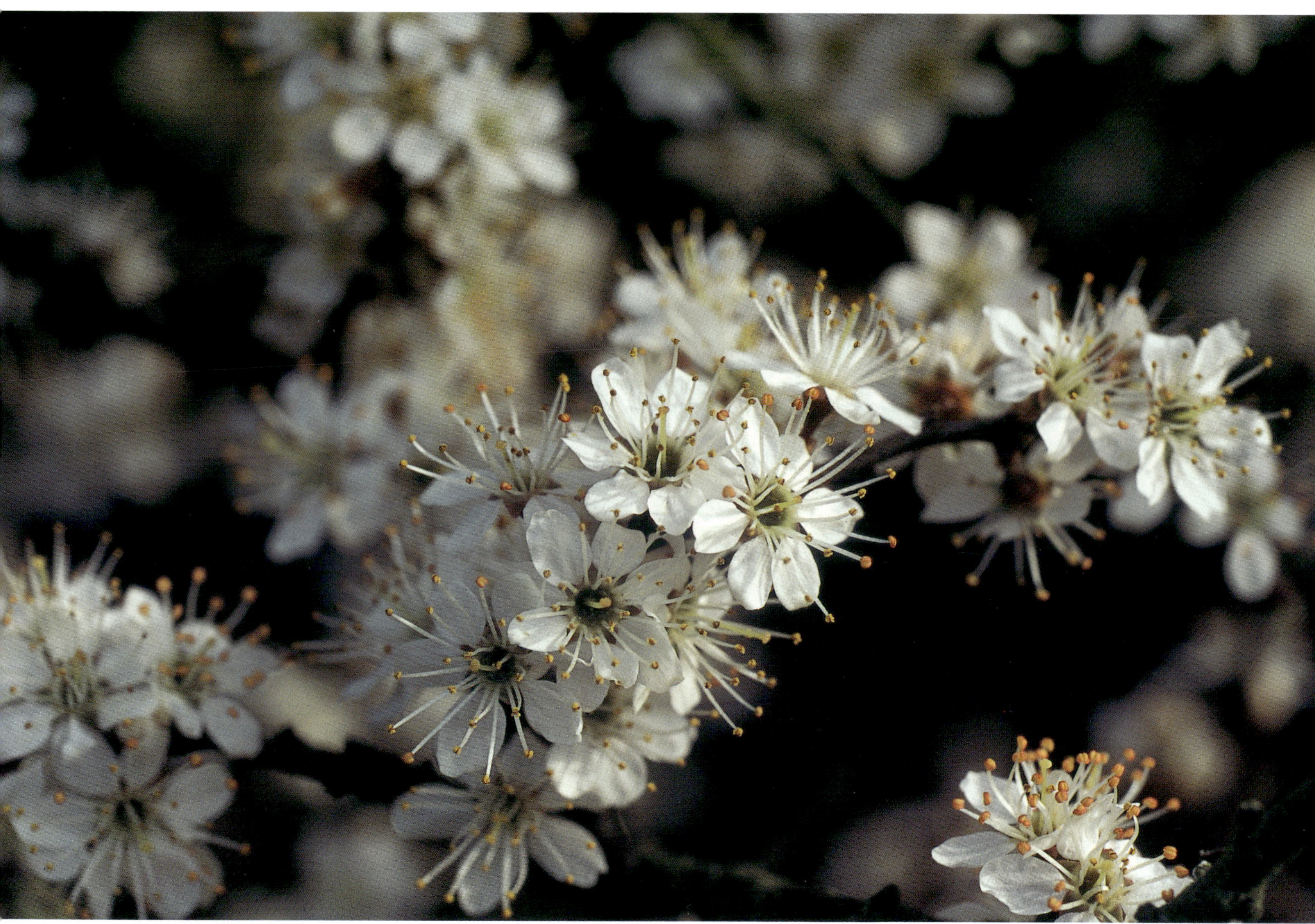

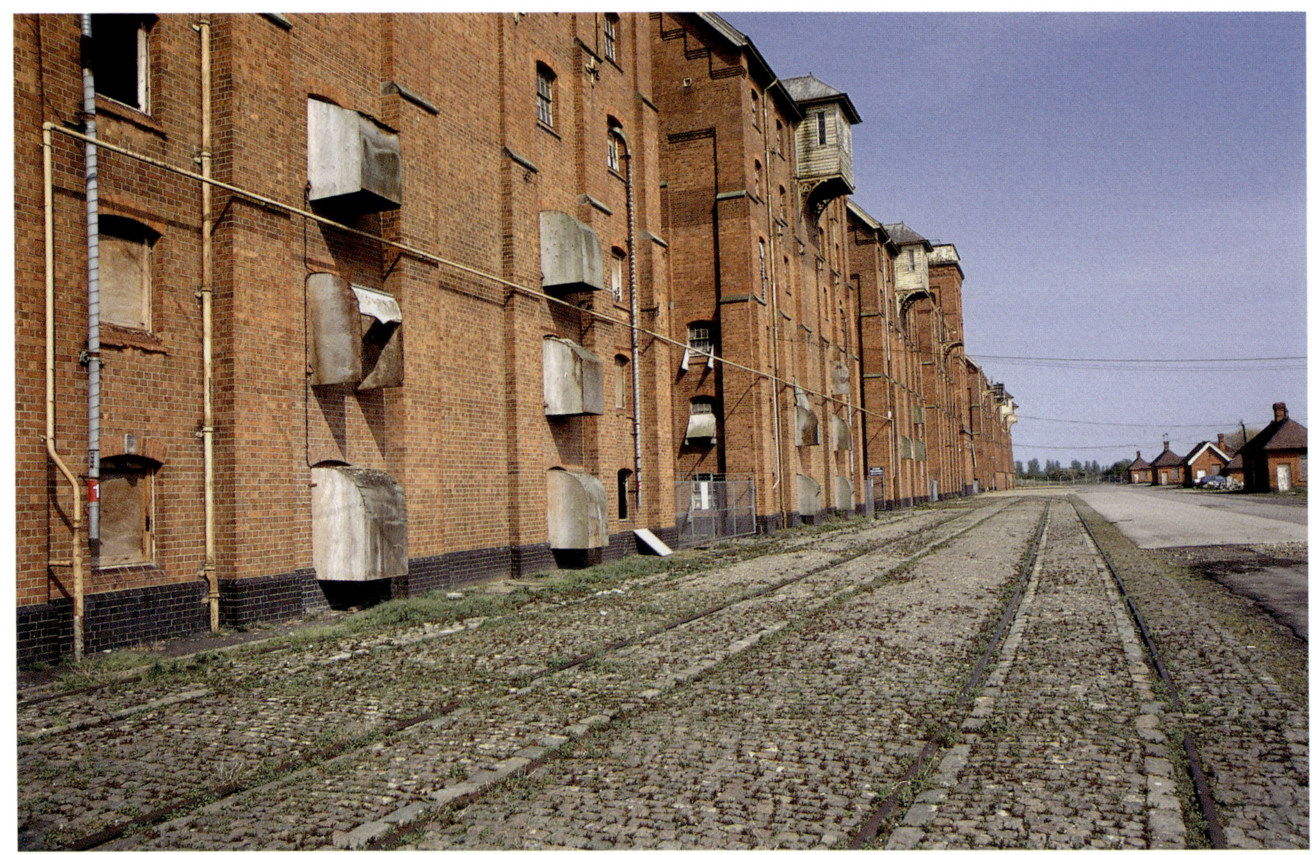

The Maltings at Sleaford
This vast range of buildings dates from the very end of the nineteenth century, but within less
than a hundred years they had become obsolete. The railway lines which once brought
in huge quantities of grain now lie unused among the granite cobbles.

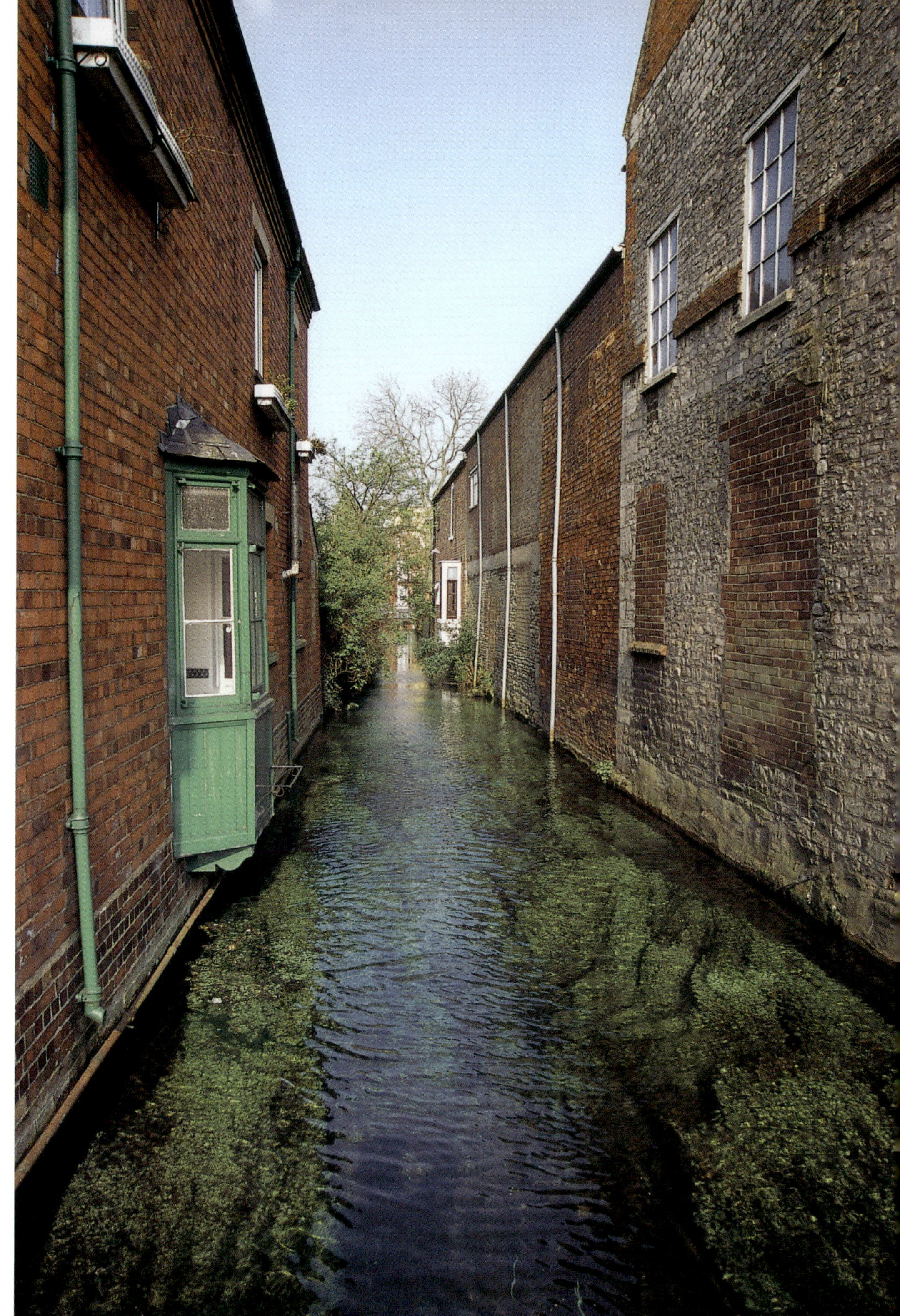

The River Slea
The town of Sleaford developed on
a crossing point on the River Slea.
Now the river flows quietly and
almost unnoticed through the
centre of the town.

Overleaf: **Lincoln Red cattle
at Harrington Hall**
A herd of Lincoln Red cattle graze
contently in the parkland around
Harrington Hall. Lincoln Reds are
a distinctive deep red-brown colour
and they are much prized as beef cattle.

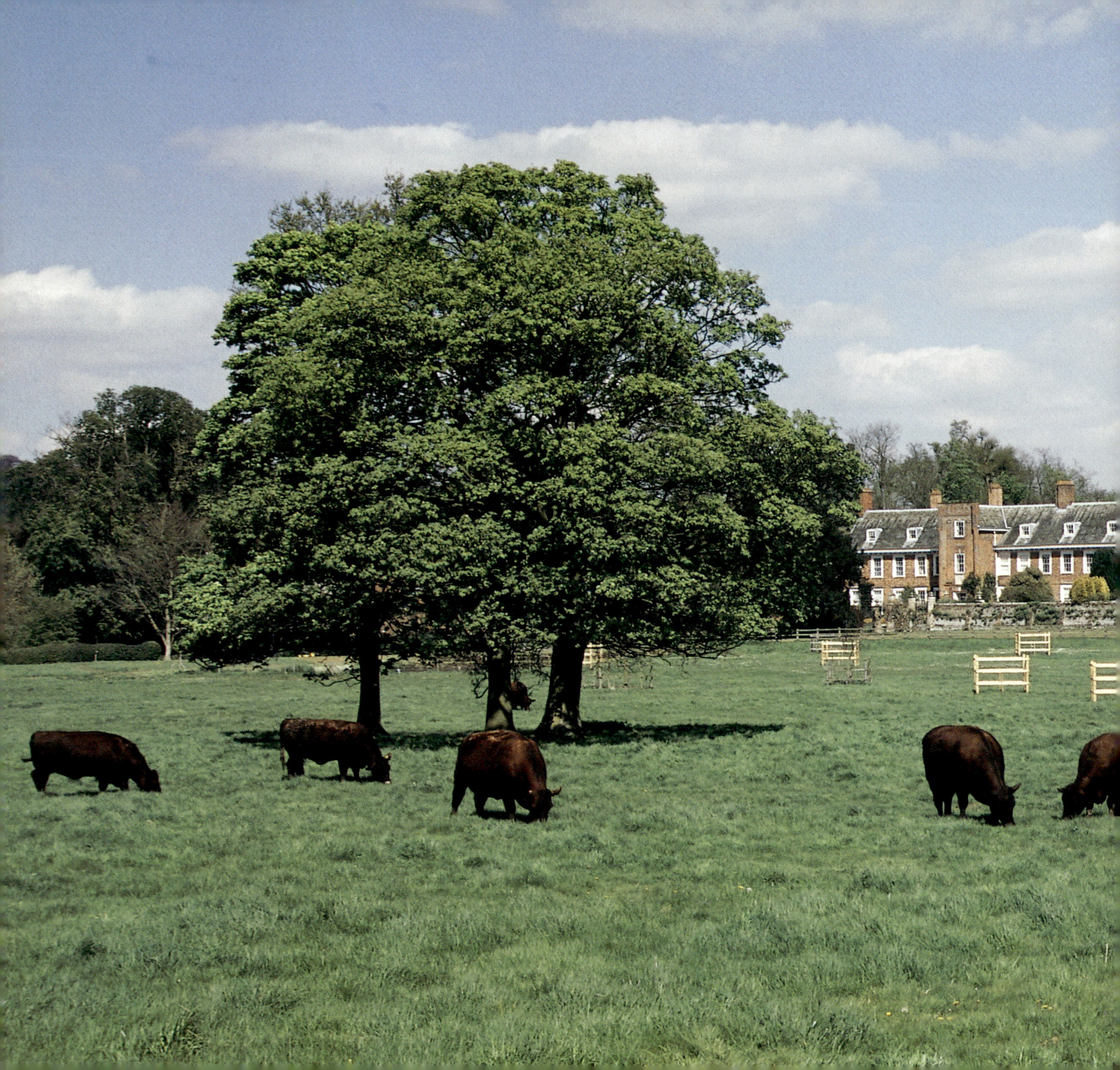

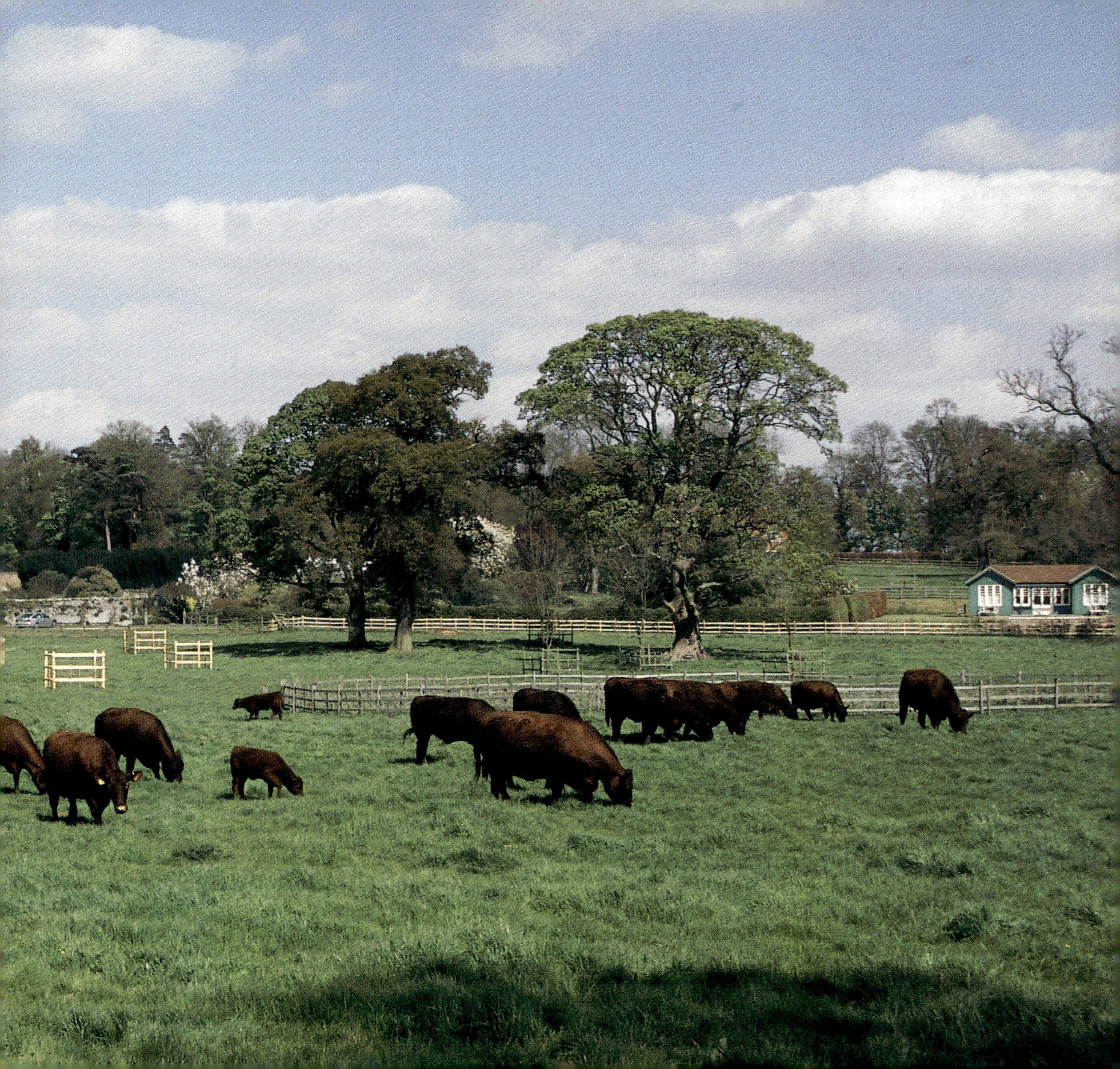

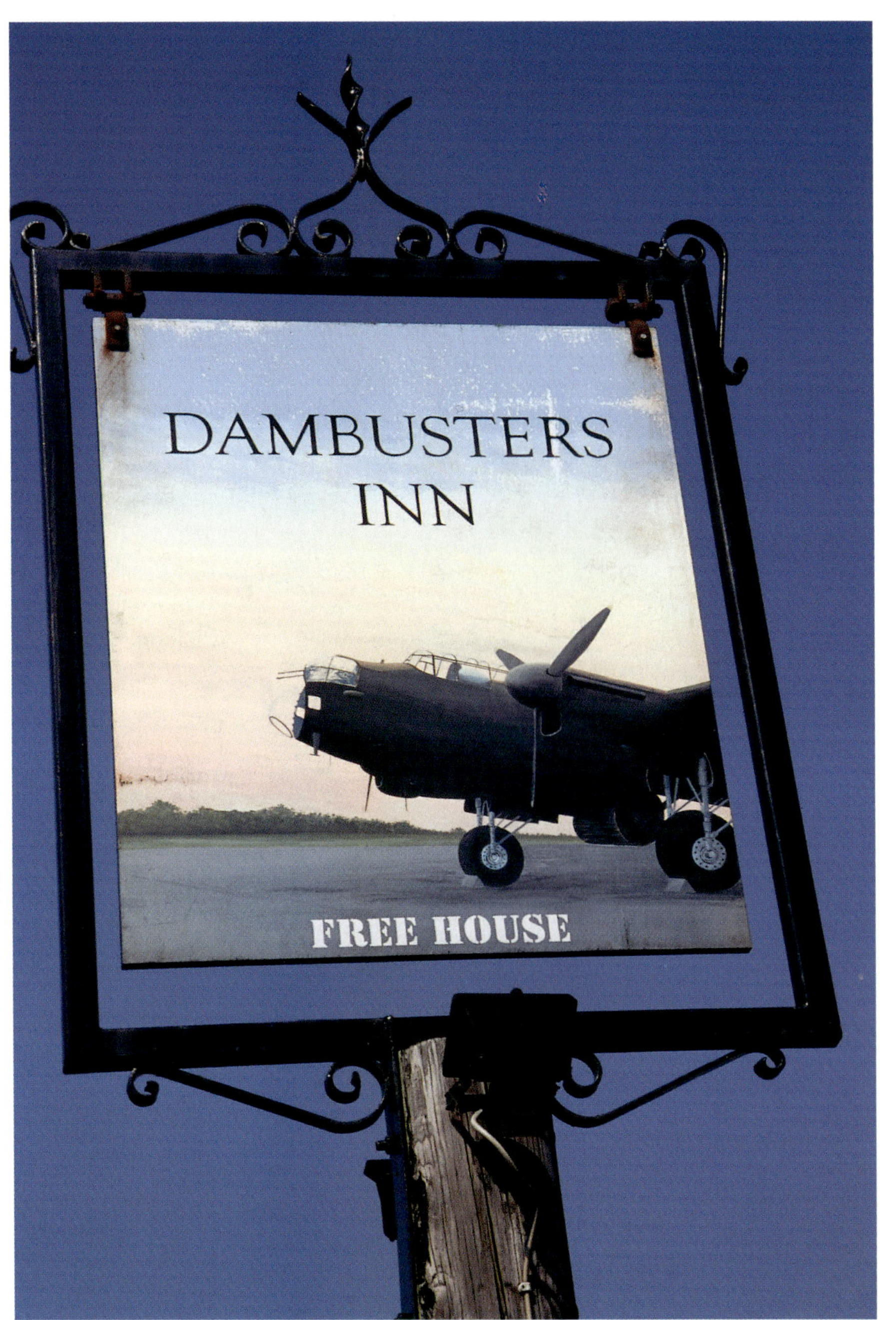

Dambuster pub sign
The public house at Scampton celebrates 617 Squadron of the RAF, which flew the famous 'Dambuster' raids against the dams of the Ruhr in 1943, while based at the nearby airfield.

Opposite: **Evening light at Hemswell Cliff**
During the Second World War, Lincolnshire became home to 46 RAF and USAAF airfields – which earned it the name of the 'Bomber County'. Disused airfields with their miles of runways and perimeter tracks are still a feature of the Lincolnshire landscape, and here at Hemswell Cliff the sun sets beyond the concrete runways.

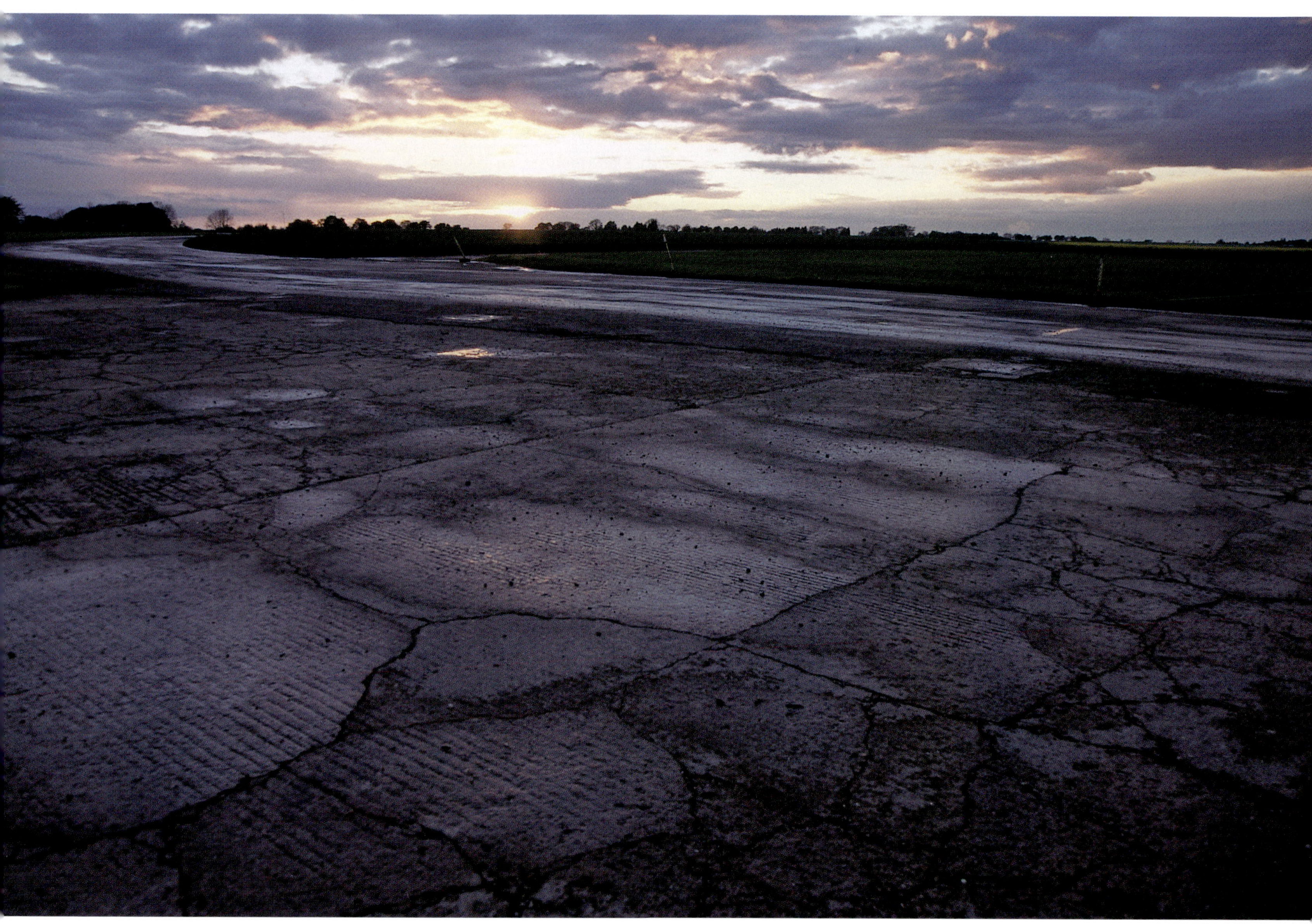

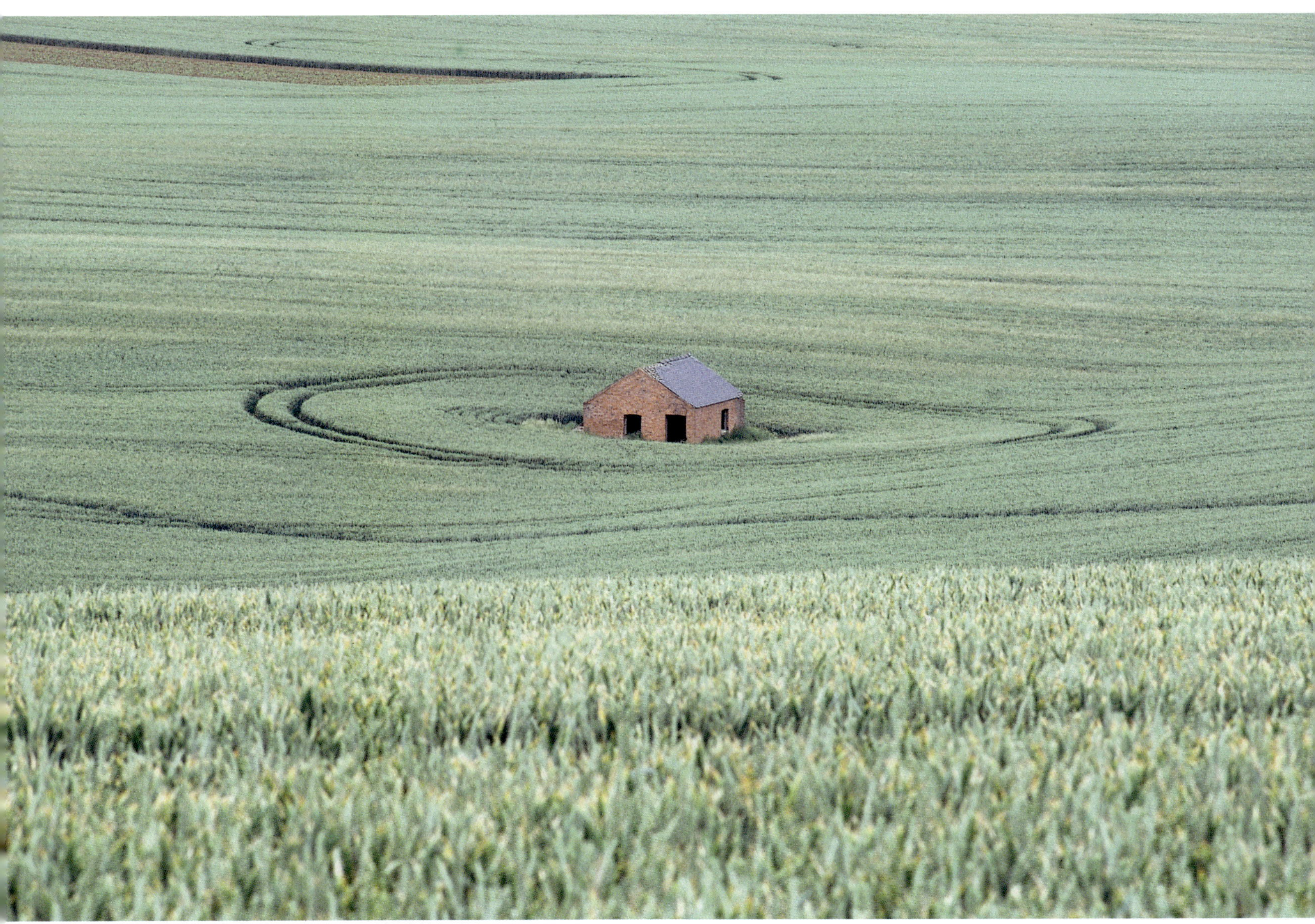

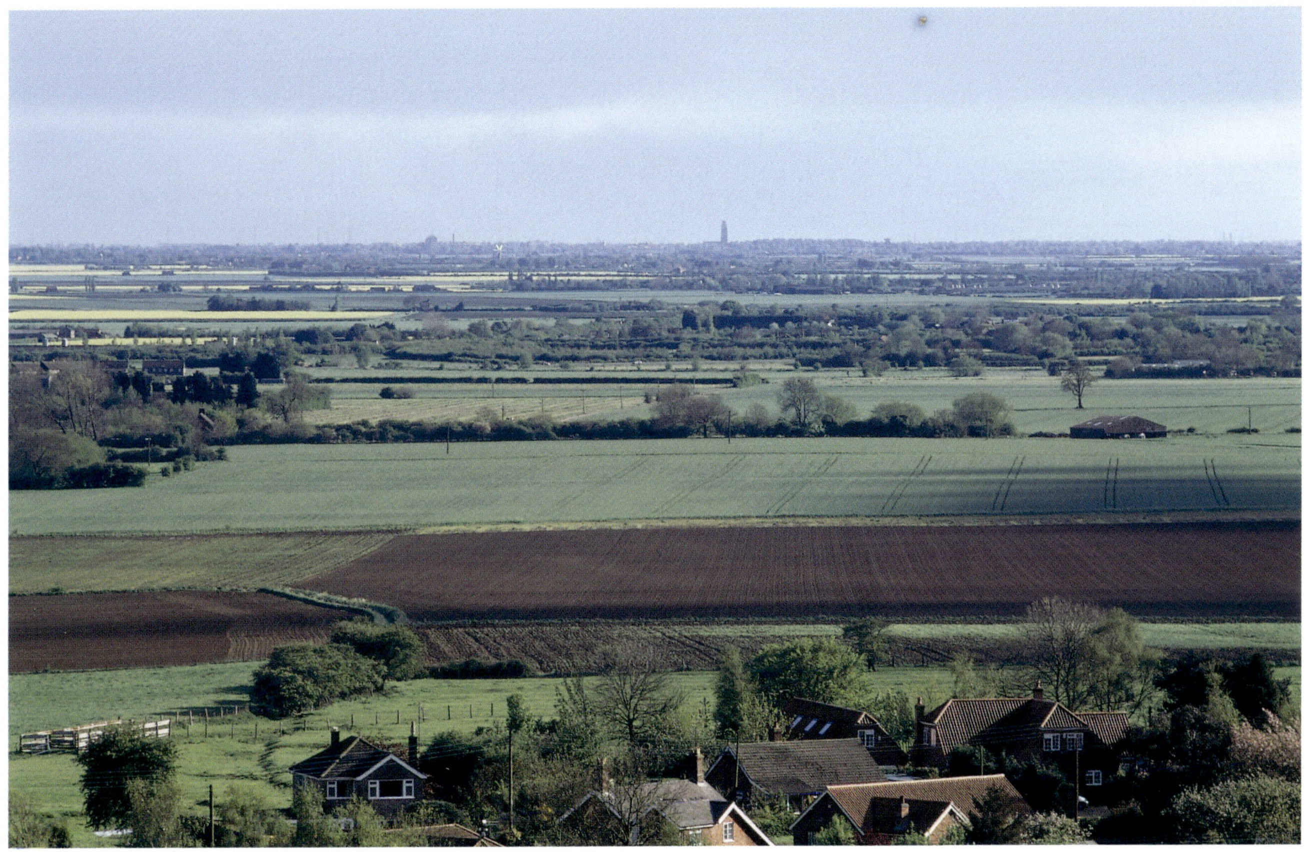

View from West Keal
This is the amazing view from the churchyard at West Keal, standing on the southern edge of the Wolds and looking across the vast expanse of East Fen towards Boston, with its tall church tower known as the 'Stump'.

Opposite: **Shed in a field near Brinkhill**
A small brick shed stands alone in a sea of winter corn, encircled by tramlines.
These are created to give access for agricultural machinery in the growing crop.

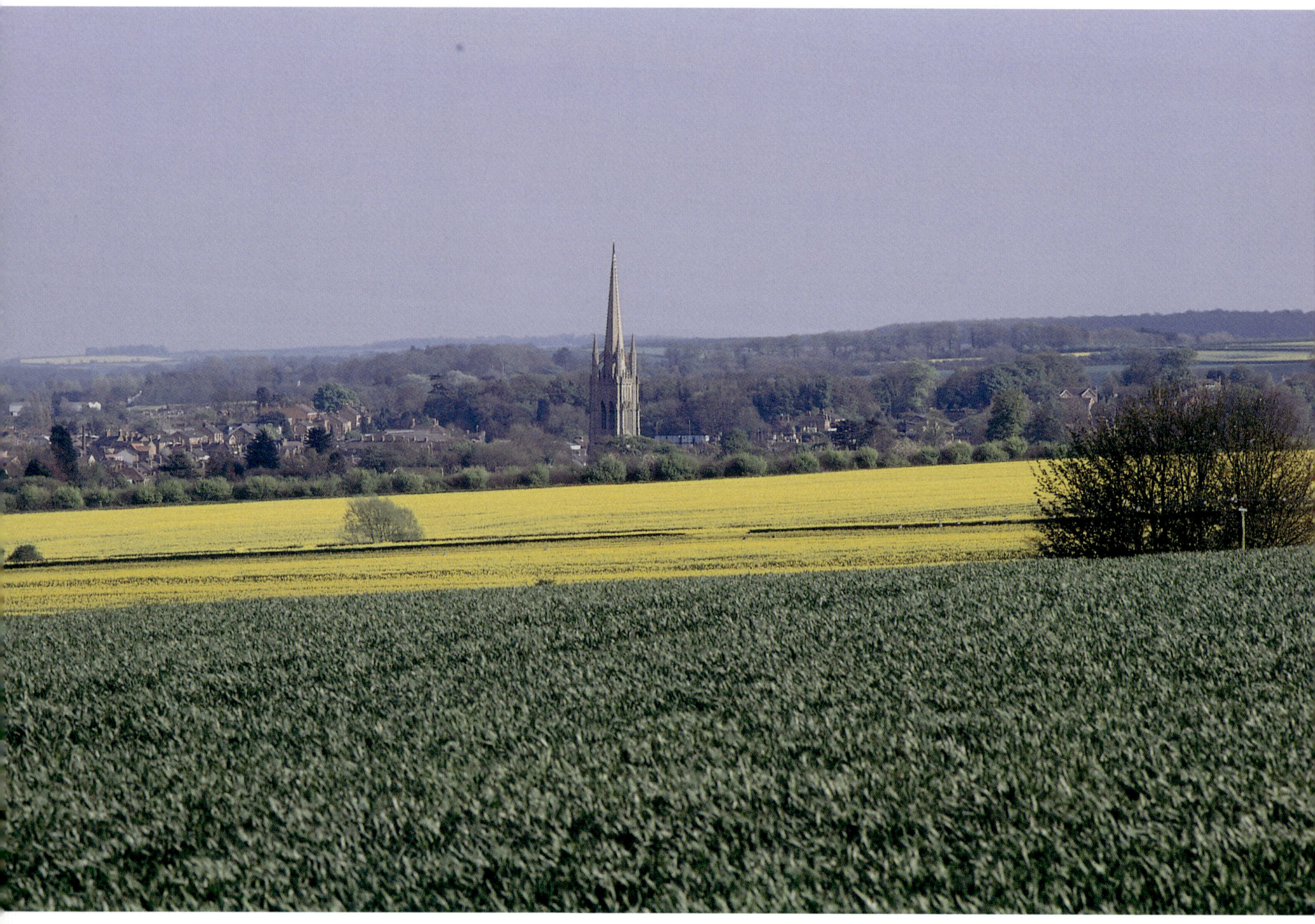

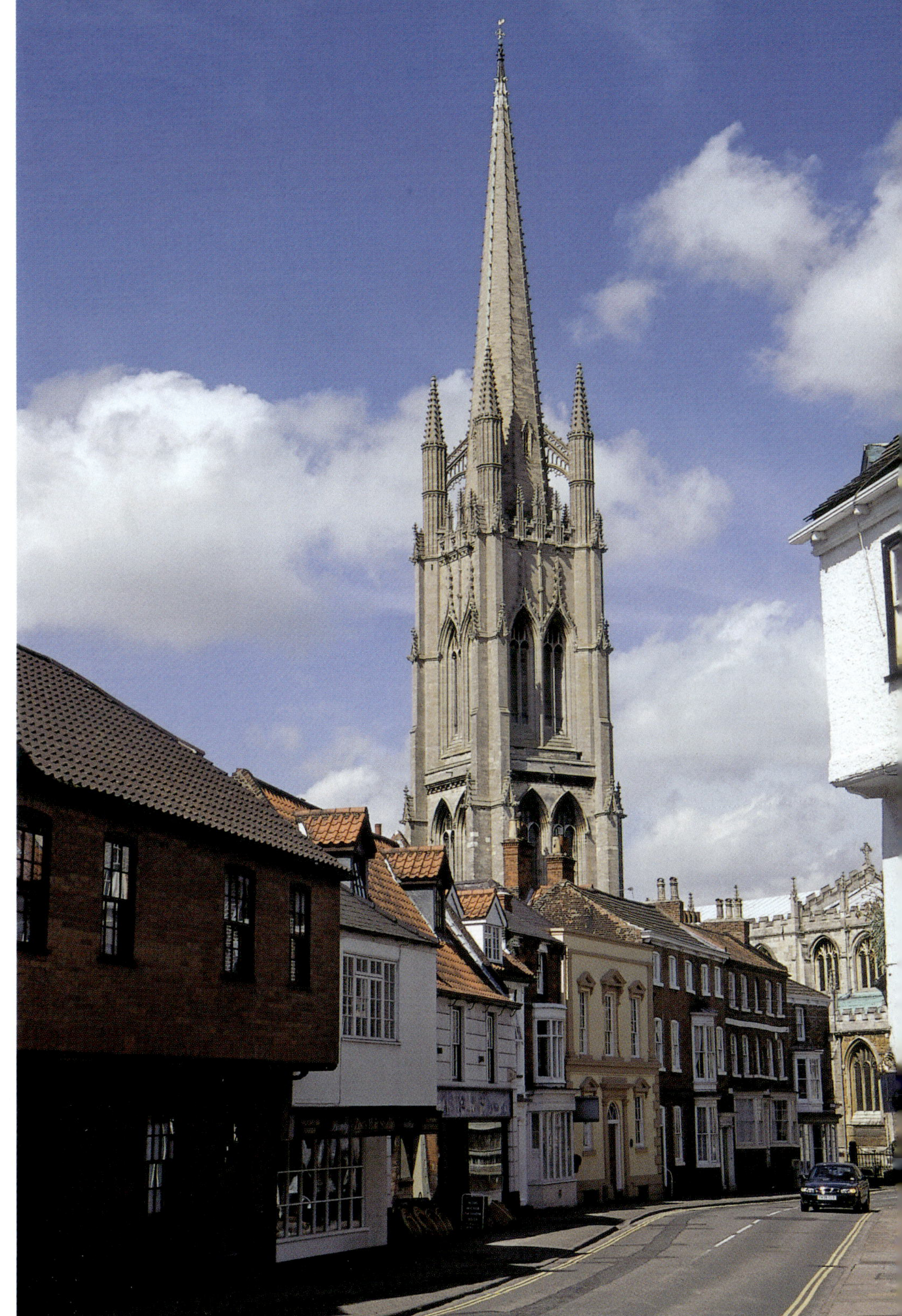

Opposite: **View of Louth from the Wolds**
The tall spire of the medieval church in Louth is a prominent feature in the surrounding landscape.

Louth church
Another view of the magnificent spire of St James's church, which rises above the elegant Georgian buildings in the market town of Louth.

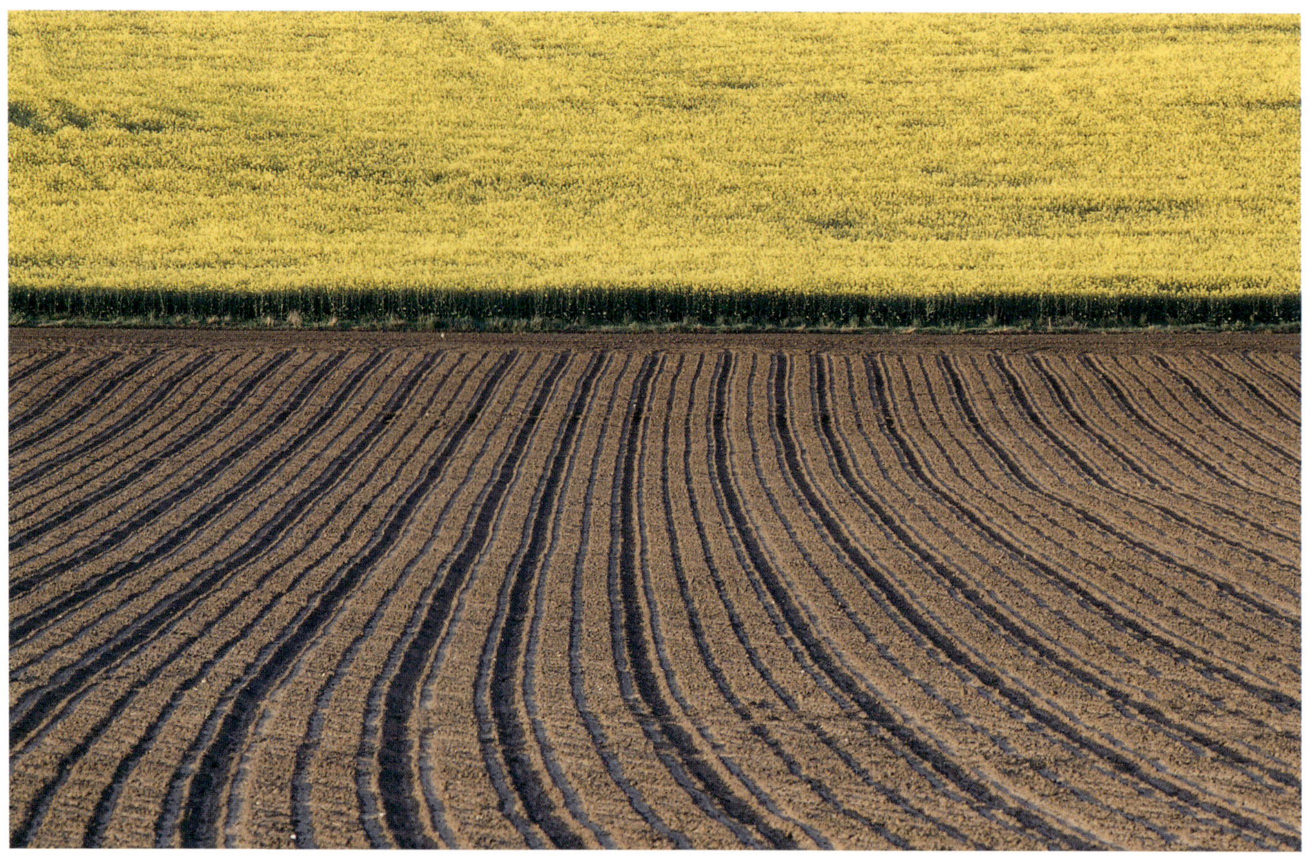

Oilseed rape and drilled sugar beet near Clixby
By the end of April, oilseed rape is in flower and here the bright yellow flowers
contrast with the brown soil and newly-drilled rows of sugar beet.

Opposite: **Footpath near Rigsby**
The footpath to Haugh crosses a field of oilseed rape under blue skies.

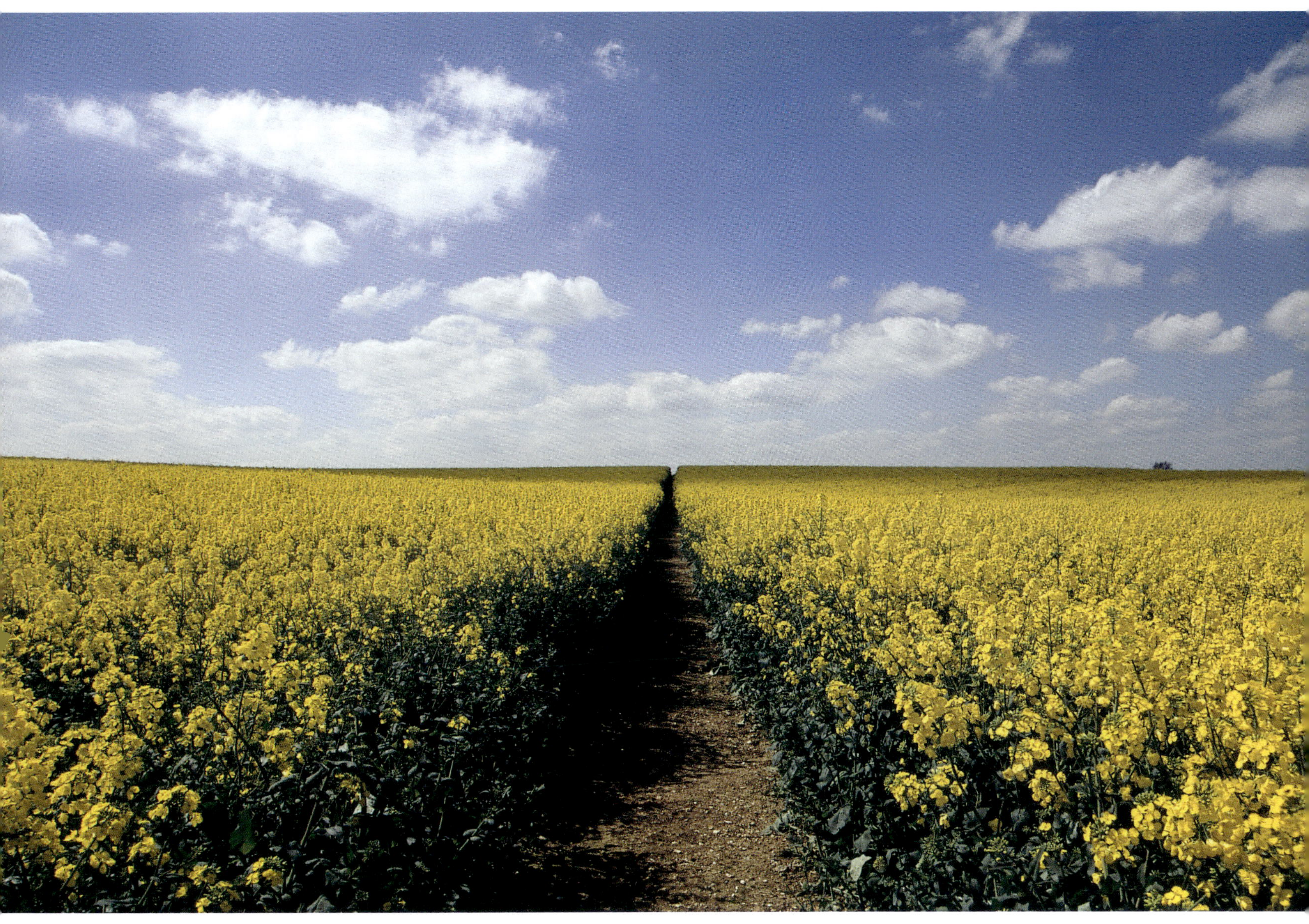

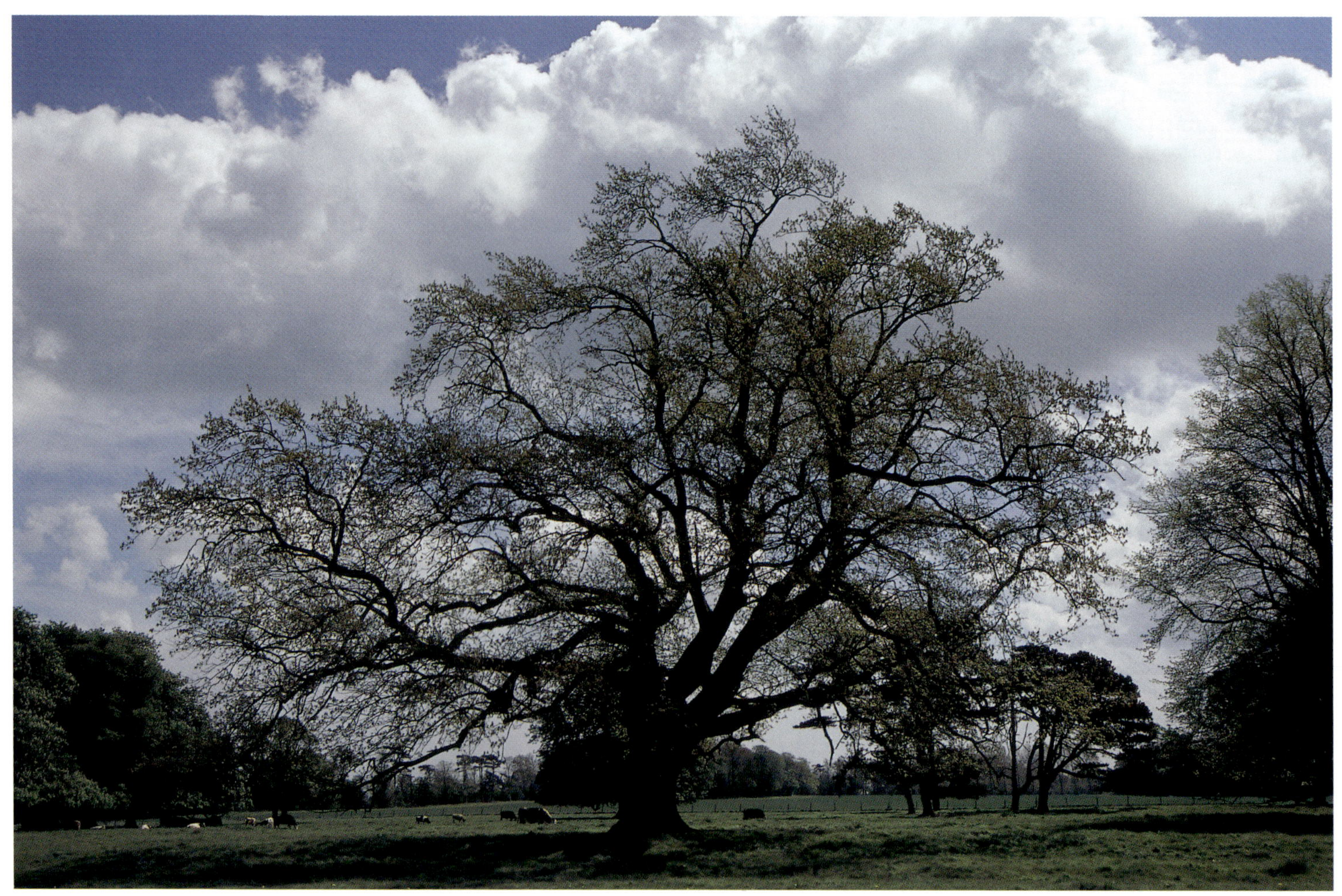

A majestic oak
Clouds gather as cattle graze beyond an ancient oak tree in parkland near Grainsby.

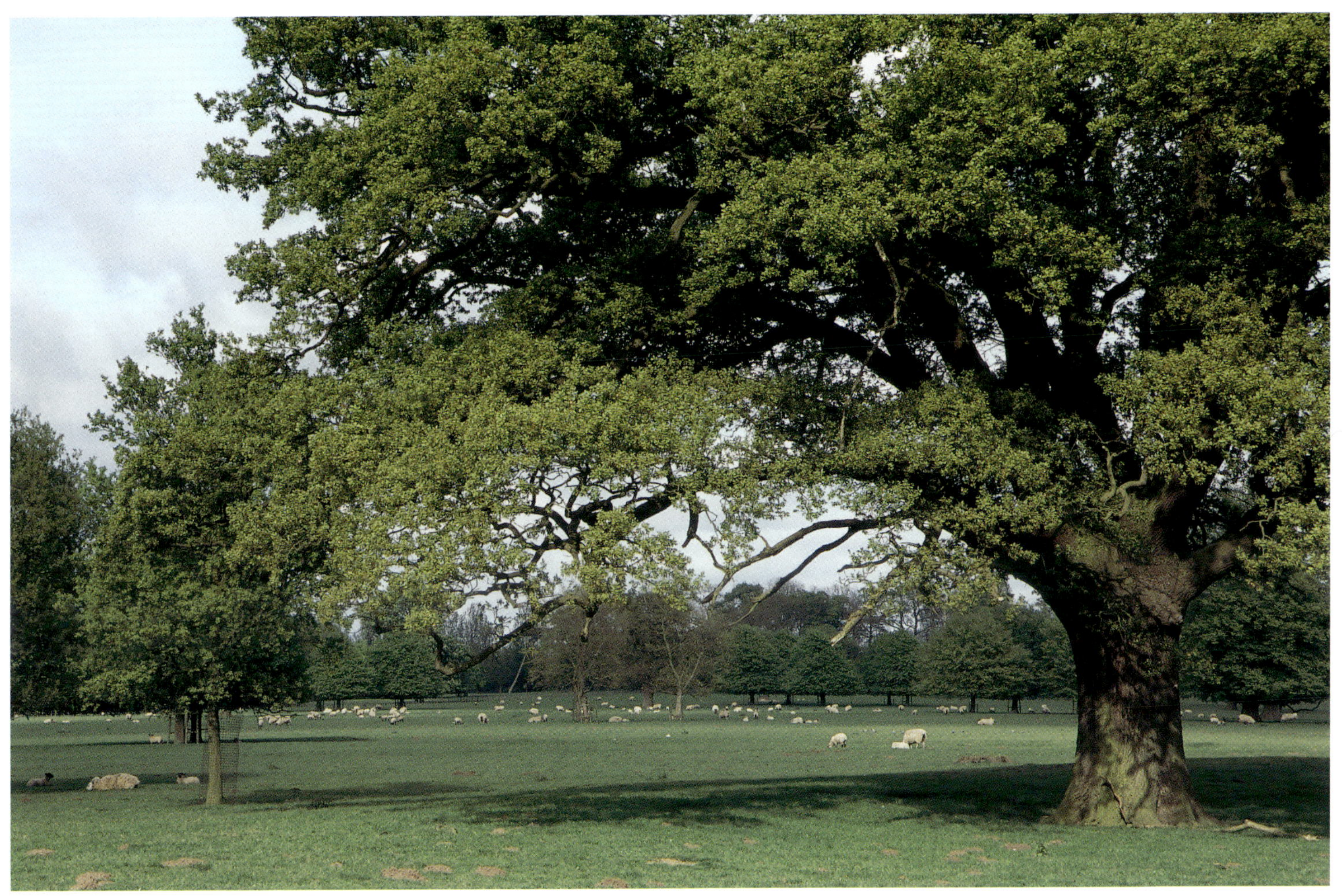

Parkland at Scrivelsby
A quiet scene of sheep grazing under the fresh green foliage of parkland trees is captured in soft evening light.

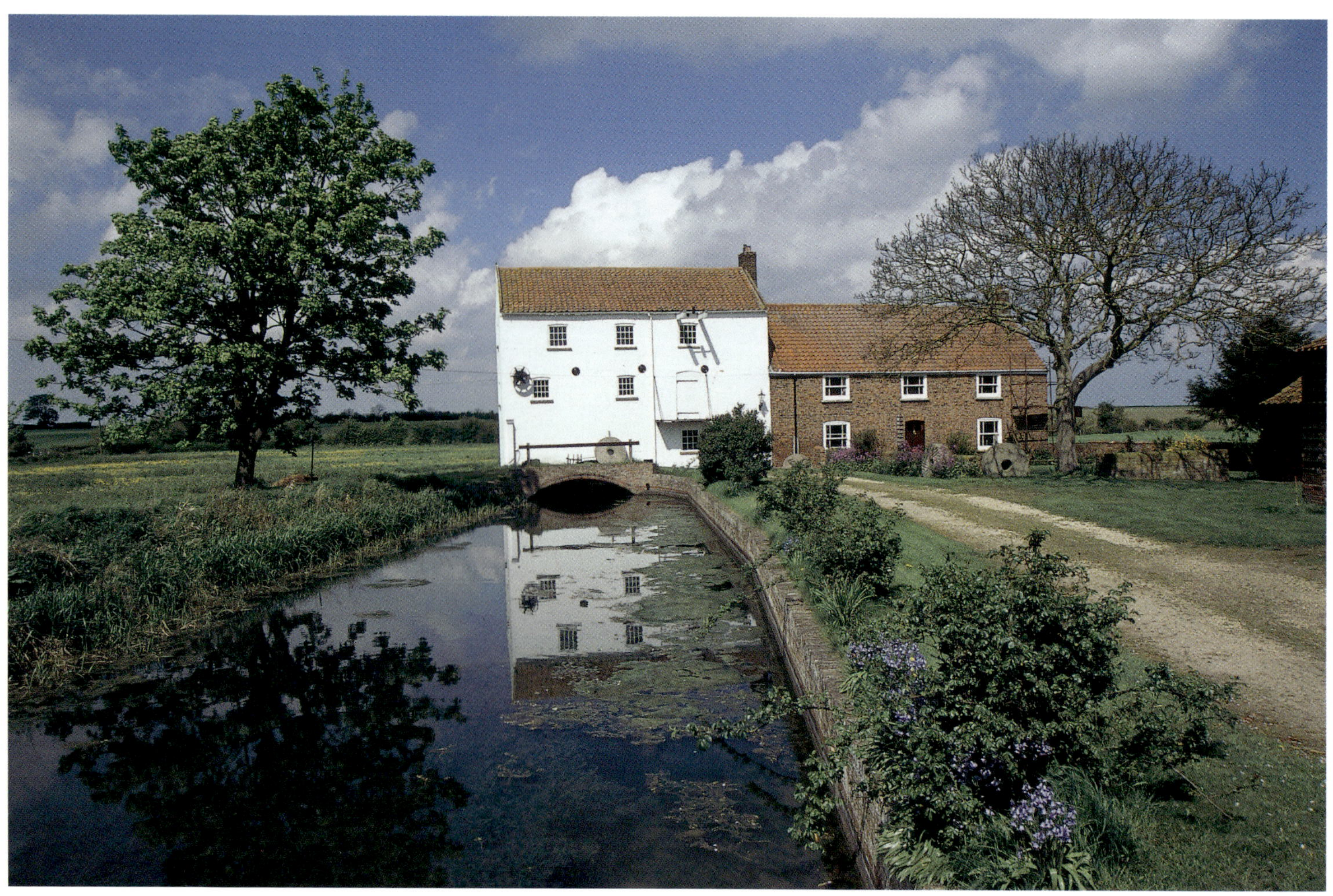

Alvingham watermill
The white-painted mill building is reflected in the clear water of the millrace.

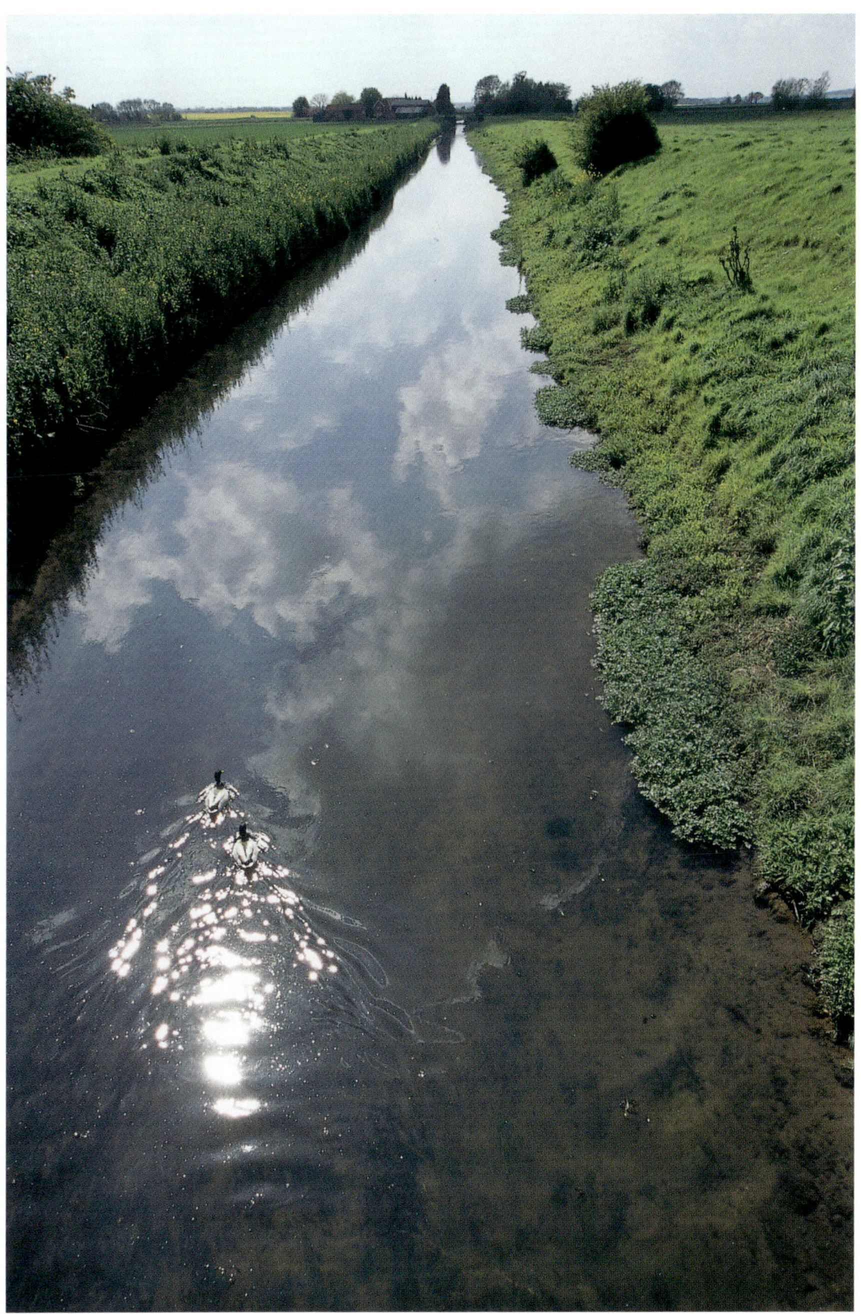

Louth canal near Alvingham
Ducks swim through the sun's reflection
in the disused canal which once linked
Louth to the sea.

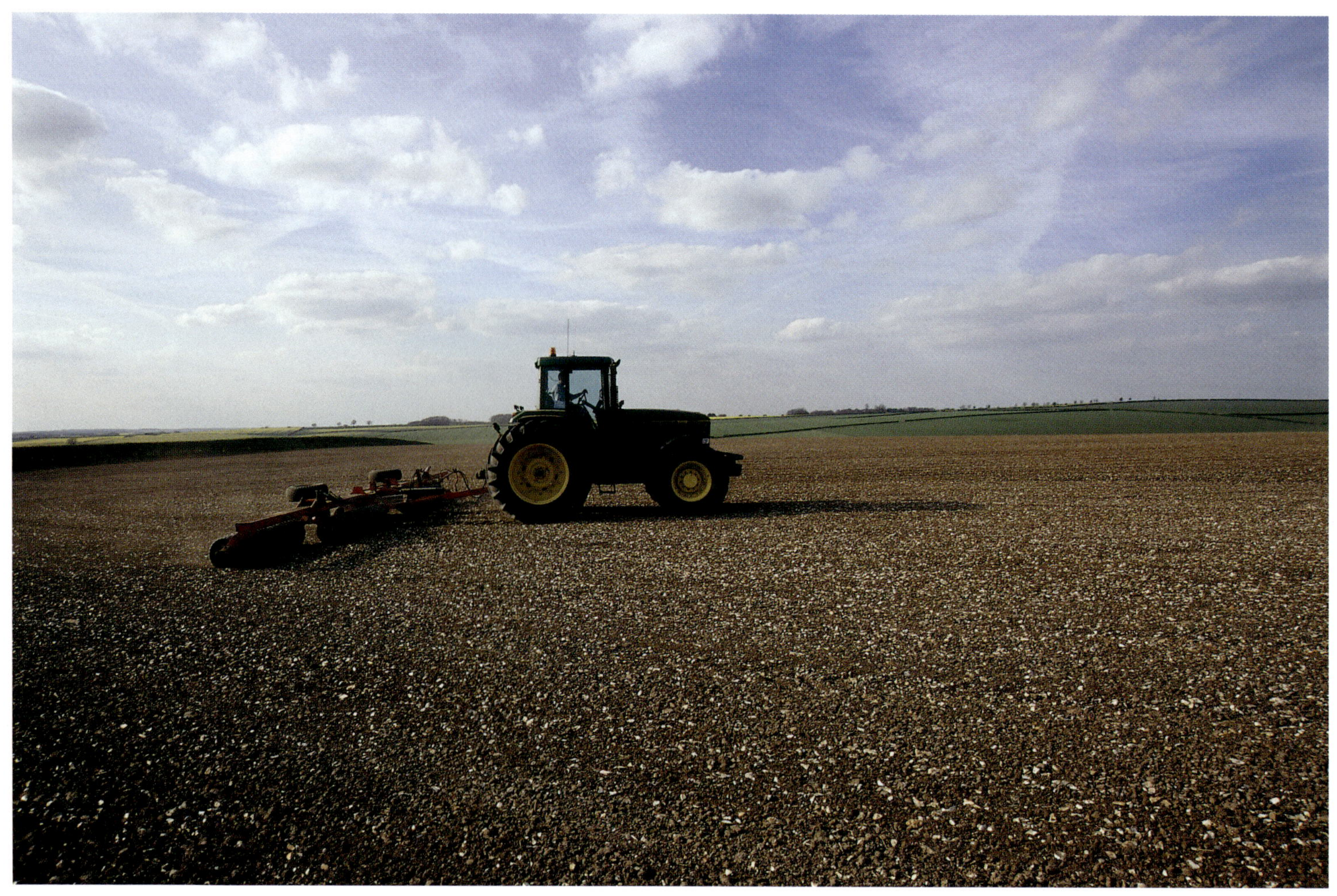

Tractor rolling near Binbrook
Rolling is almost complete on this recently-drilled cornfield, high up on top of the Wolds.

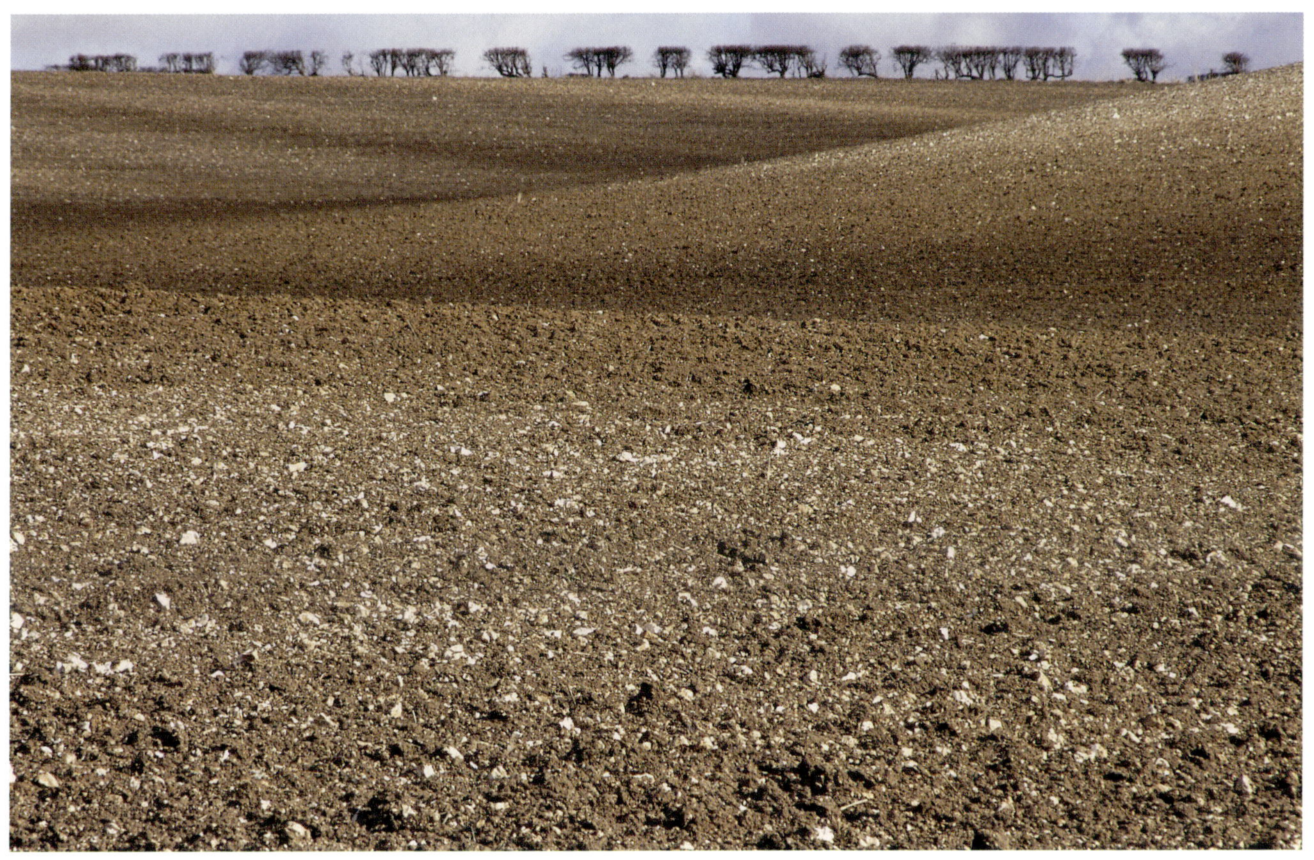

Chalky soils on the Wolds
The white chalk shows through the thin soils of the Lincolnshire Wolds.

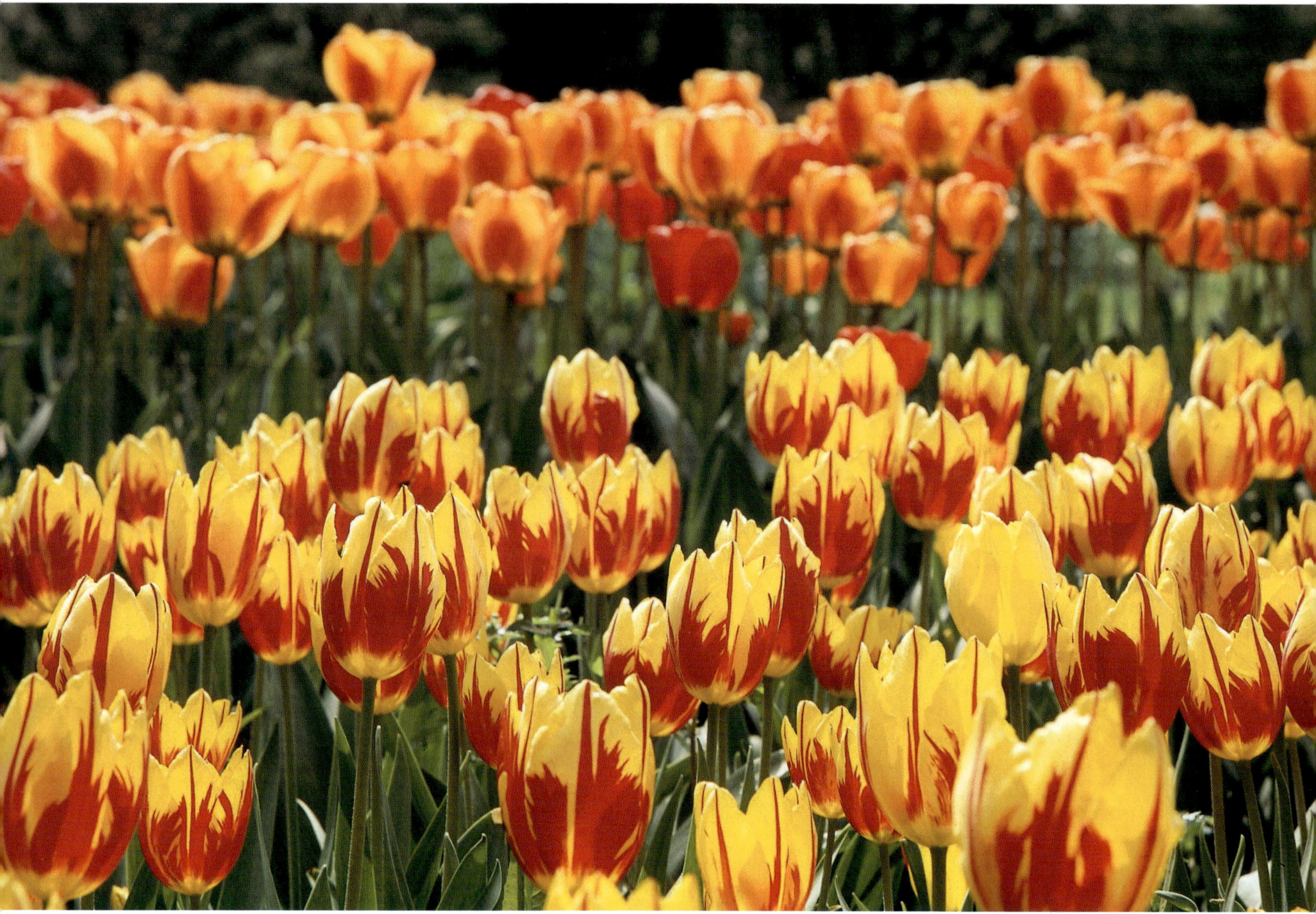

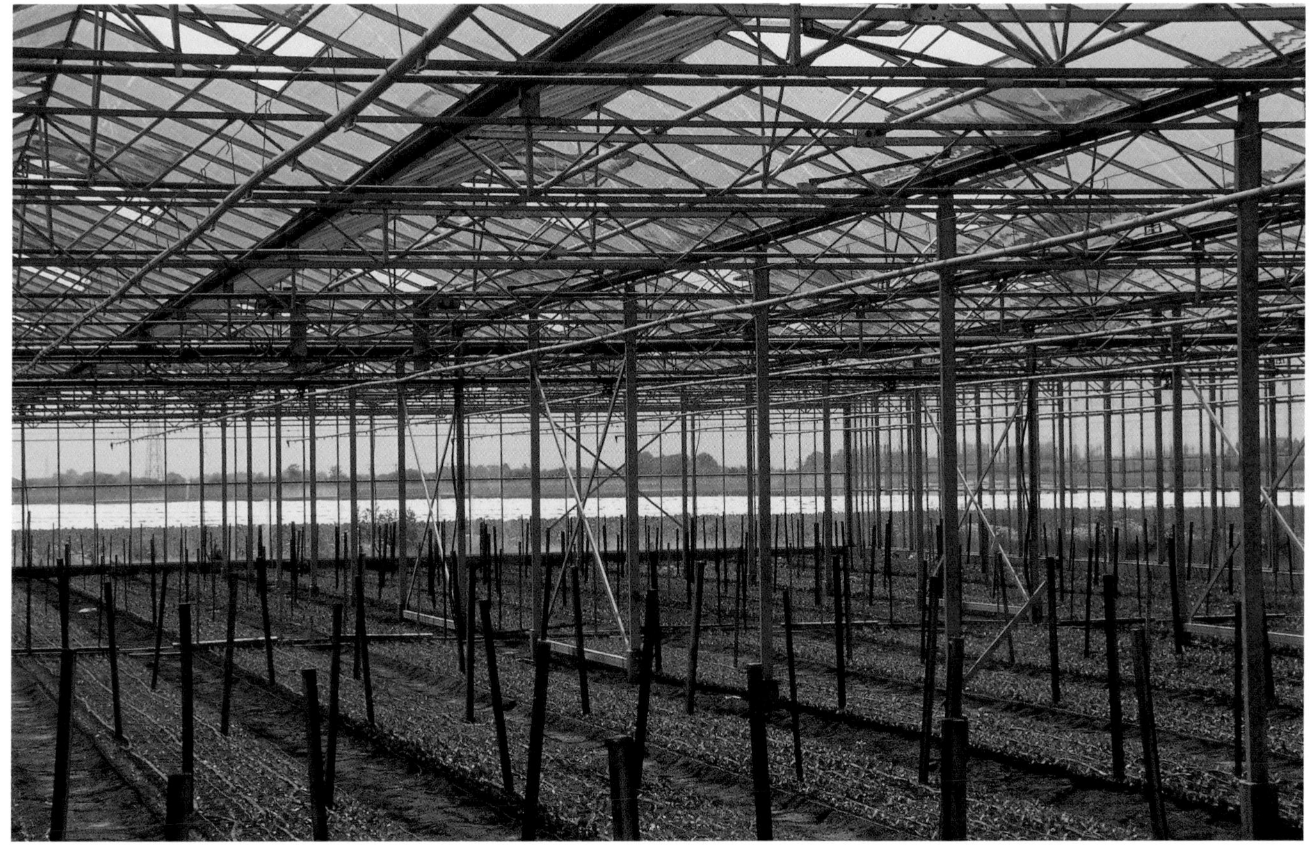

Greenhouse near Long Sutton
A variety of vegetable and flower plants are encouraged into early growth in the controlled
environment of the greenhouses which are found across the Fens.

Opposite: **Tulips**
Once grown in profusion in the Fens, tulips are now rarely seen beyond
display planting, like these at Springfields Gardens in Spalding.

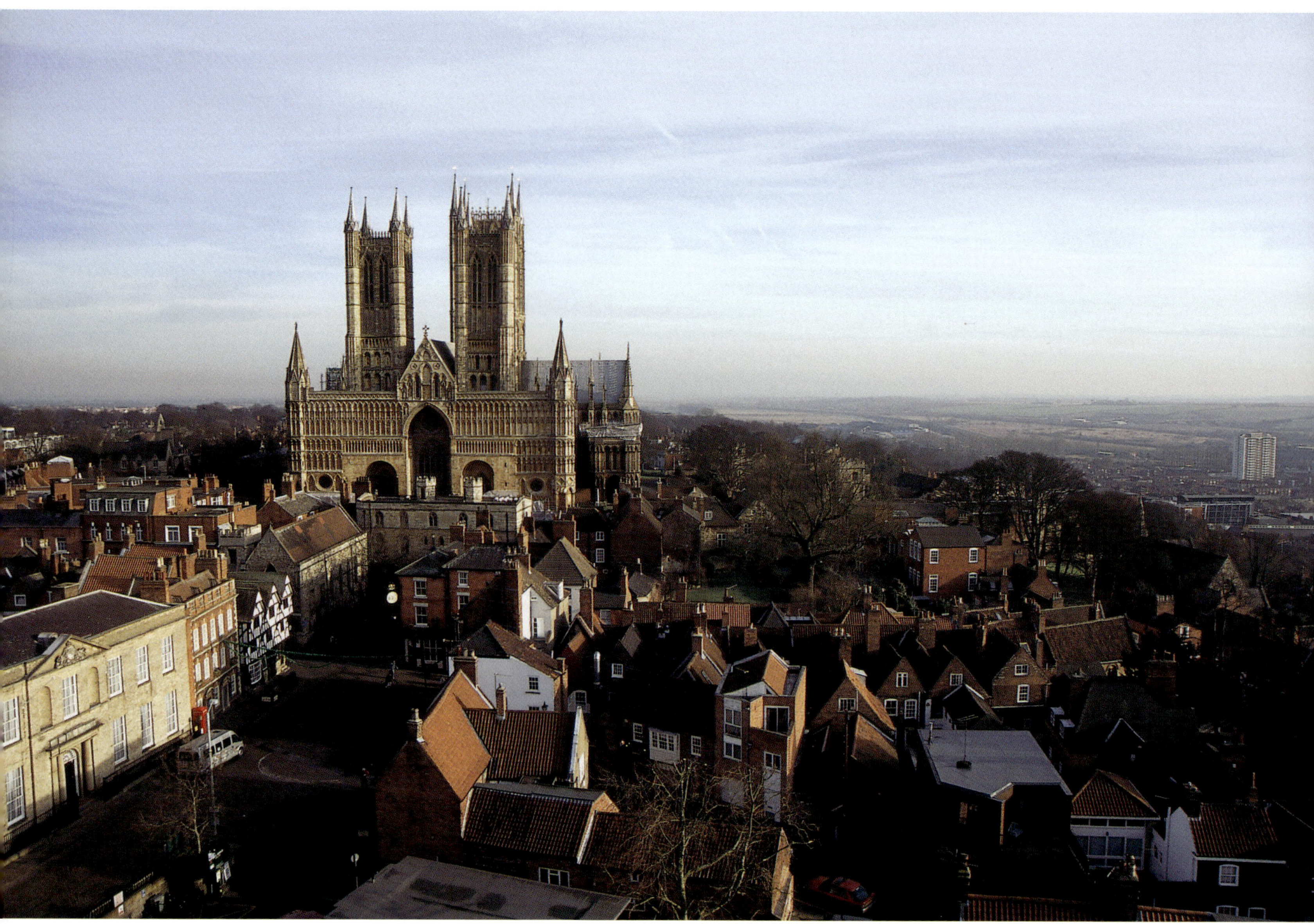

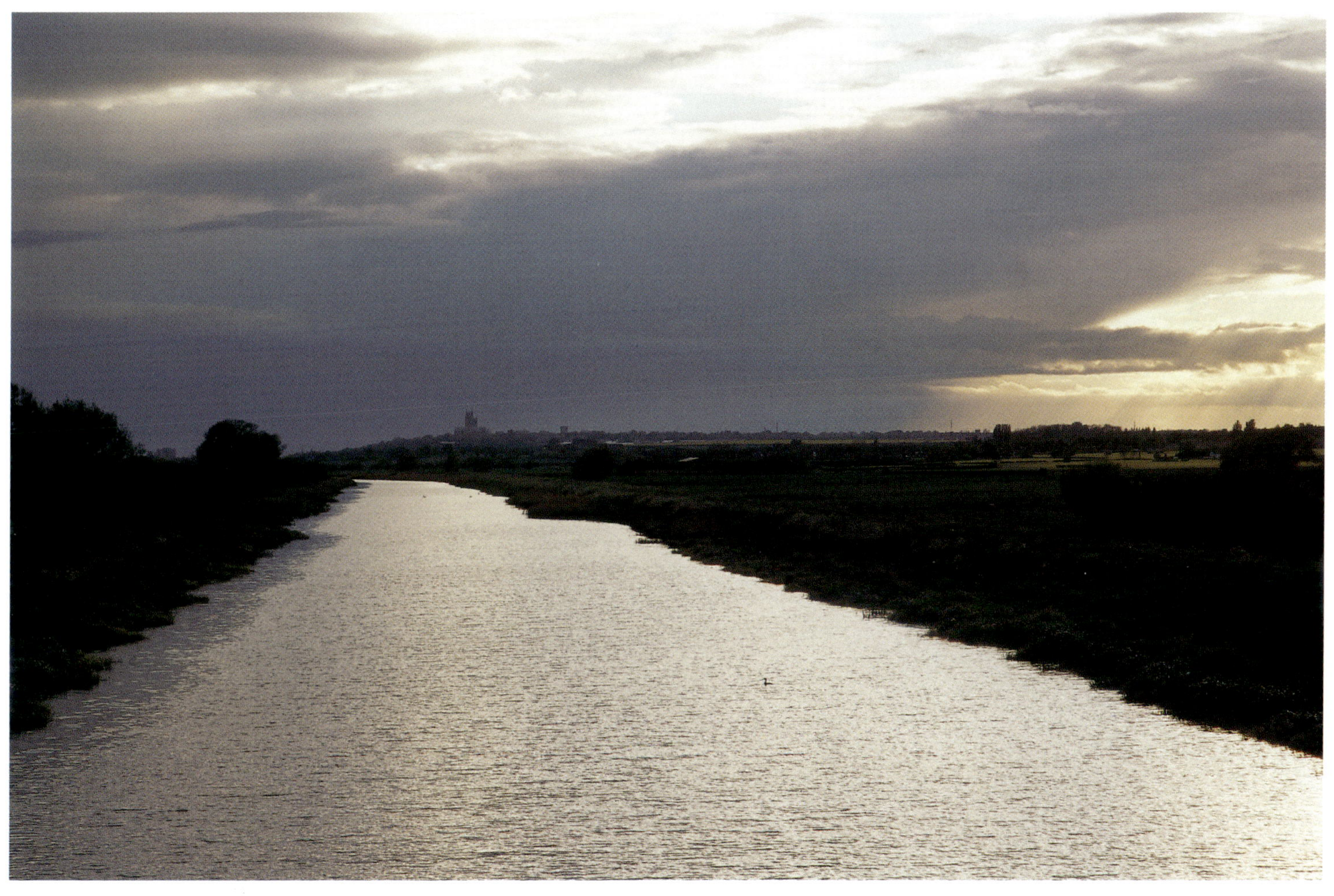

River Witham
Evening light reflects on the River Witham, with the unmistakeable outline of Lincoln Cathedral in the distance.

Opposite: **Lincoln Cathedral**
Viewed from the Observatory Tower at the castle, the magnificent medieval cathedral rises above the city.

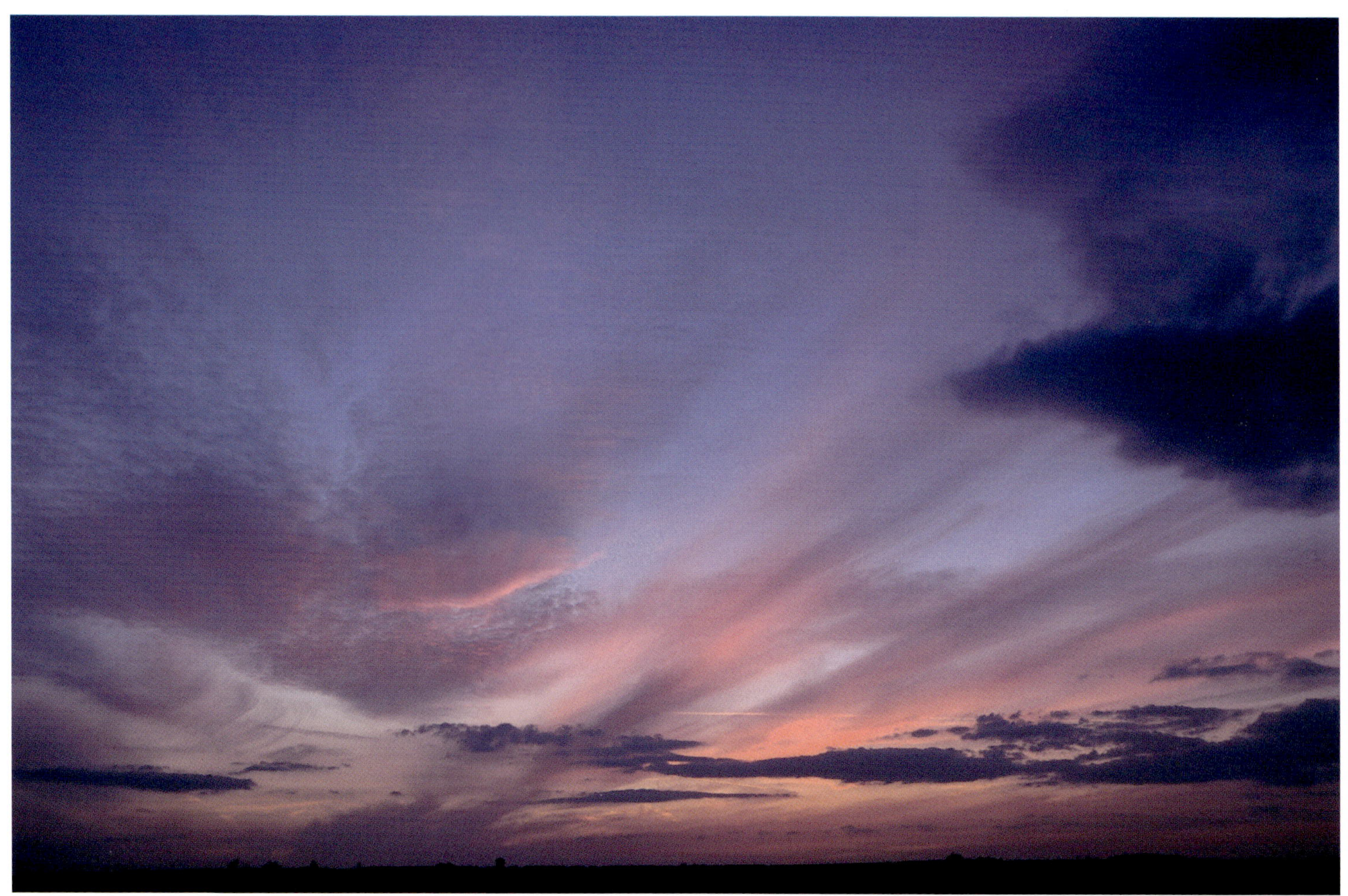

Evening sky
The sky is lit by pastel shades of mauve and pink as the sun sets beyond Elsham Hill.

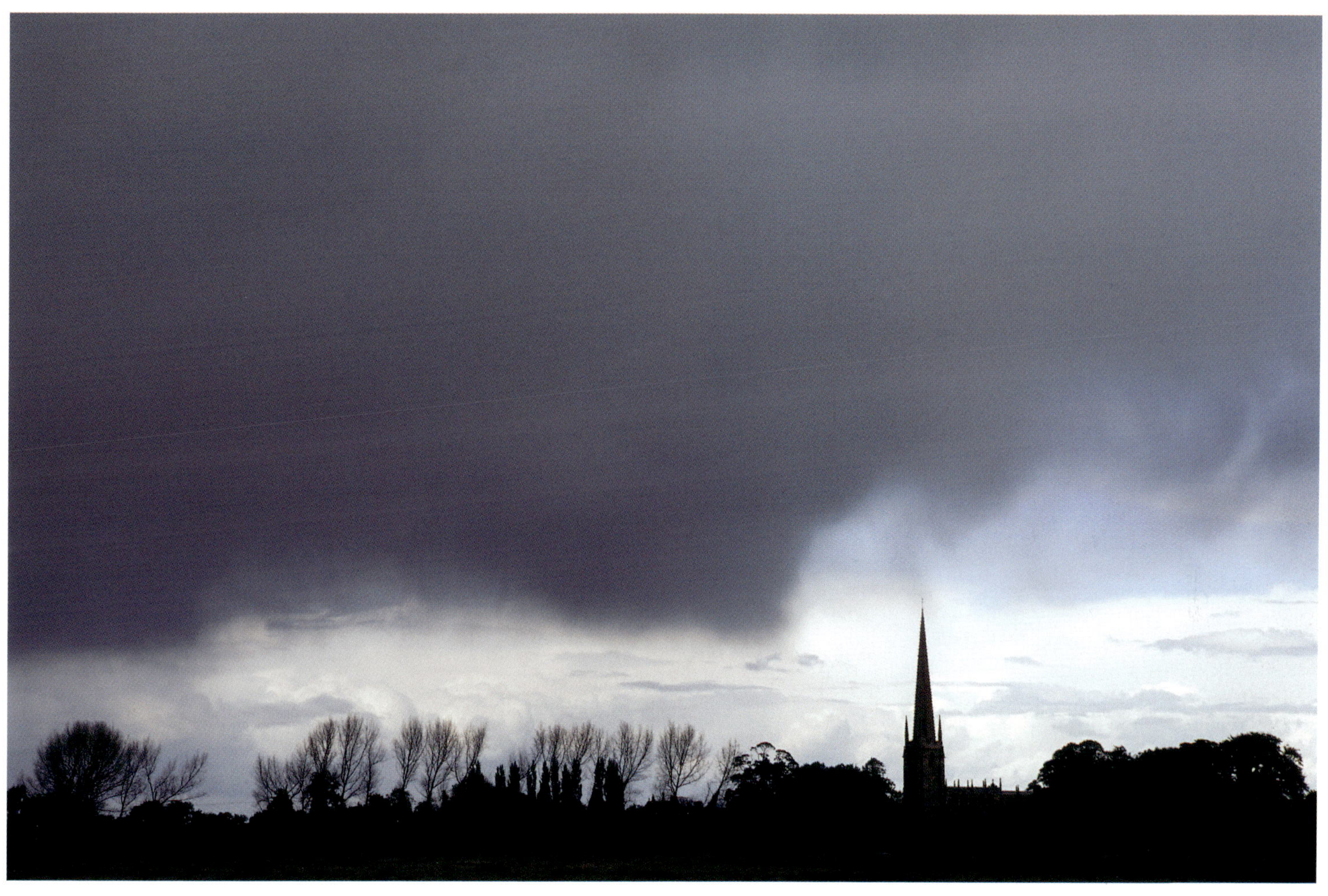

Brant Broughton church
Dark storm clouds gather over the slim spire of St Helen's church at Brant Broughton.

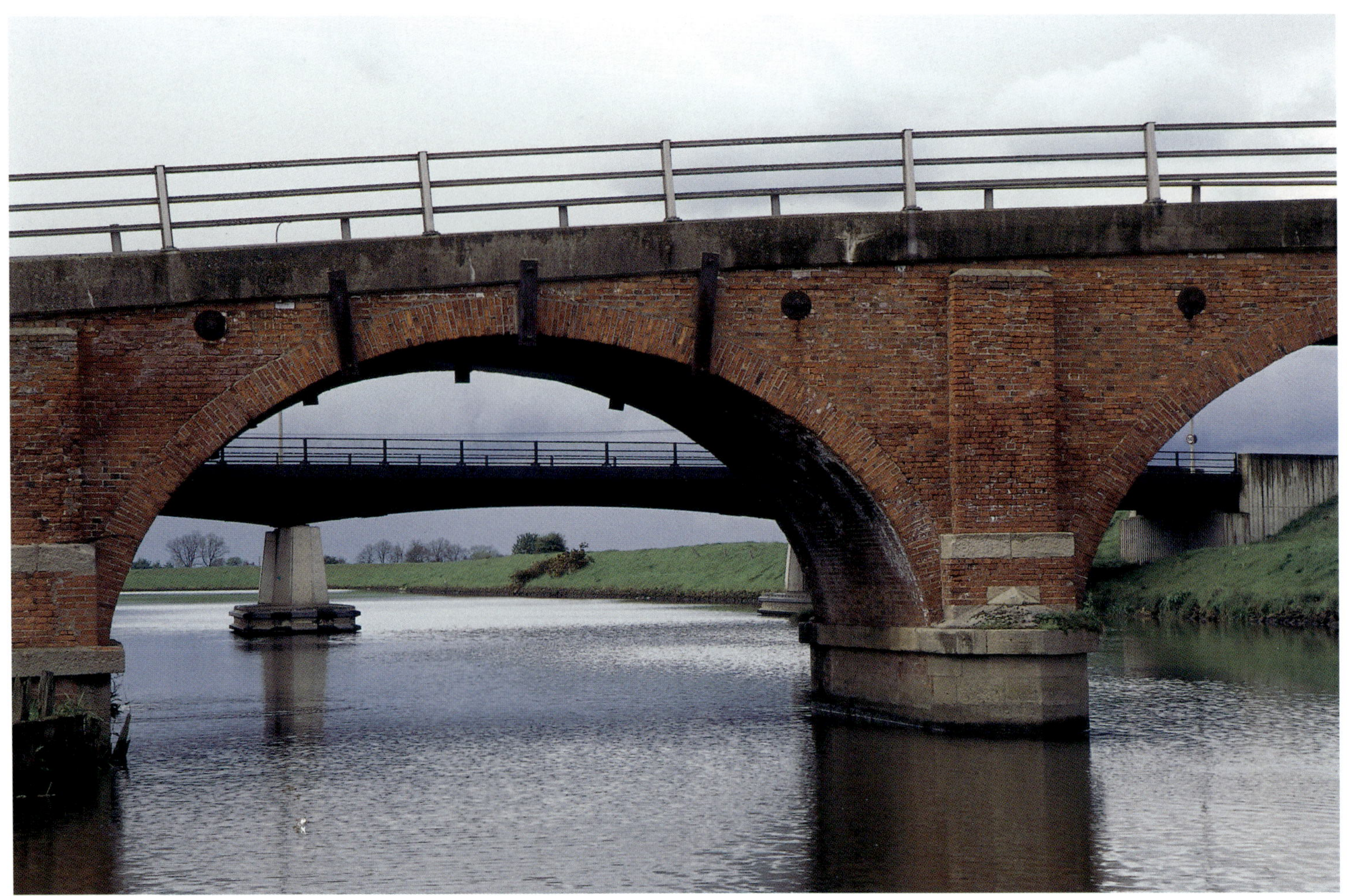

Tattershall bridges
The contrasting shapes of the old and new road bridges are reflected in the River Witham
as it flows through the village of Tattershall Bridge.

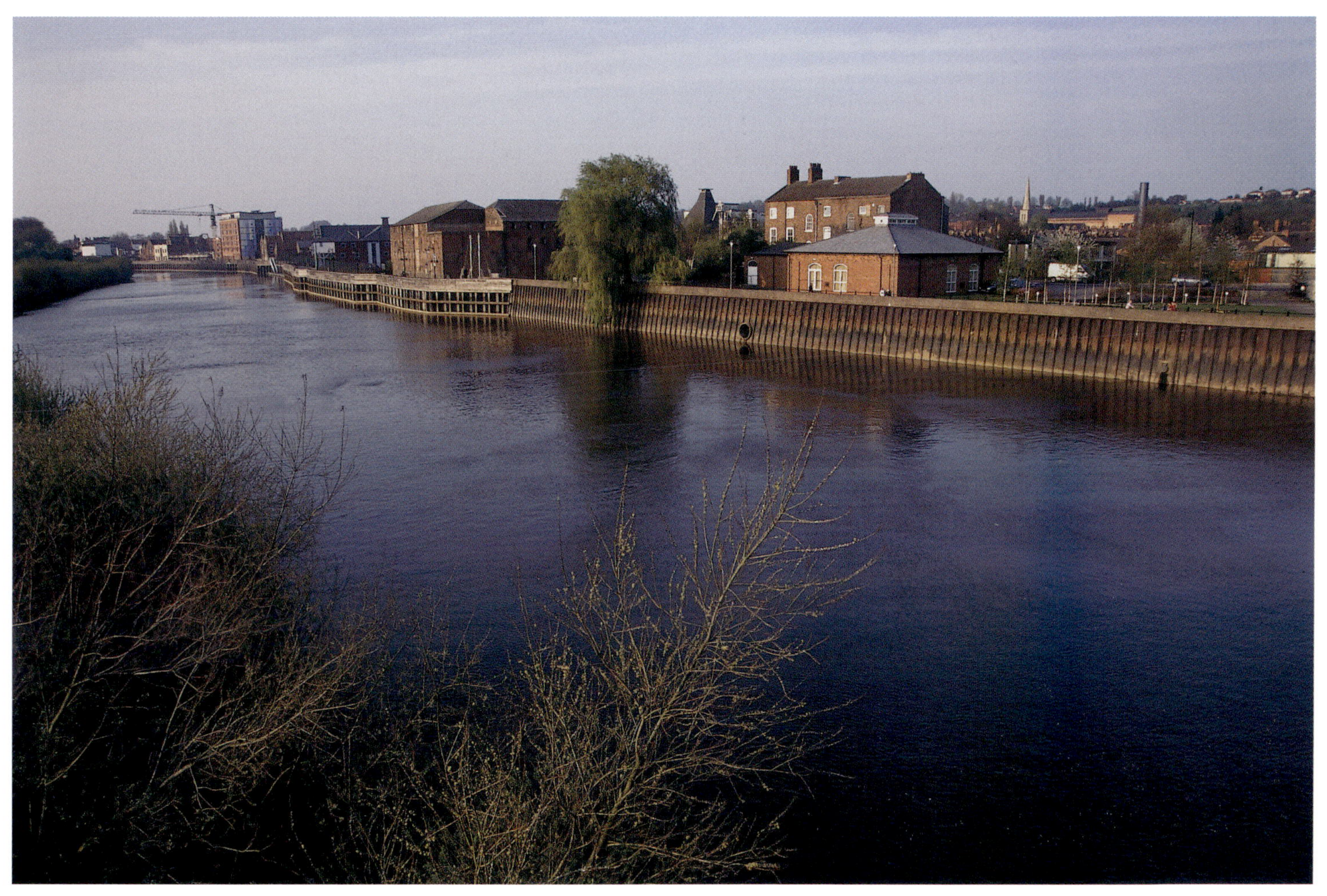

The River Trent at Gainsborough
Warm evening light catches the old warehouses and maltings along the eastern bank of the River Trent.

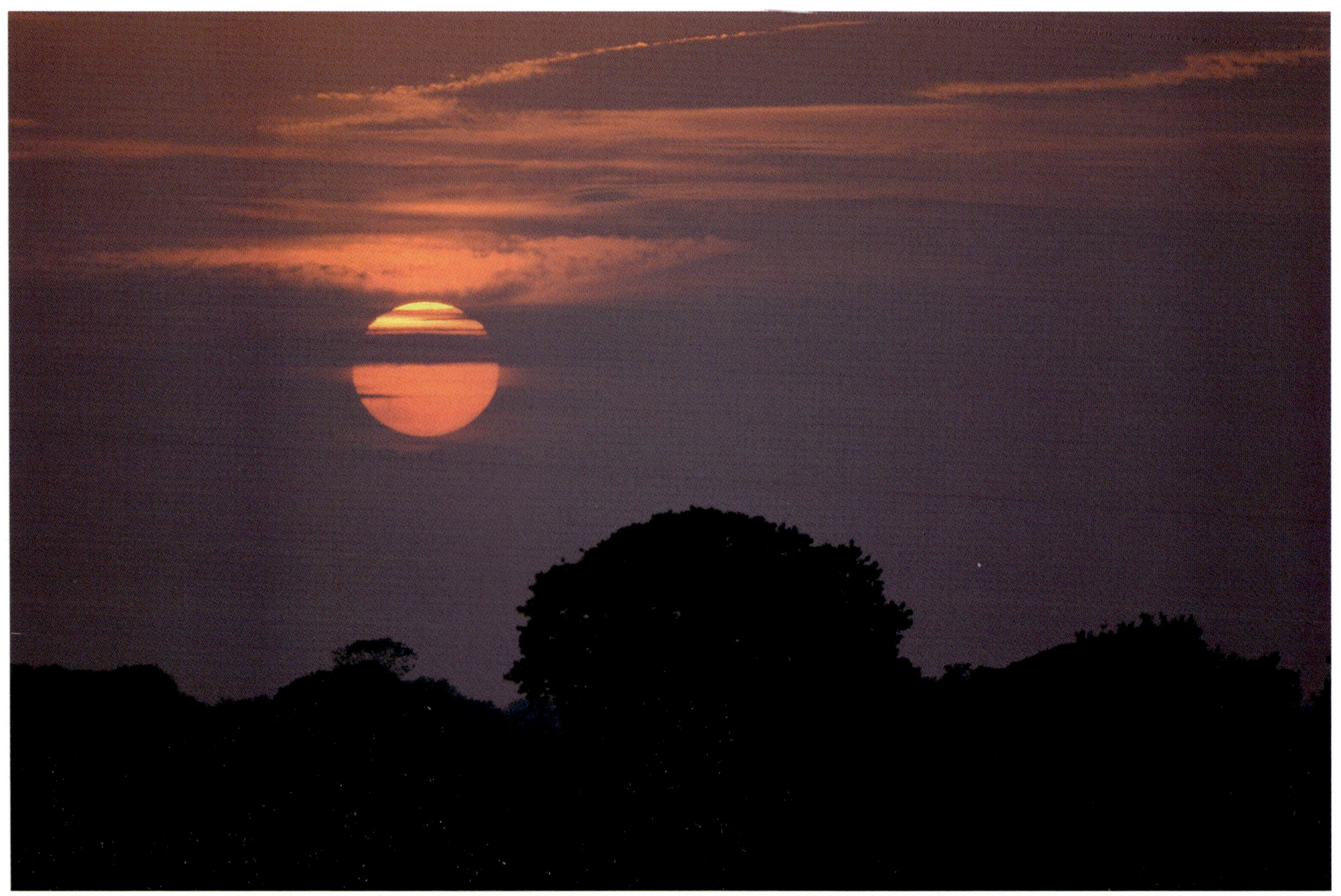

Sunset near Market Rasen
The sun descends through a veil of cloud on a summer evening.

Opposite: **Hare's-tail cottongrass at sunset**
The sun sets behind the fluffy seed heads of hare's-tail cottongrass, photographed on Crowle Moors Nature Reserve.

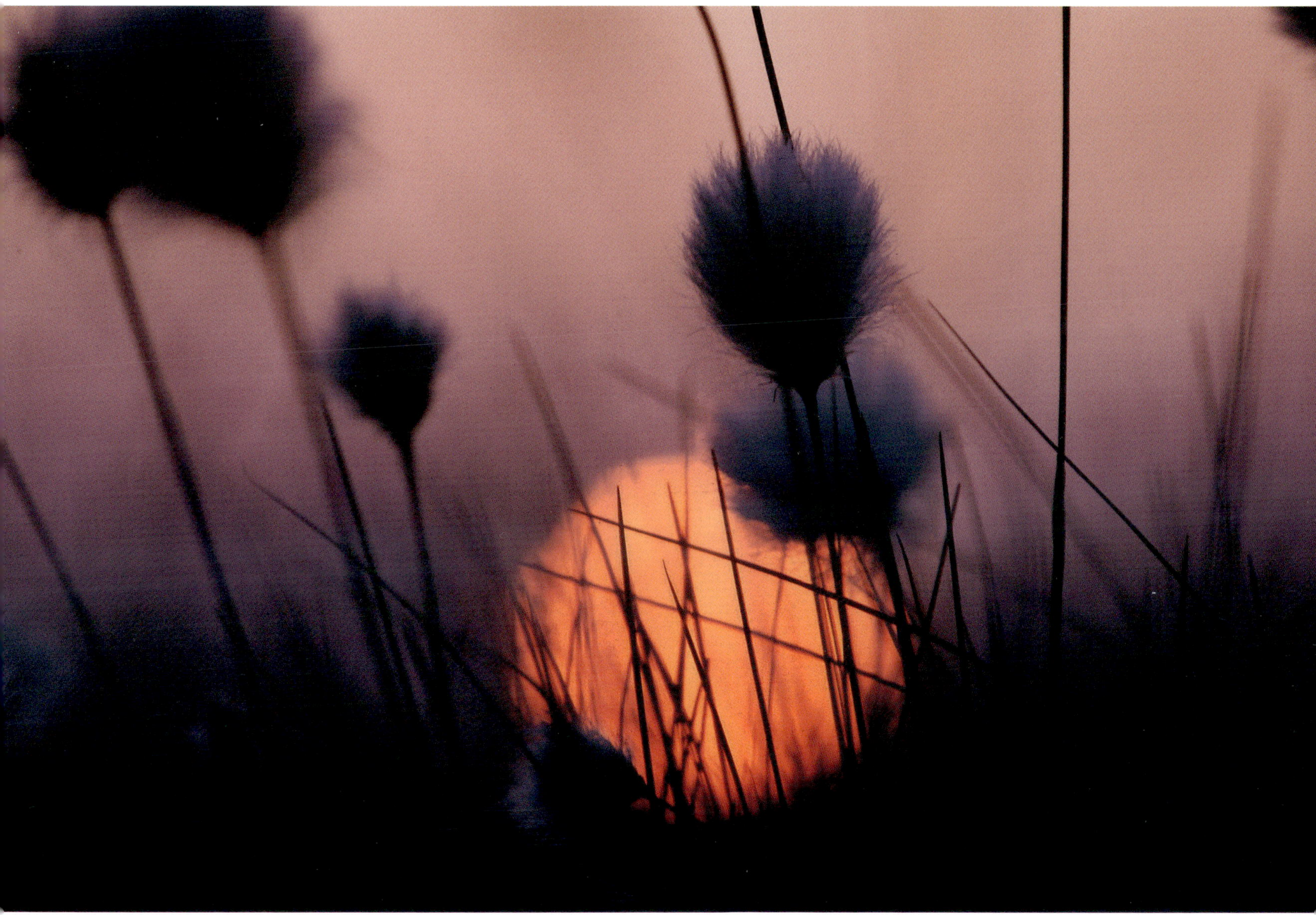

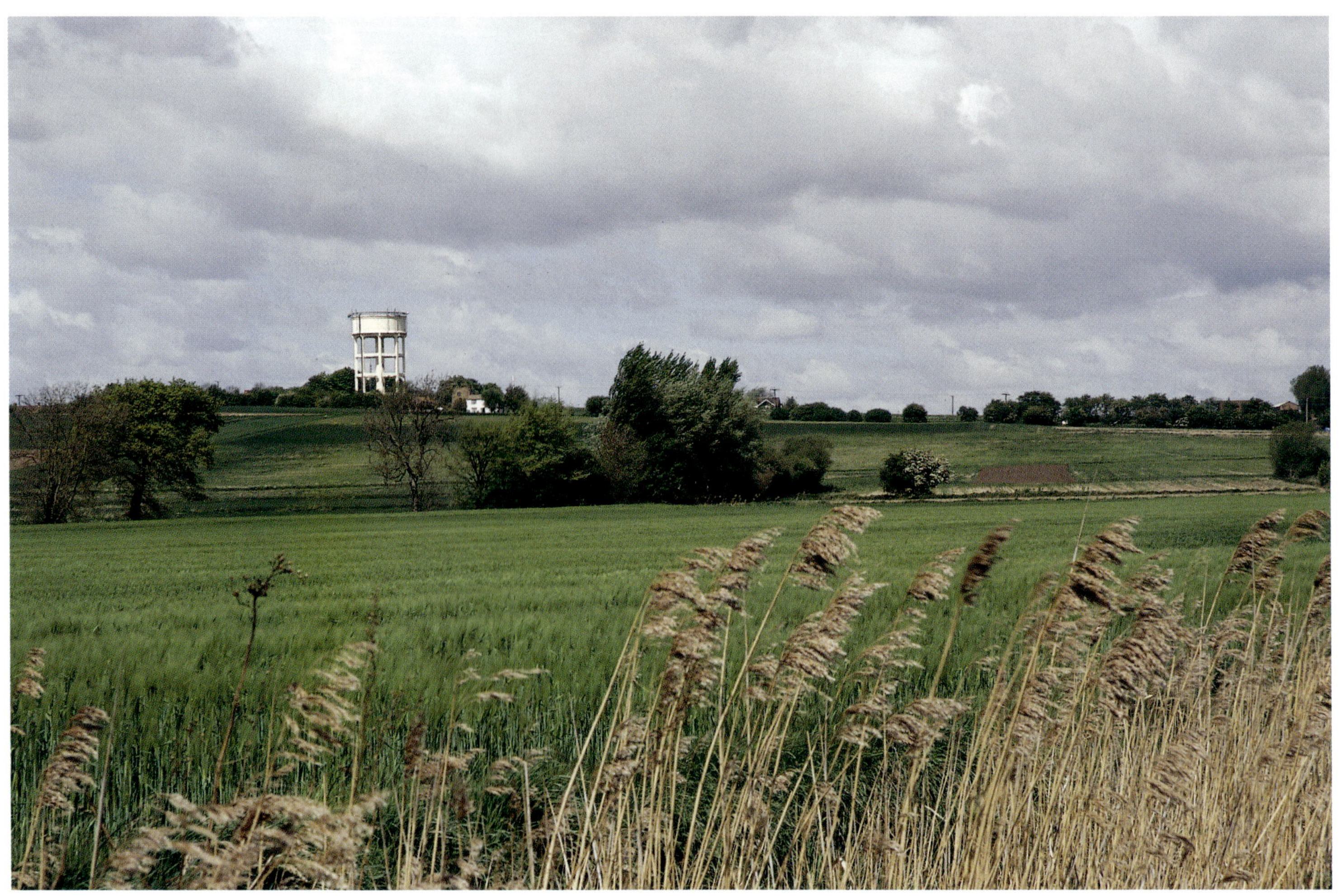

Water tower
The water tower is a prominent feature on its hilltop site between the villages
of Haxey and Westwoodside in the Isle of Axholme.

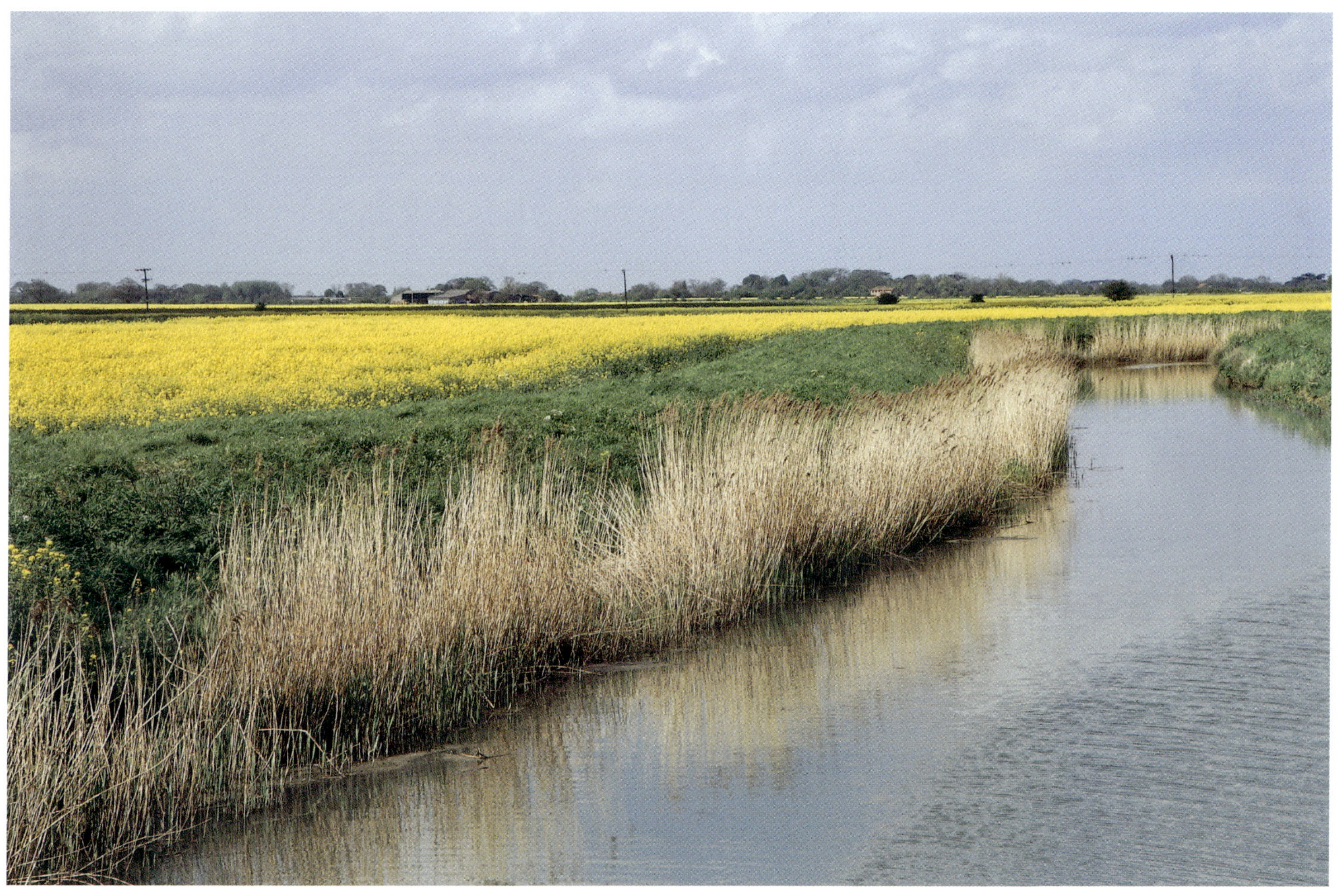

The Great Eau
Reeds fringe the bank of the Great Eau, one of the many drains which cross the marshland east of Louth.

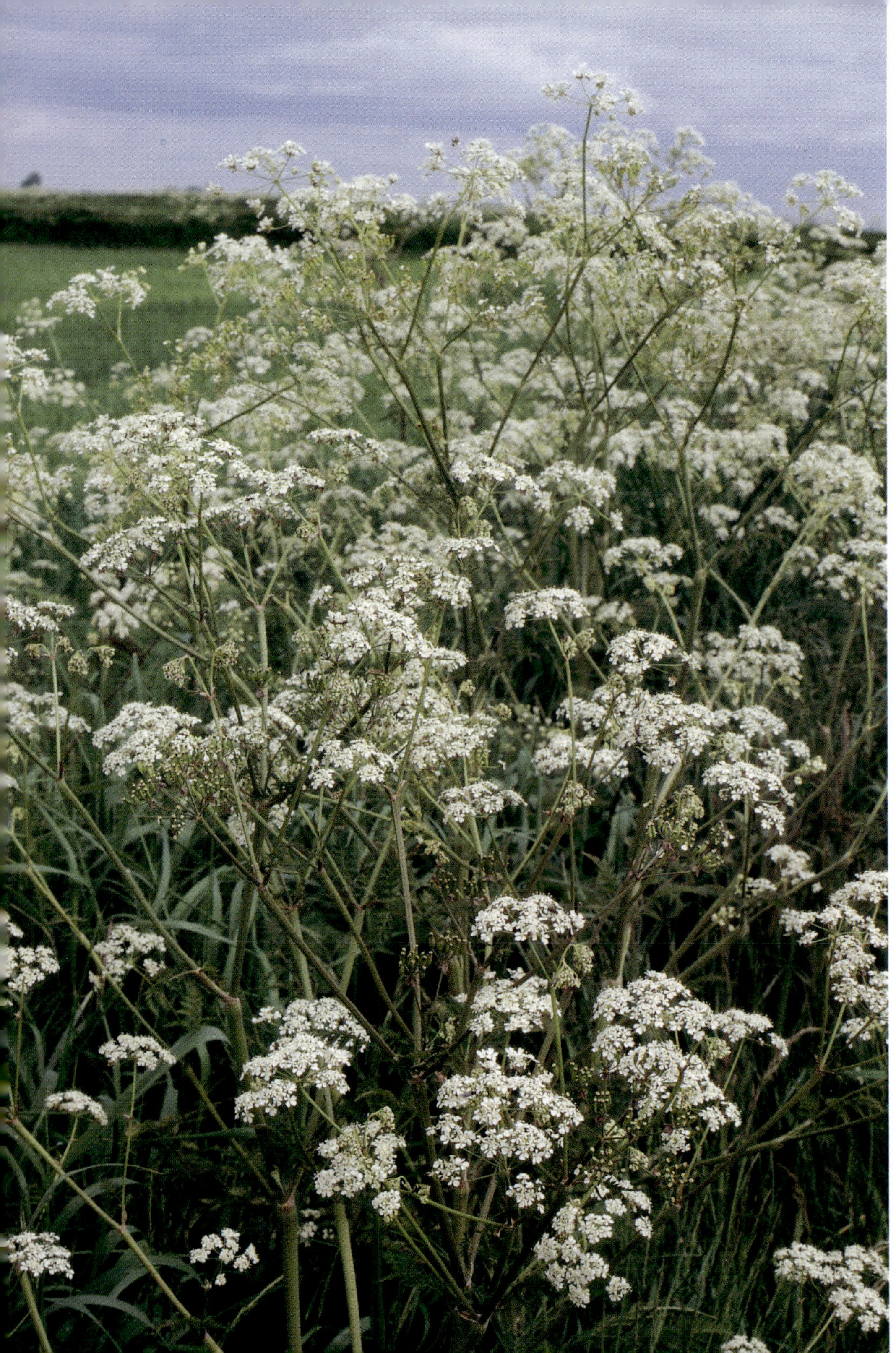

Cow parsley
The frothy white flowers of cow parsley
are a familiar sight on roadside verges
in May and early June.

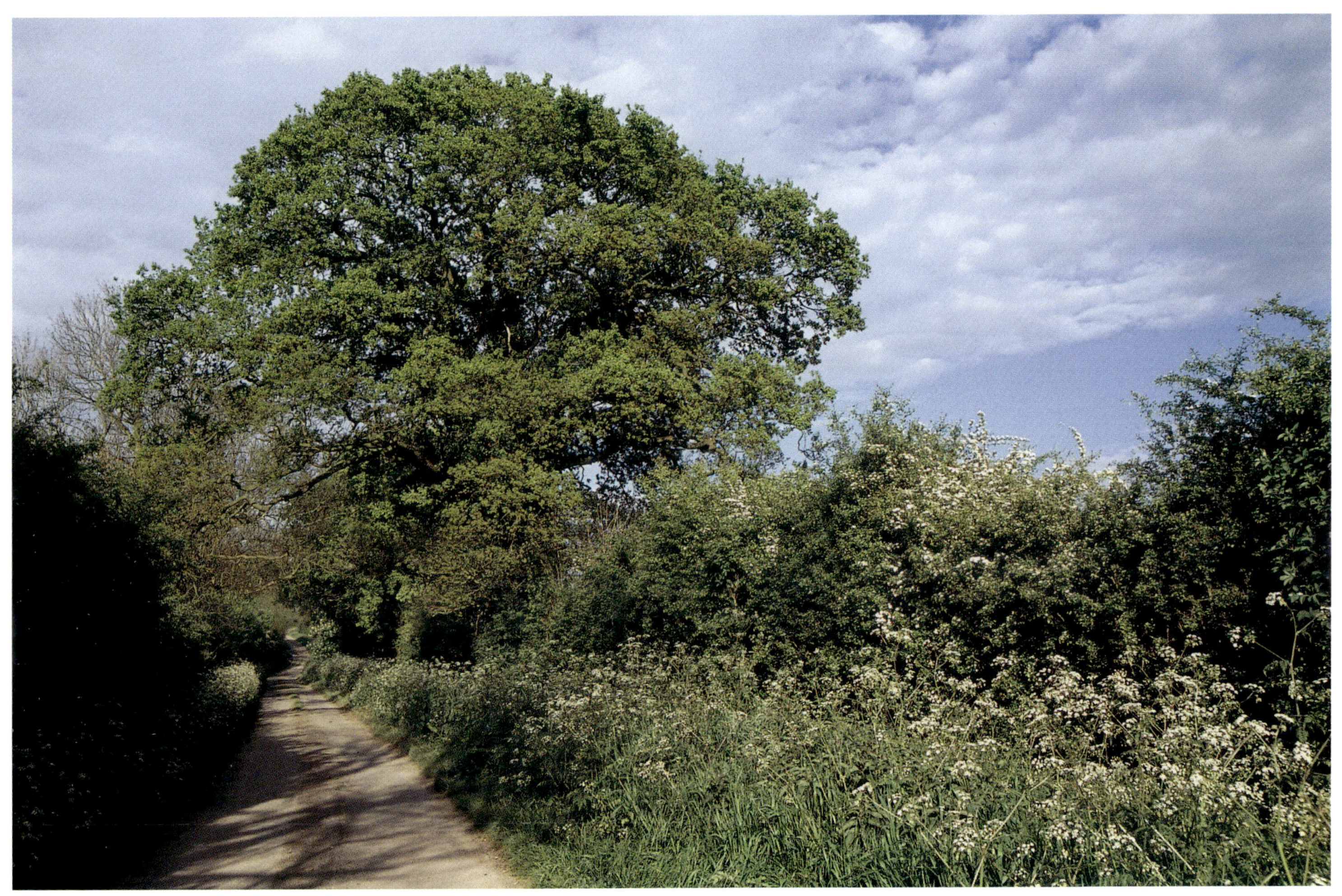

Country lane
The fresh green foliage of an oak tree, together with the white flowers of
hawthorn blossom and cow parsley, line this country lane near Edenham.

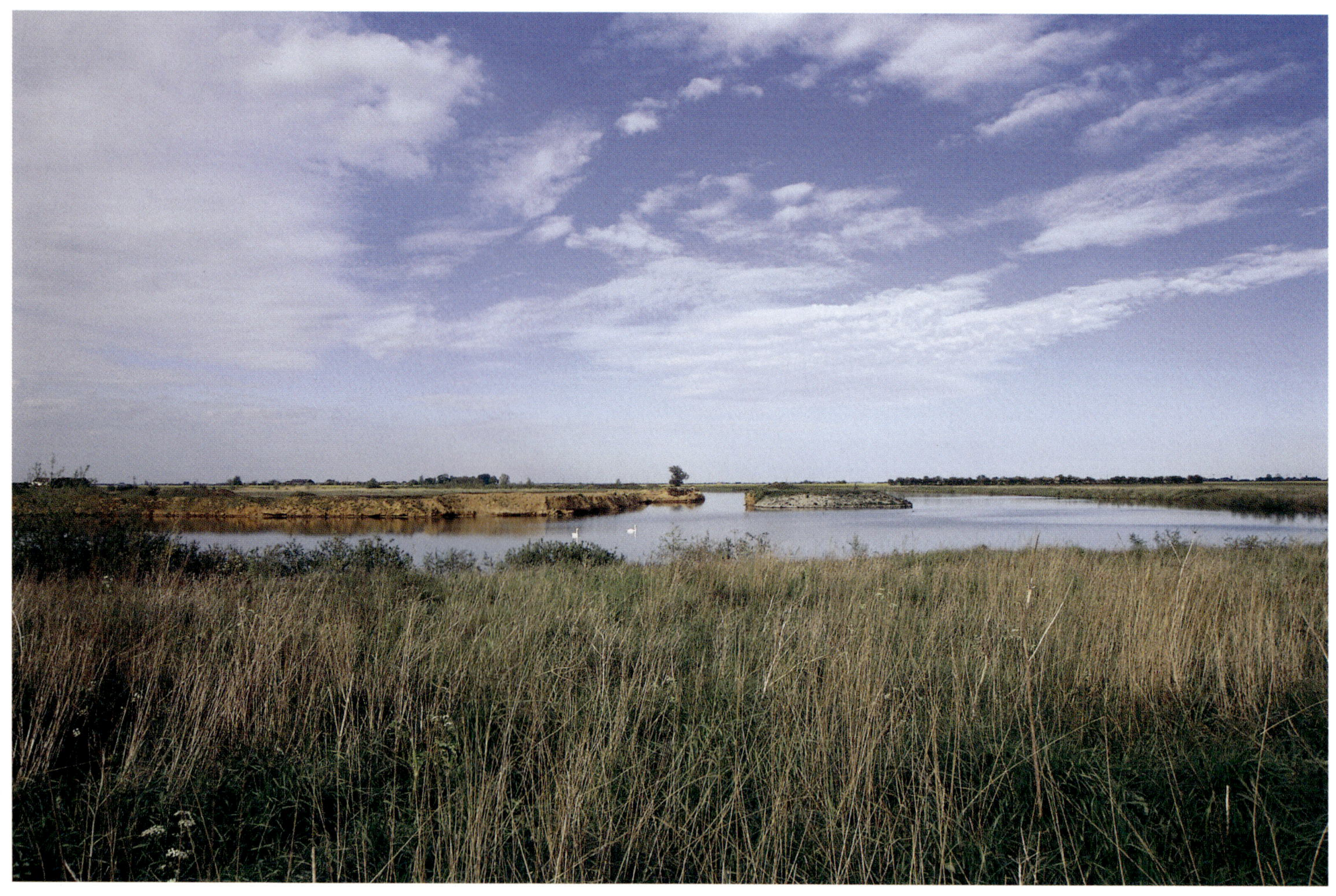

Swans at Langtoft
Abandoned gravel pits, like this one at Langtoft in the south of the county, provide a haven for wildlife.

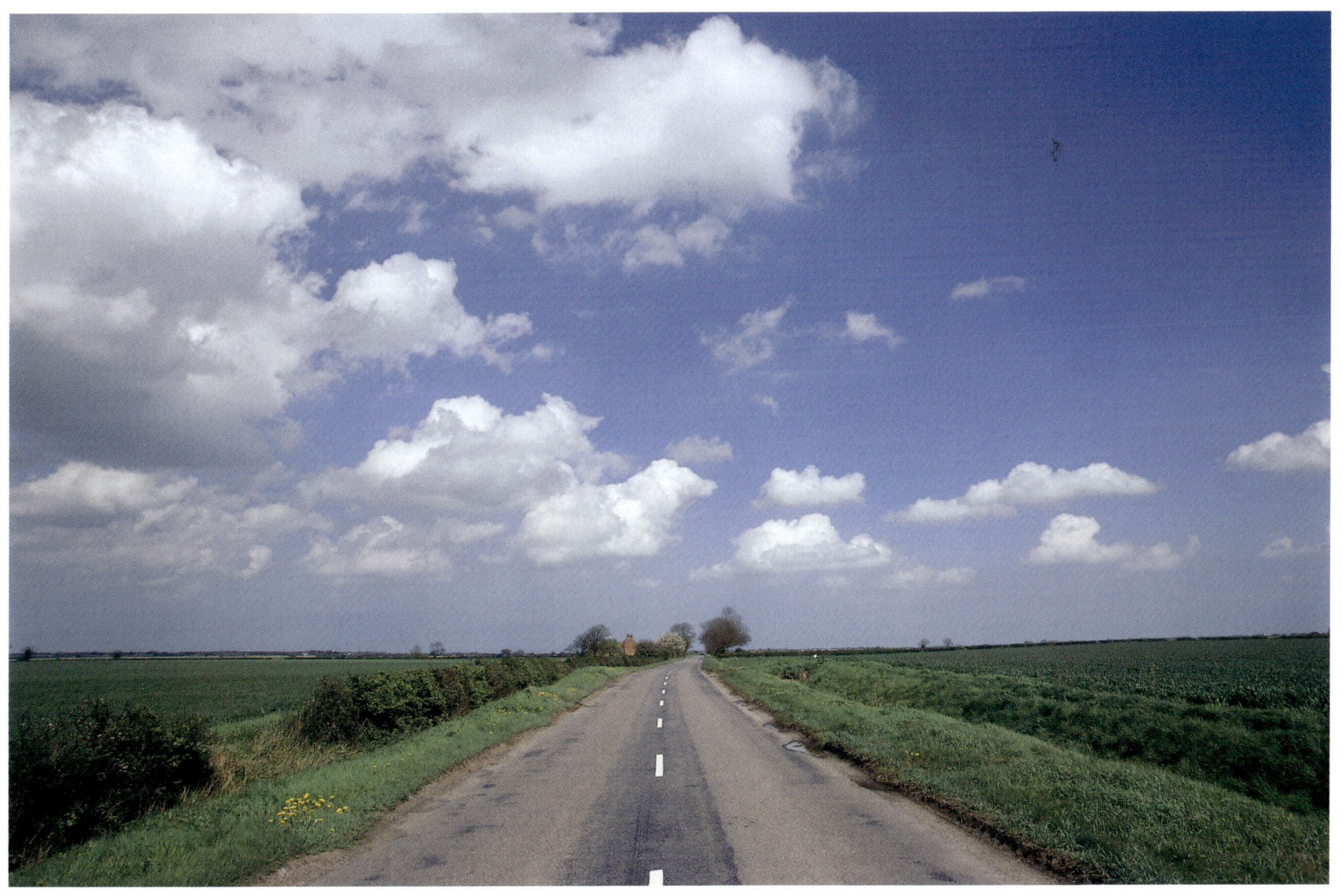

Road through the marshes
Cotton wool clouds drift over the road from South Cockerington to Saltfleet.

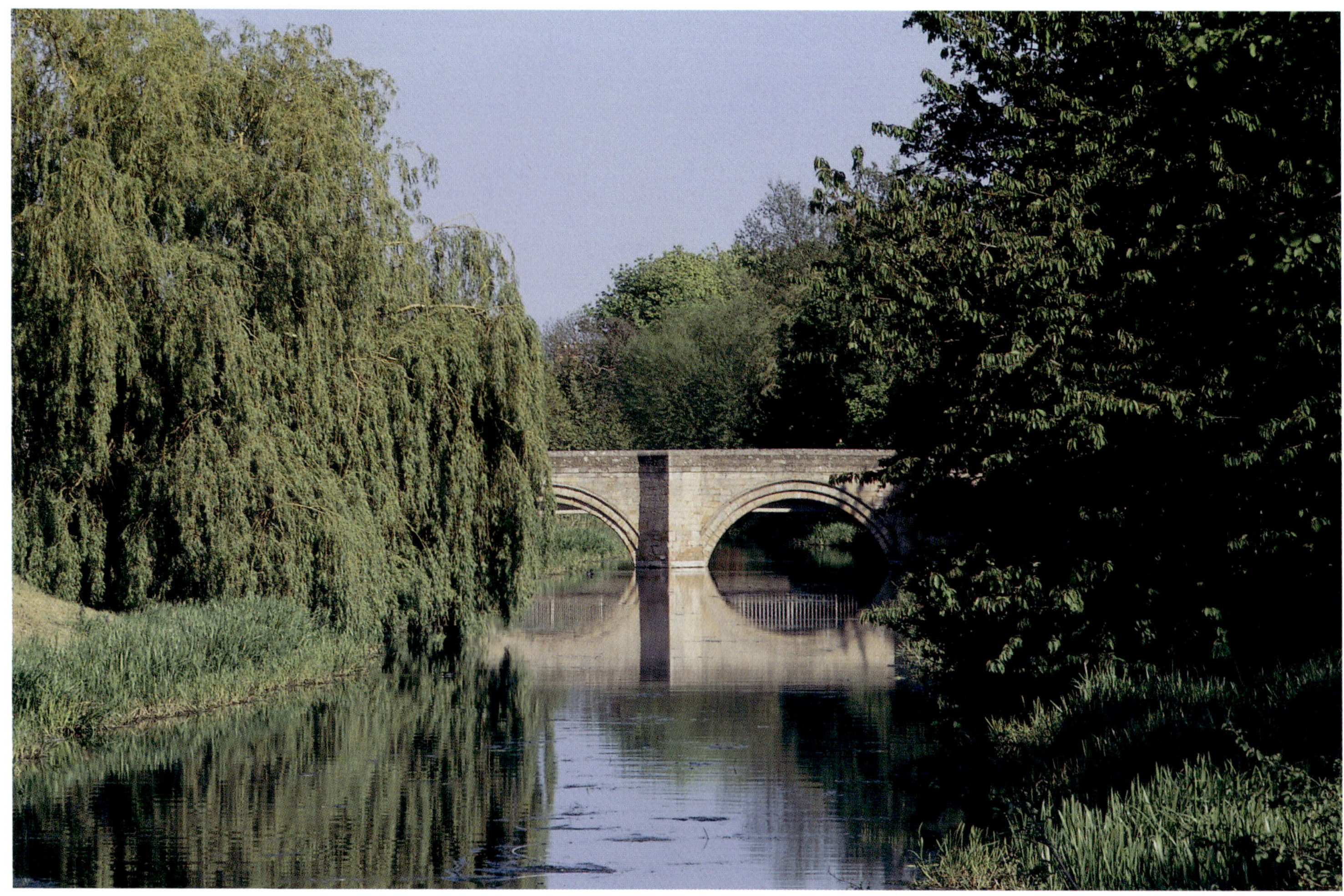

The River Welland at Deeping Gate
This tranquil scene at Deeping Gate is made by the reflection of the bridge and the waterside trees.

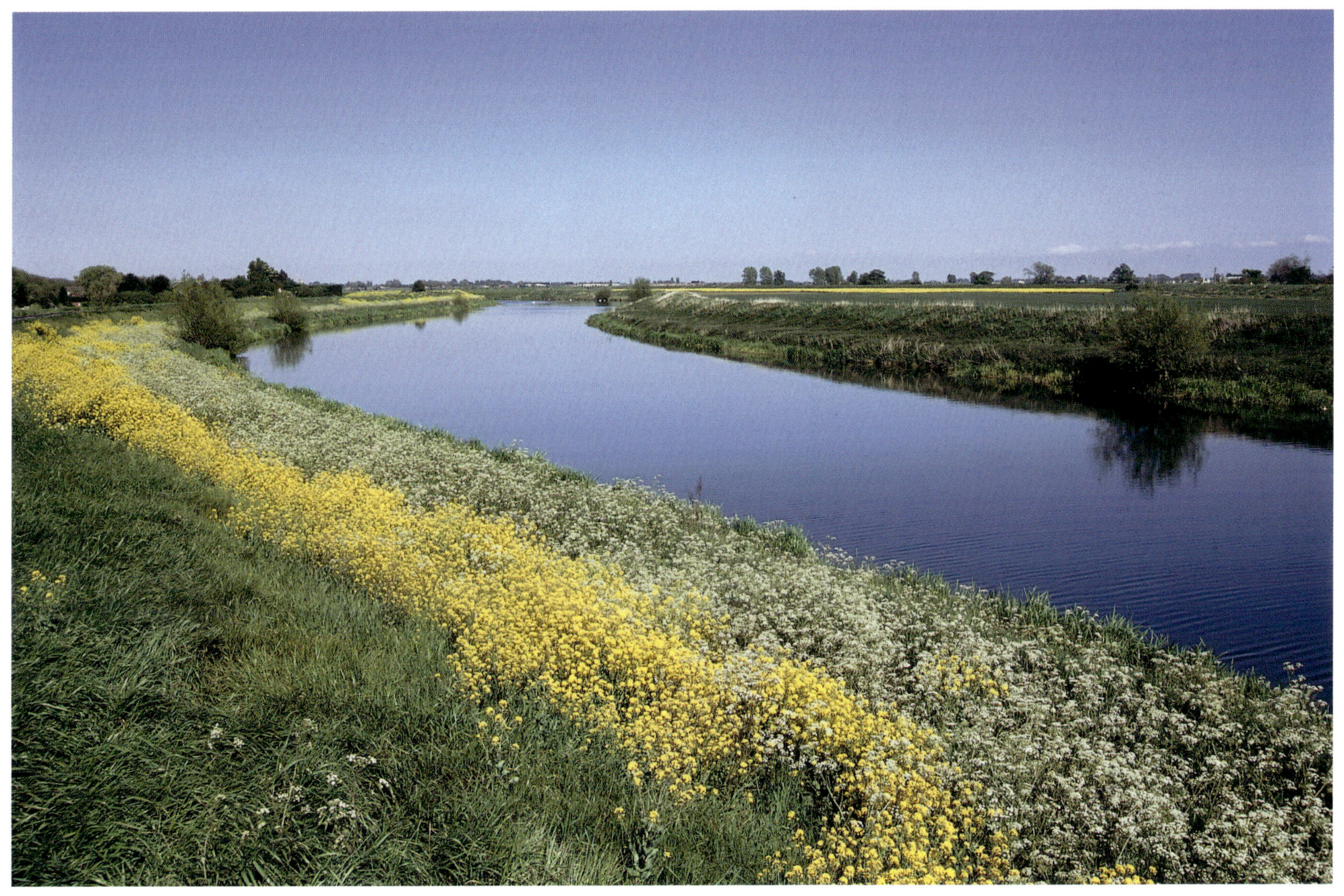

The River Welland near Crowland
Broad swathes of yellow and white flowers line the banks of the River Welland
as it flows through the Fens under cloudless summer skies.

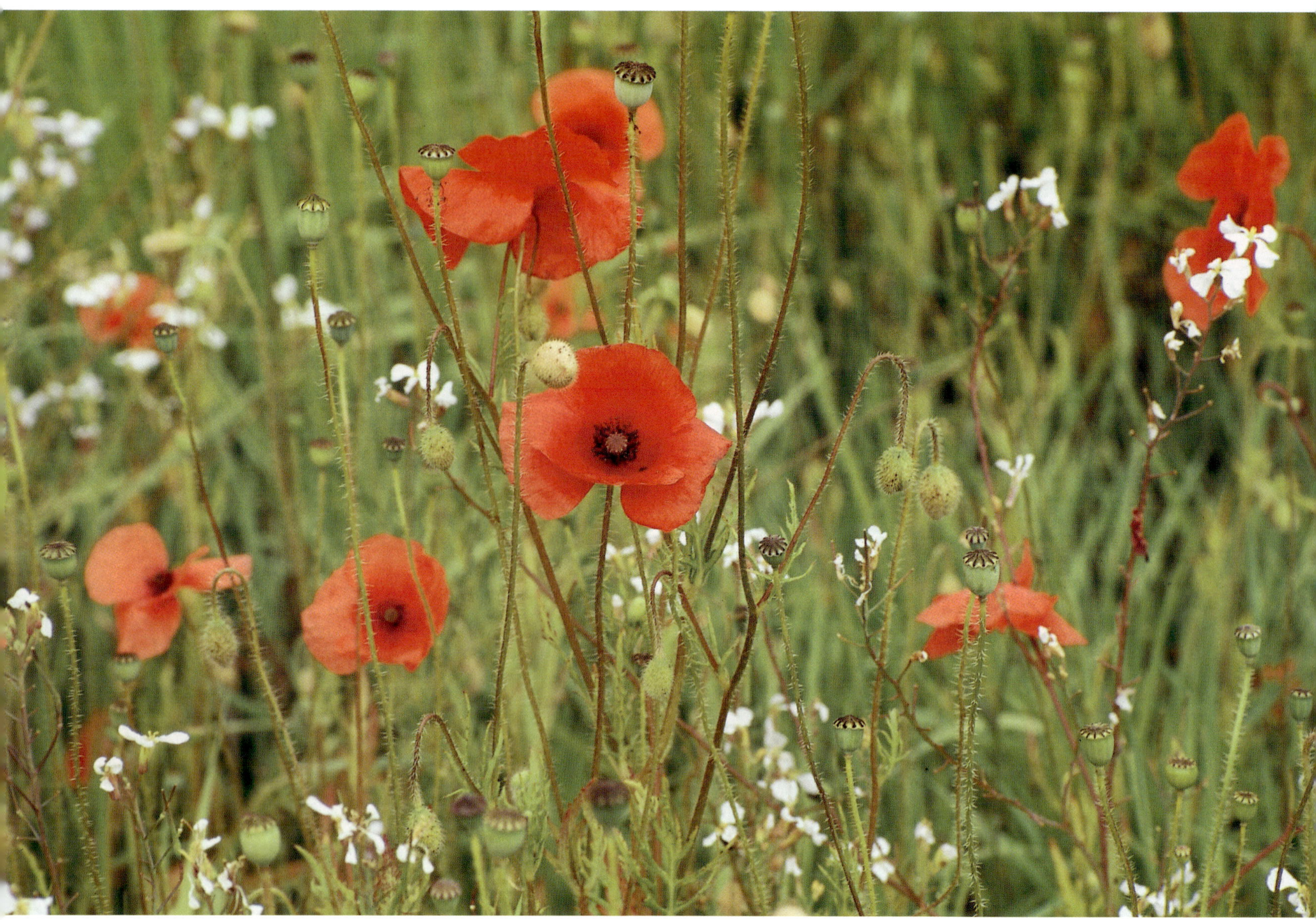

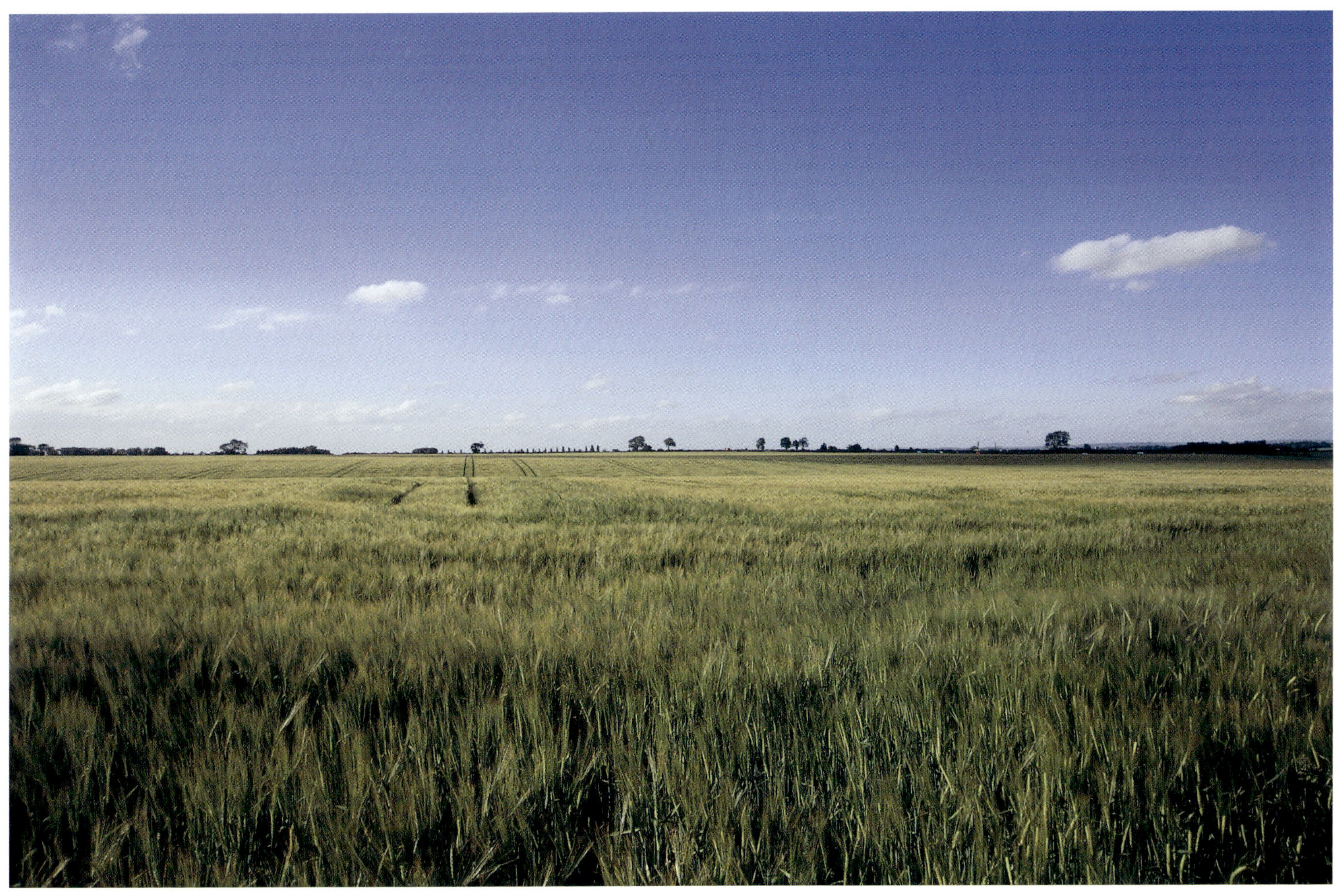

Barley field on Willoughton Cliff
The whiskered ears of barley catch the early evening sunlight on a warm June day.

Opposite: **Poppies**
Once a common weed on arable land, poppies are now making an appearance on conservation headlands —
strips of ground around arable fields which are sown with wild flowers.

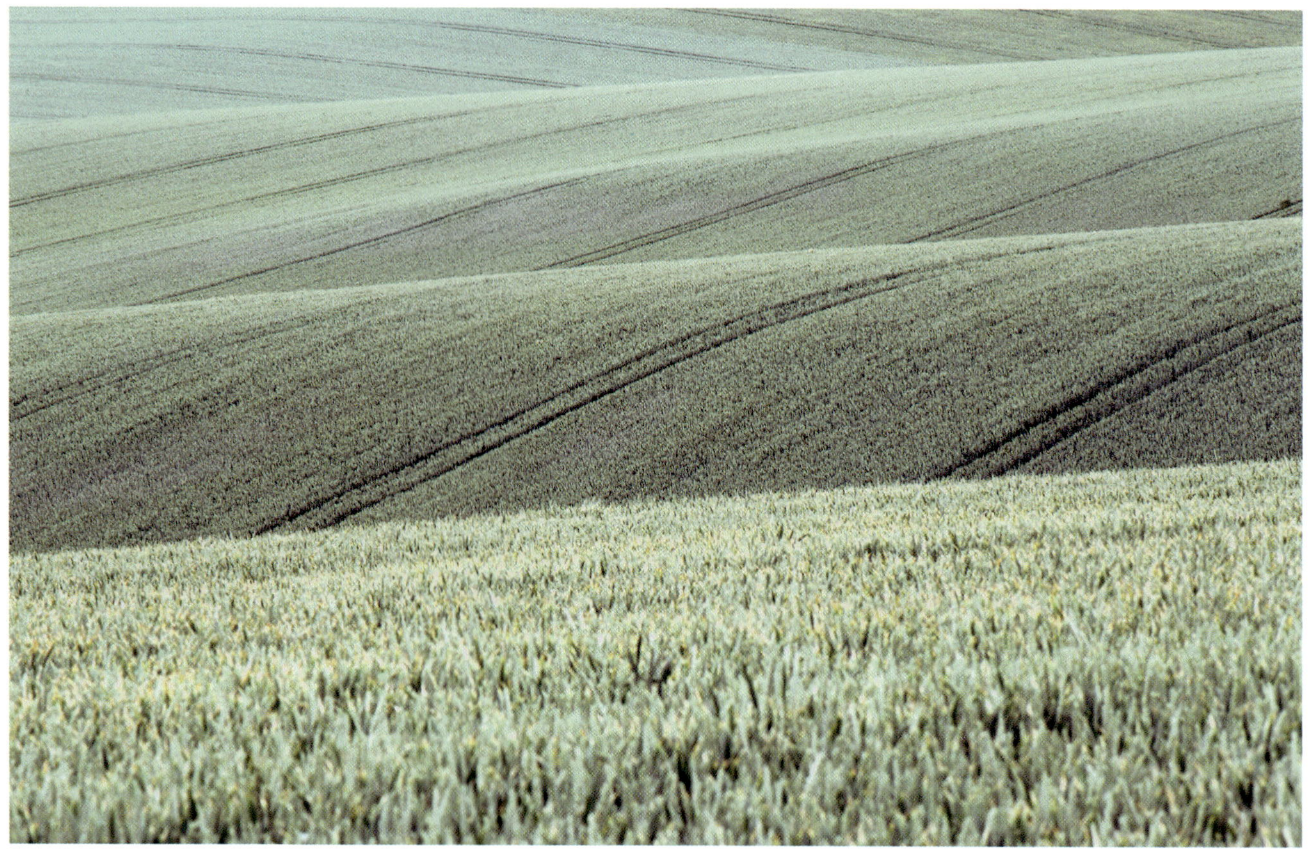

Wheat field near Brinkhill
The blue-green colour of growing wheat, interrupted by the regular pattern of tramlines,
covers this undulating field on the Wolds.

Opposite: **Poppies near Riseholme**
Poppies flowering in a field of oilseed rape provide a vivid splash of colour.

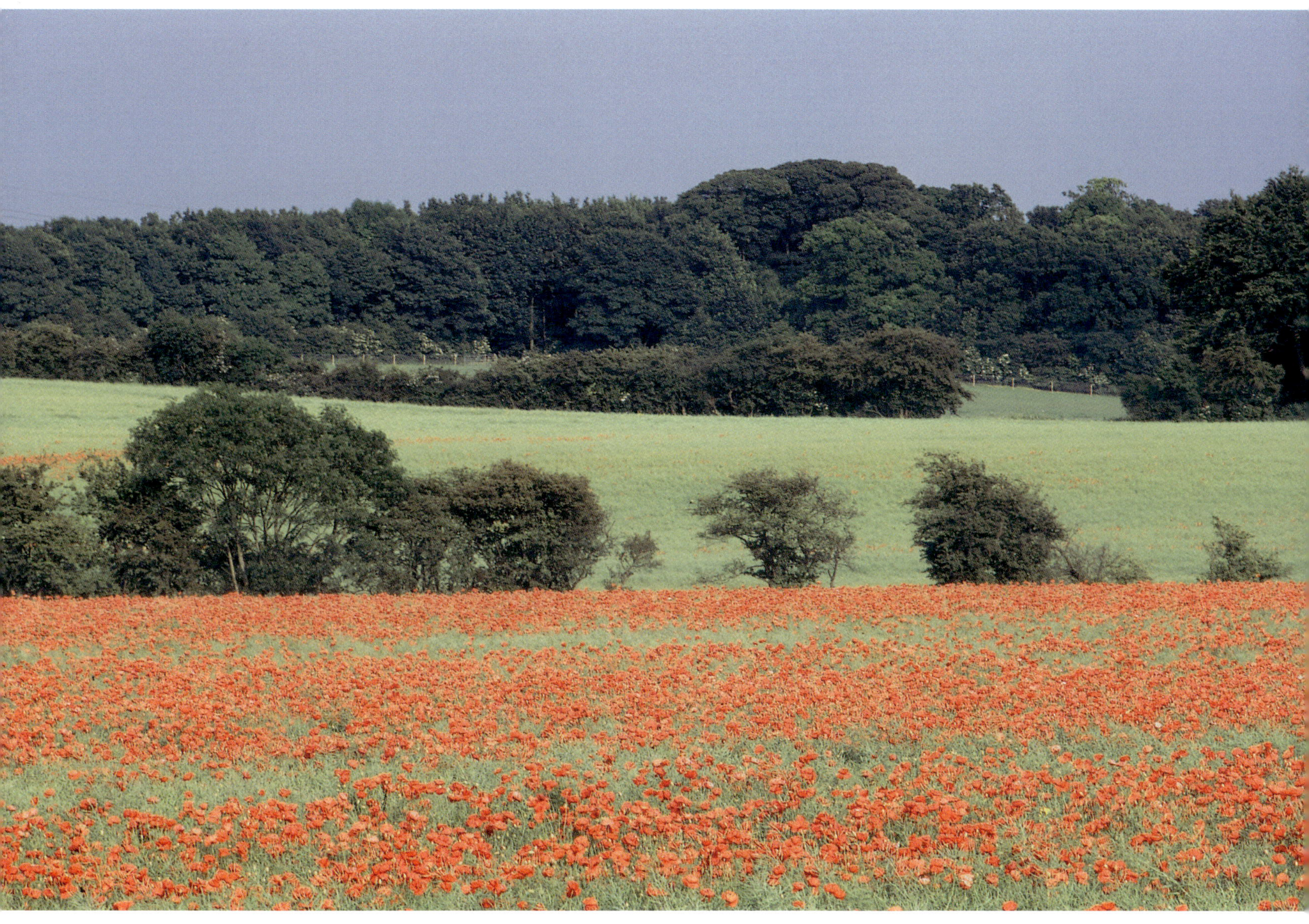

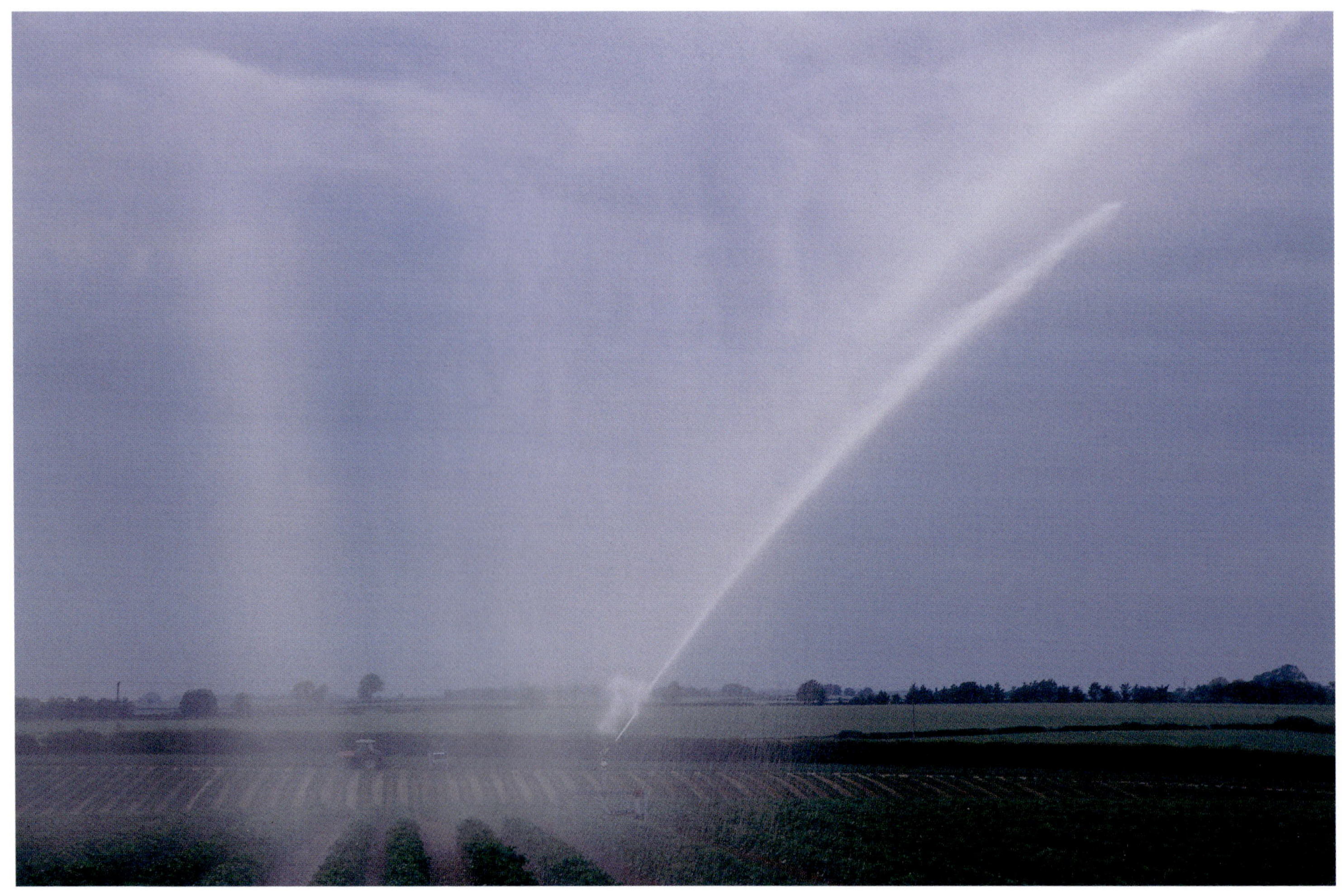

Irrigating potatoes near Welton
The enormous jets of water from this irrigator are still visible as the light fades at the end of another warm day.

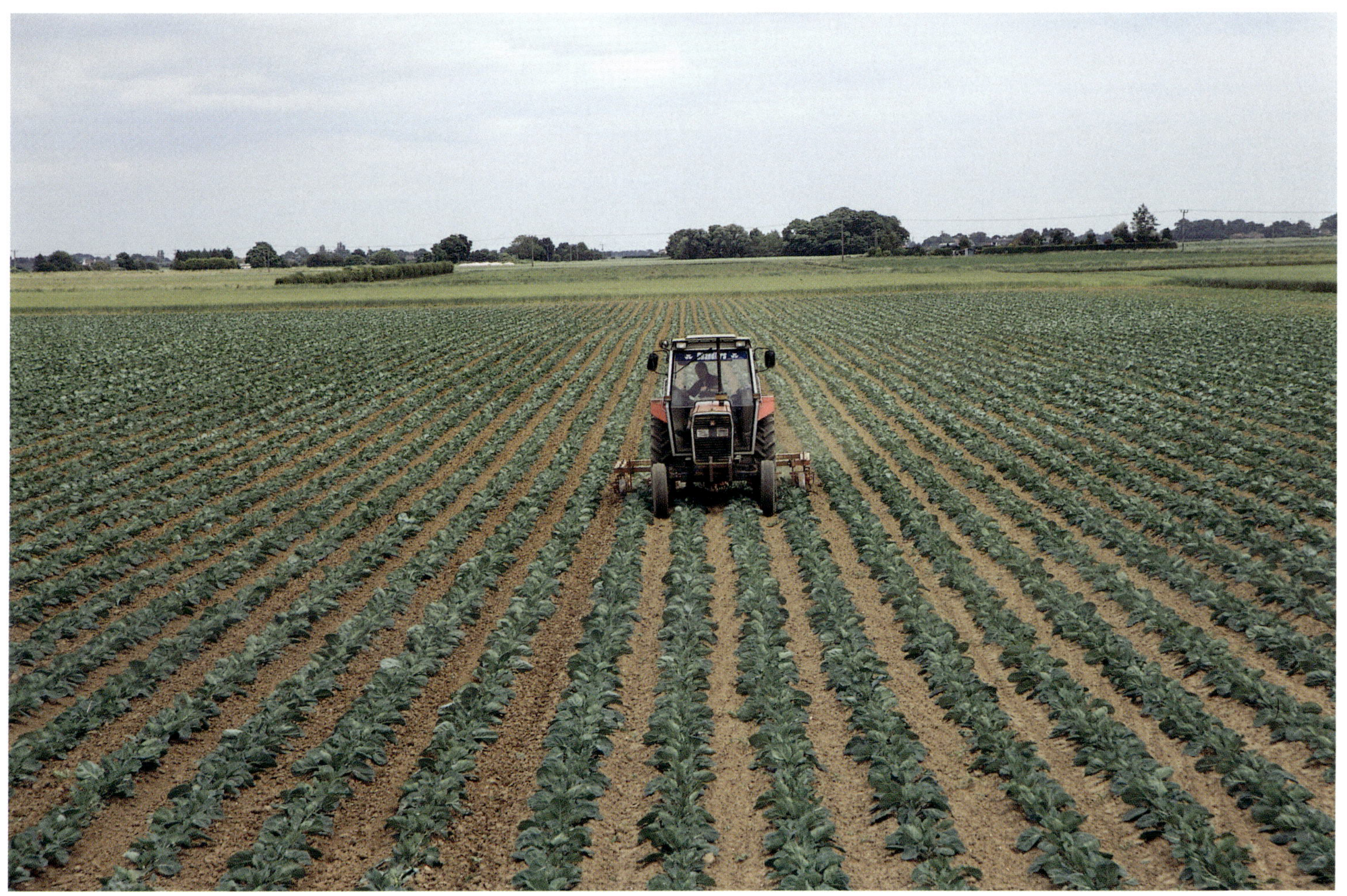

Hoeing brassicas
A tractor hoes out the weeds in these long rows of brassicas growing alongside the Hobhole Drain on East Fen.

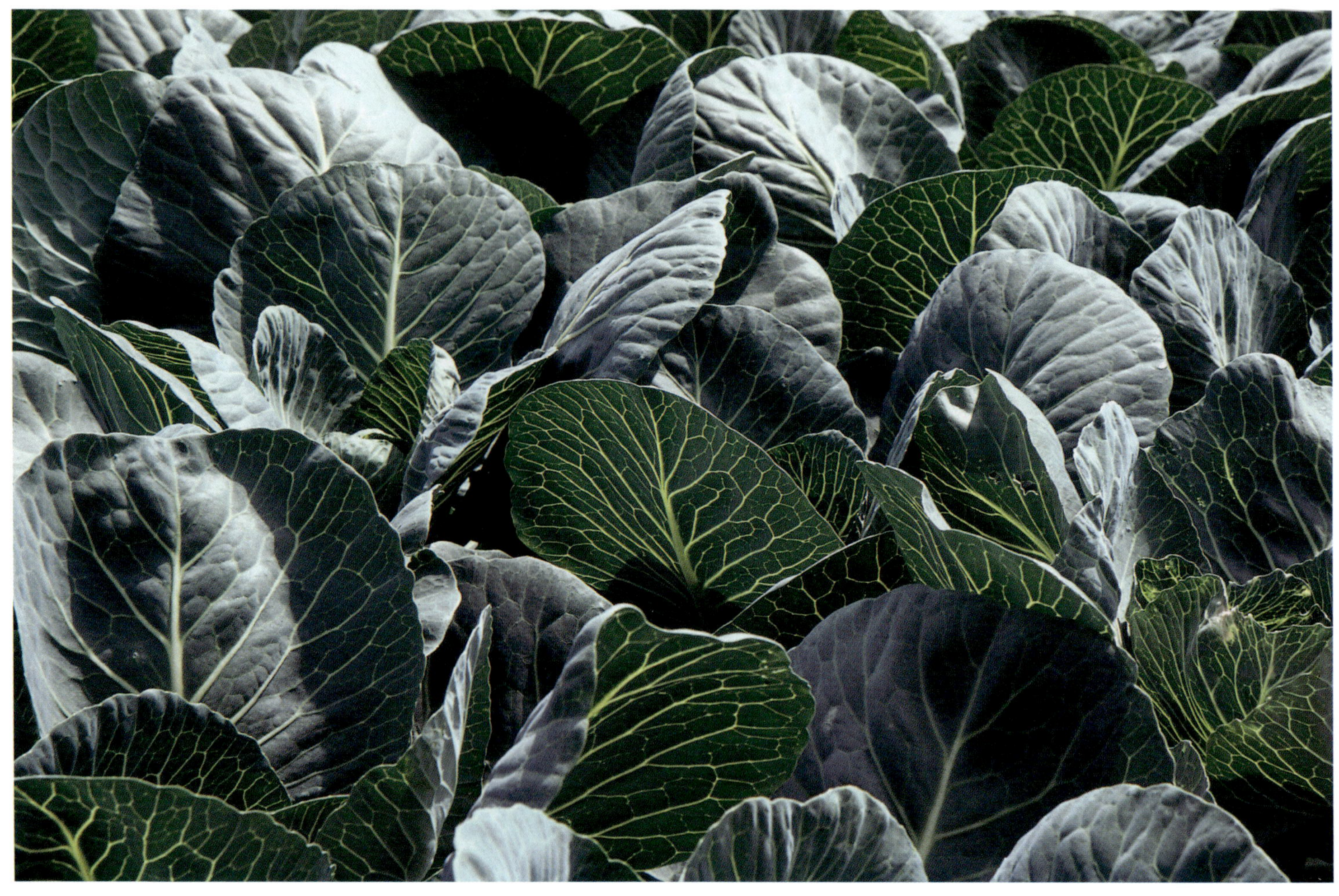

Cabbage crop
Back-lighting highlights the veins in the leaves of this crop of cabbages growing near Kirton in Holland.

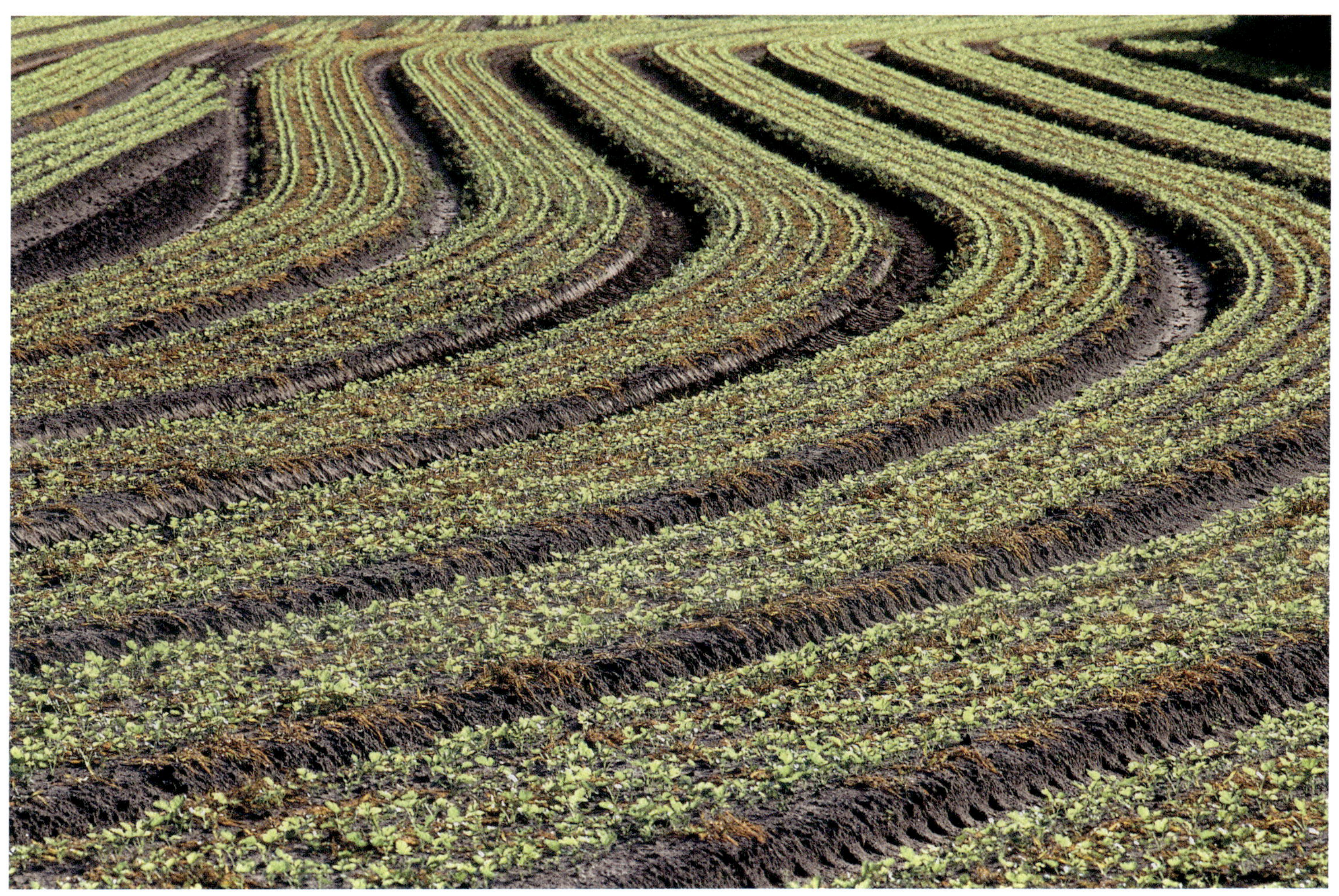

Parsnip beds near Messingham
The beds of young parsnips curve around as they follow the pattern of the field boundary.

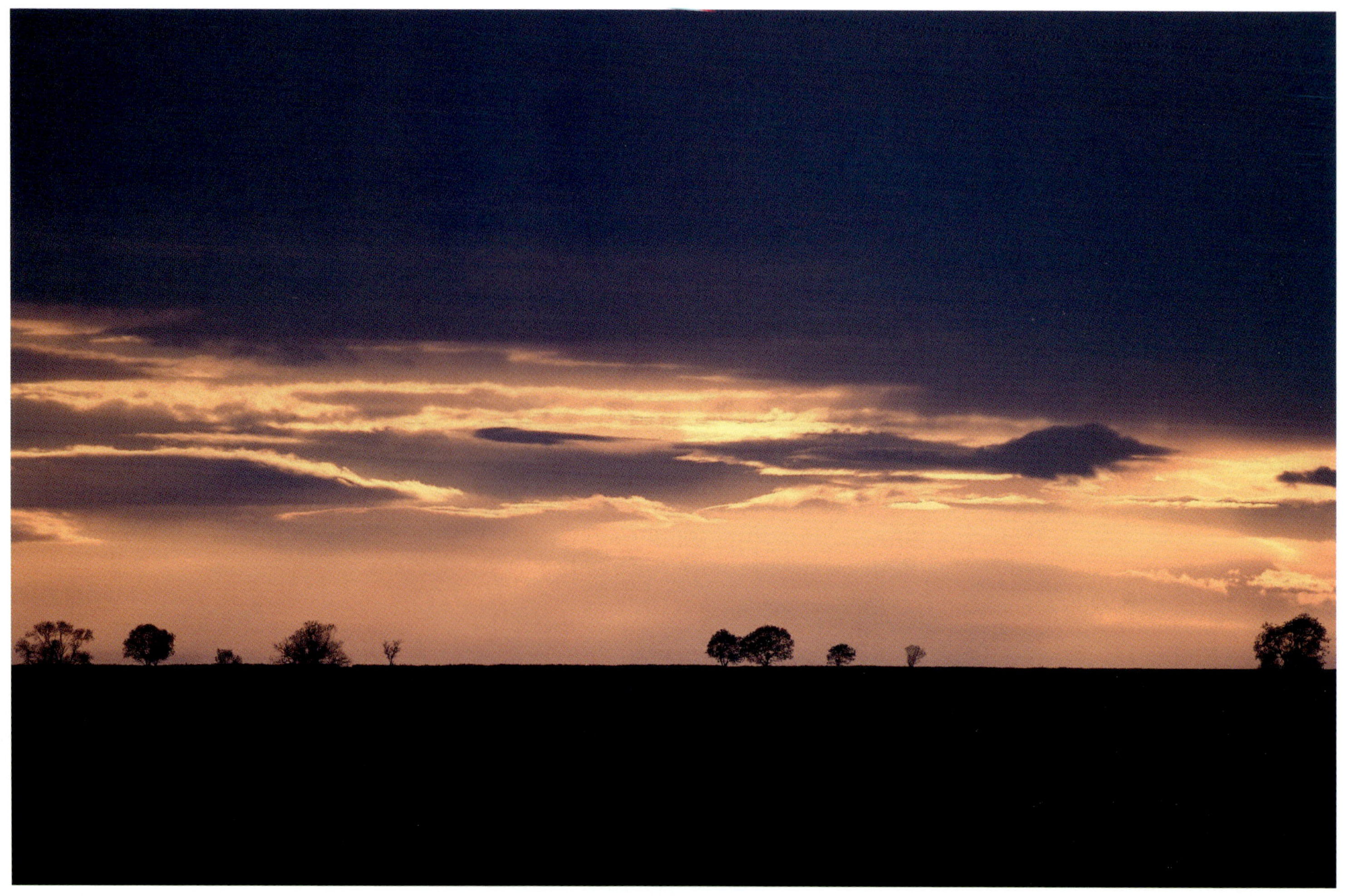

Sunset near Walesby
Rich evening light gives a backcloth to scattered trees on the western edge of the Wolds.

Opposite: **Evening sky**
The sun, low in the sky, highlights the speckled pattern of the clouds.

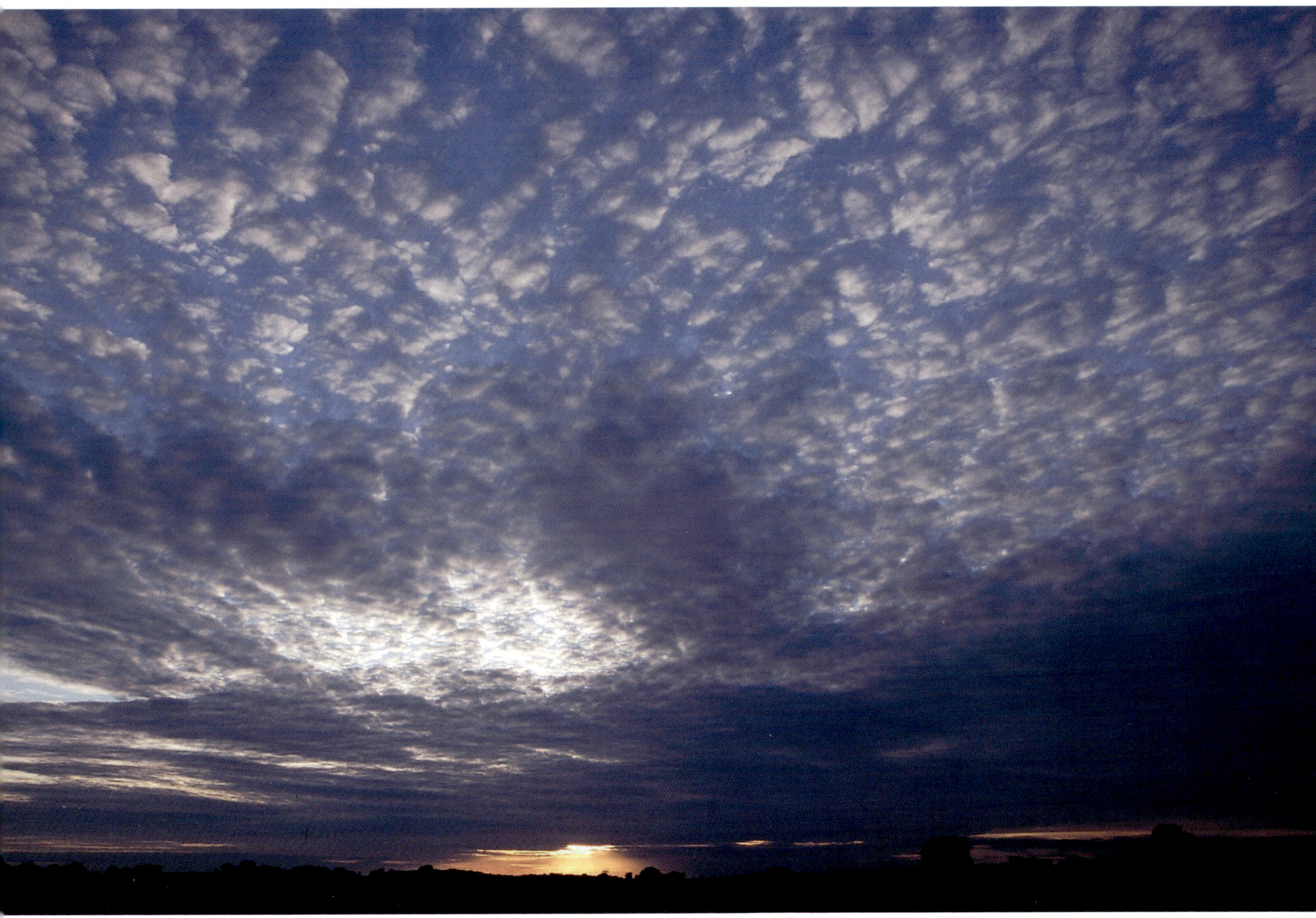

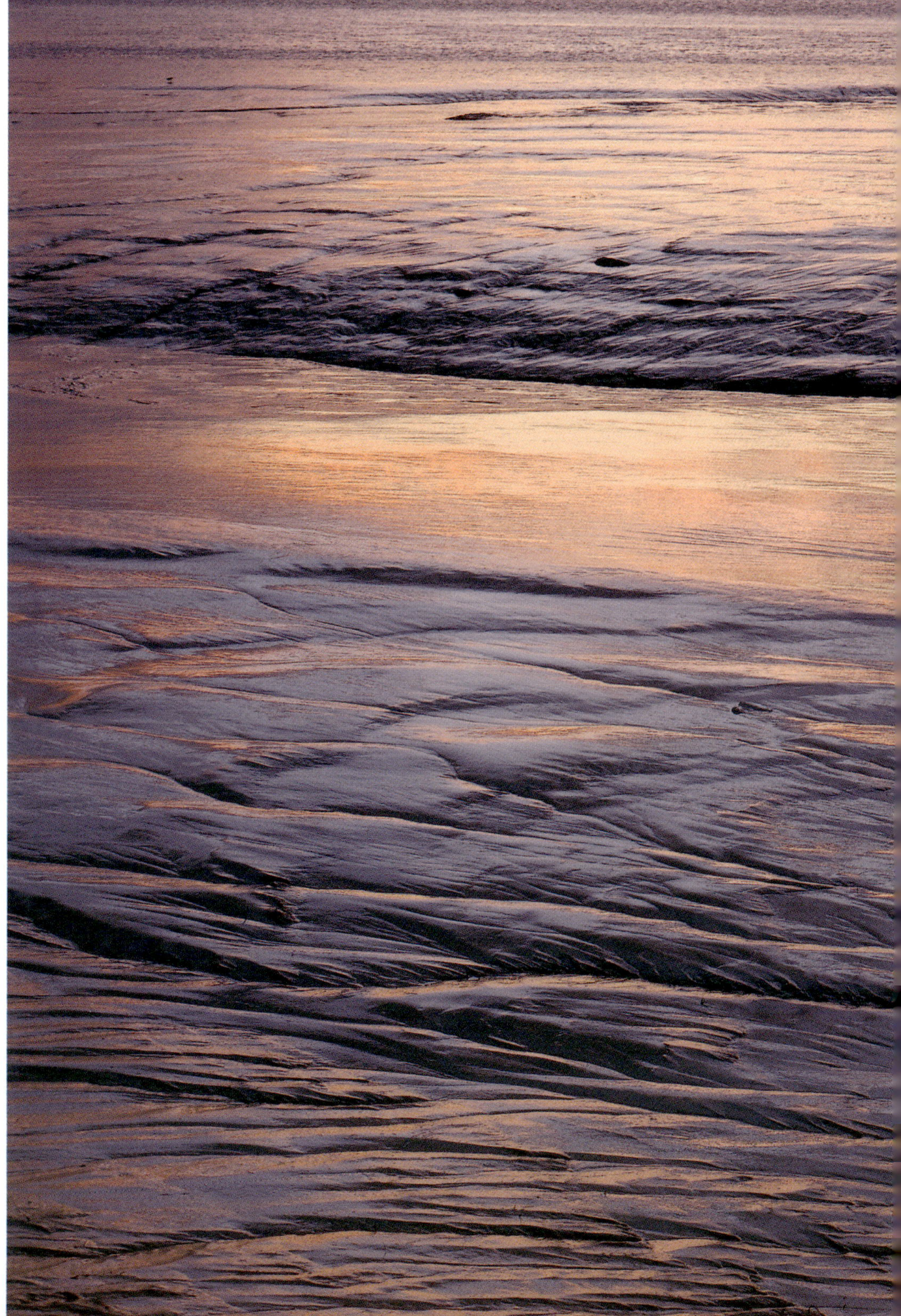

Opposite: **Sunset over the Wash**
In this view of the Lincolnshire
coast from Norfolk, on the eve of mid-
summer, the sun sets over the Wash and
a golden glow lights up the sea.

Mudflats
Early morning light is reflected in the
mudflats which line the Lincolnshire
shore of the Wash.

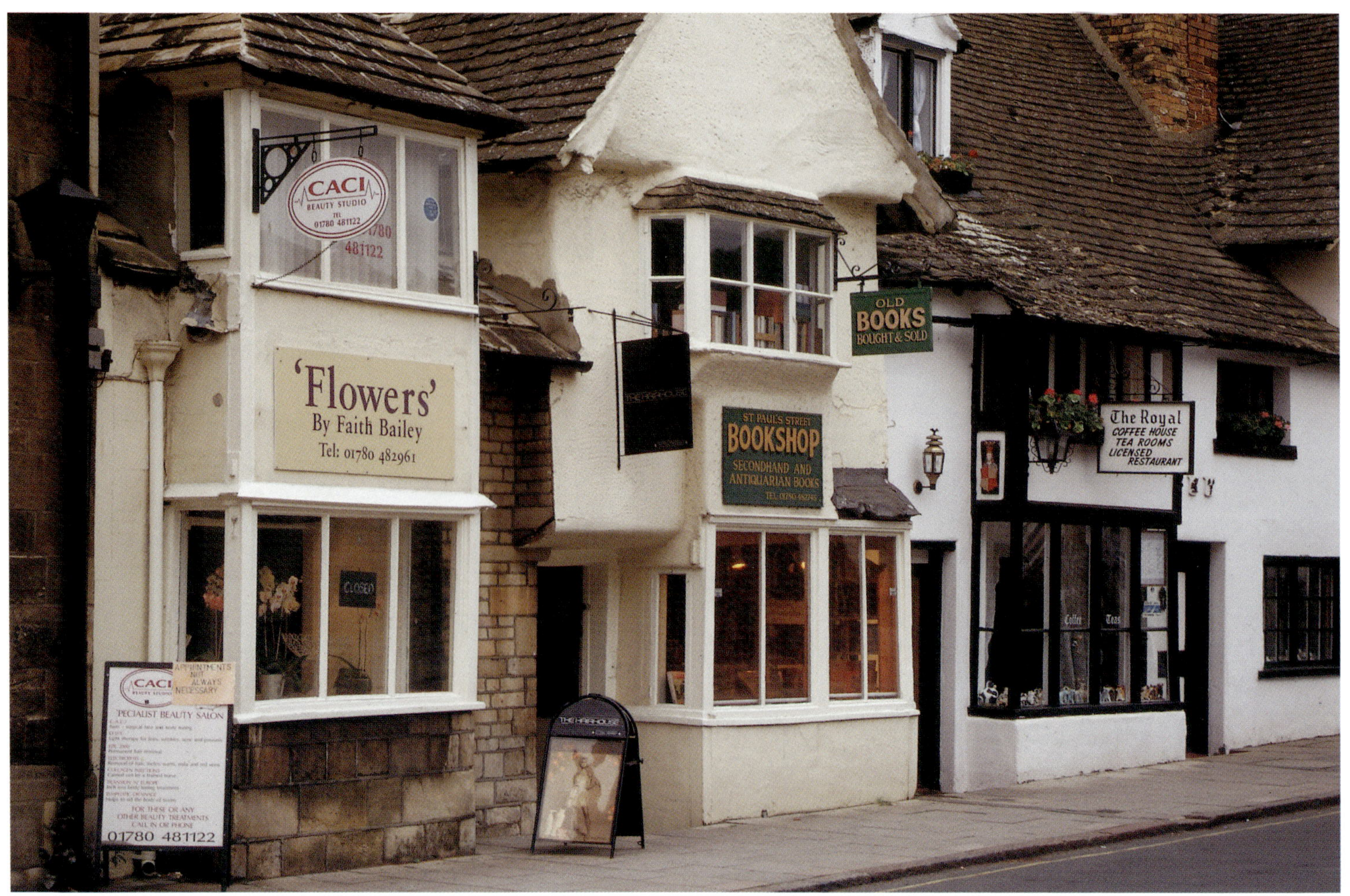

Stamford shopfronts
A mix of mellow limestone and timber-framing fronts these ancient buildings on St Paul's Street in Stamford.

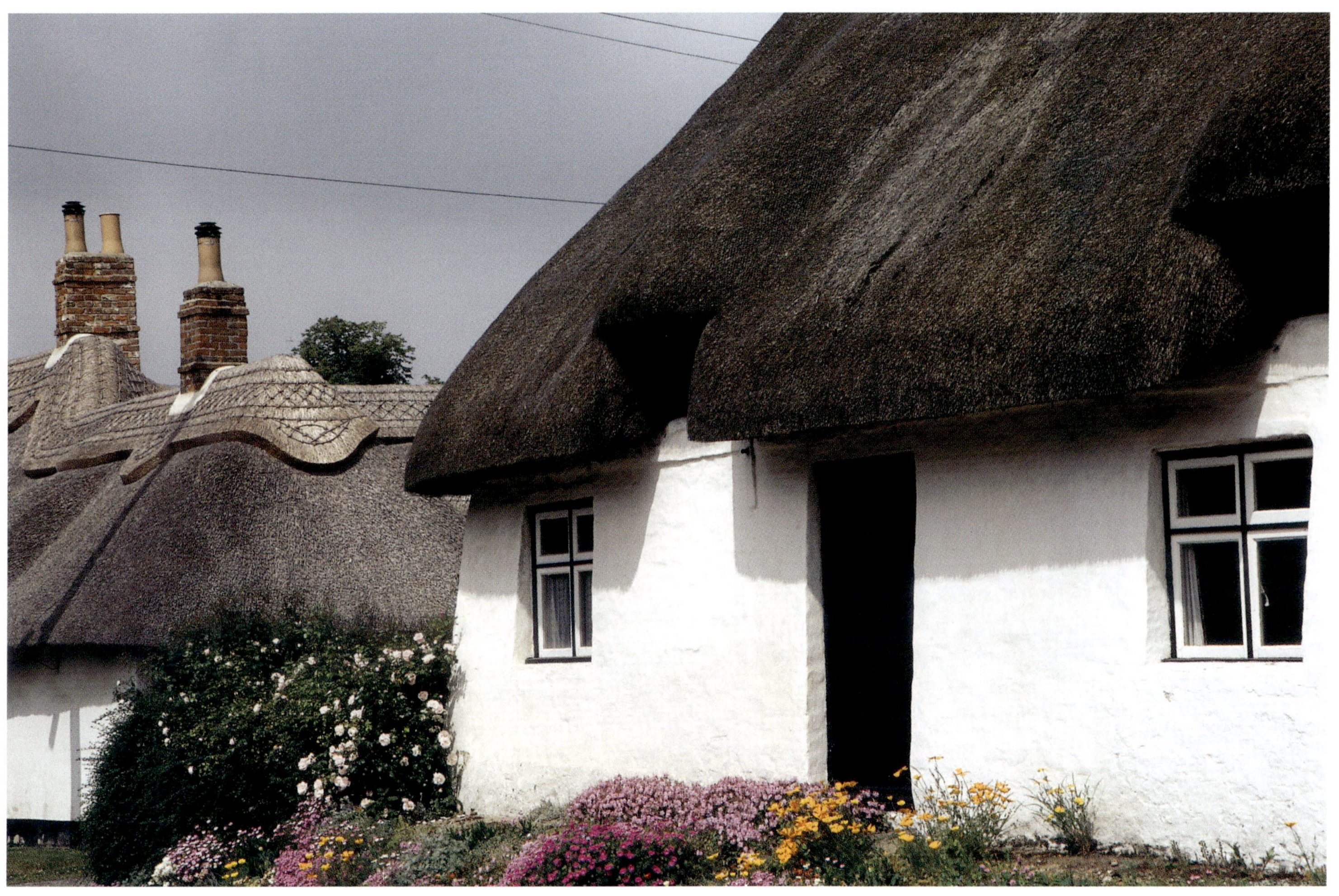

Thimbleby
These mud and stud cottages with their thatched roofs and pretty gardens make a picture-postcard scene.

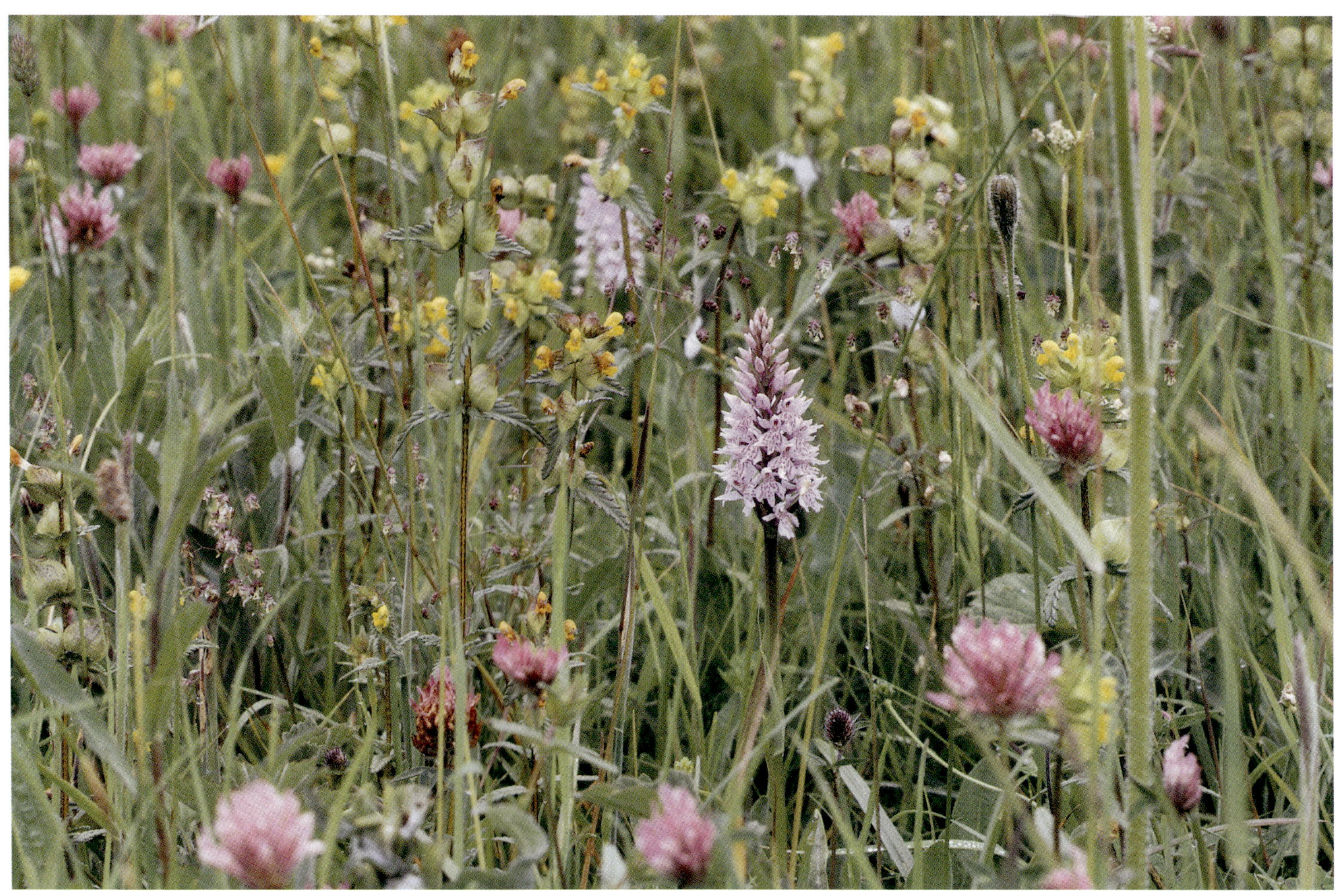

Meadow flowers
Common spotted orchids, red clover and yellow hay-rattle flower in a traditional hay meadow near Sotby.

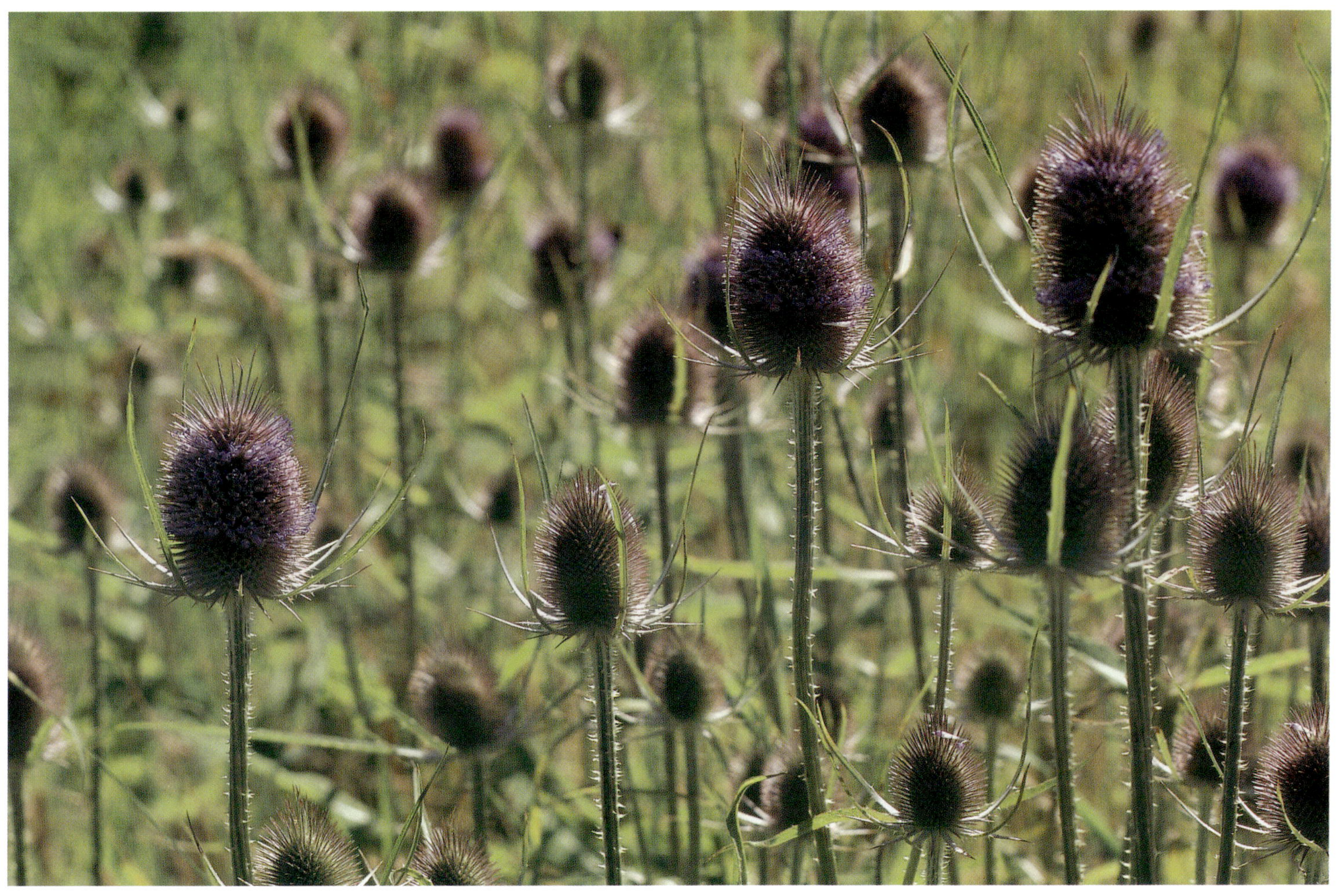

Teasels
Backlighting highlights the prickly heads of teasels flowering on waste ground near Scunthorpe.

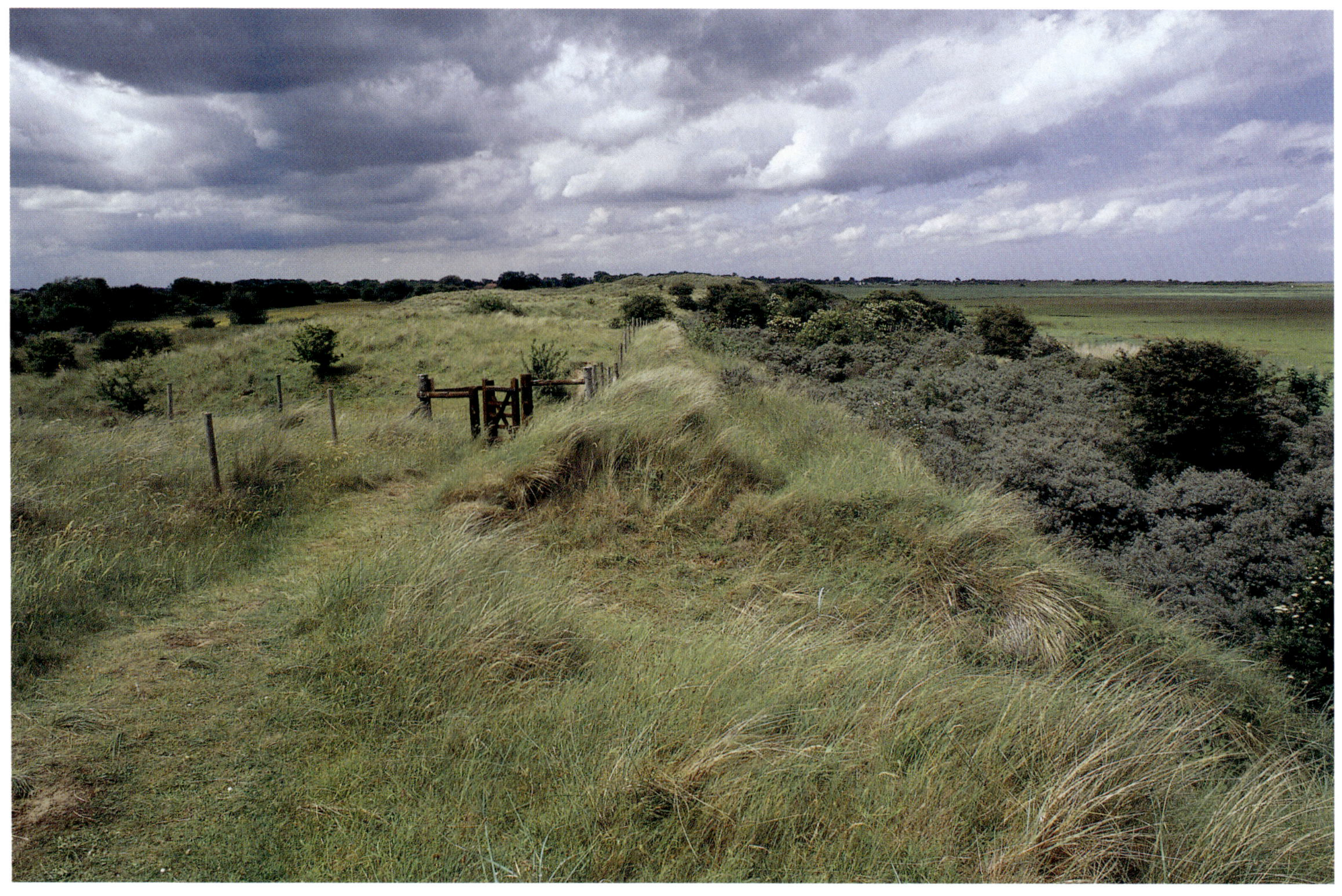

Sand dunes at Saltfleetby
Summer clouds sweep over the scrub and salt marsh at Saltfleetby and Theddlethorpe Dunes National Nature Reserve.

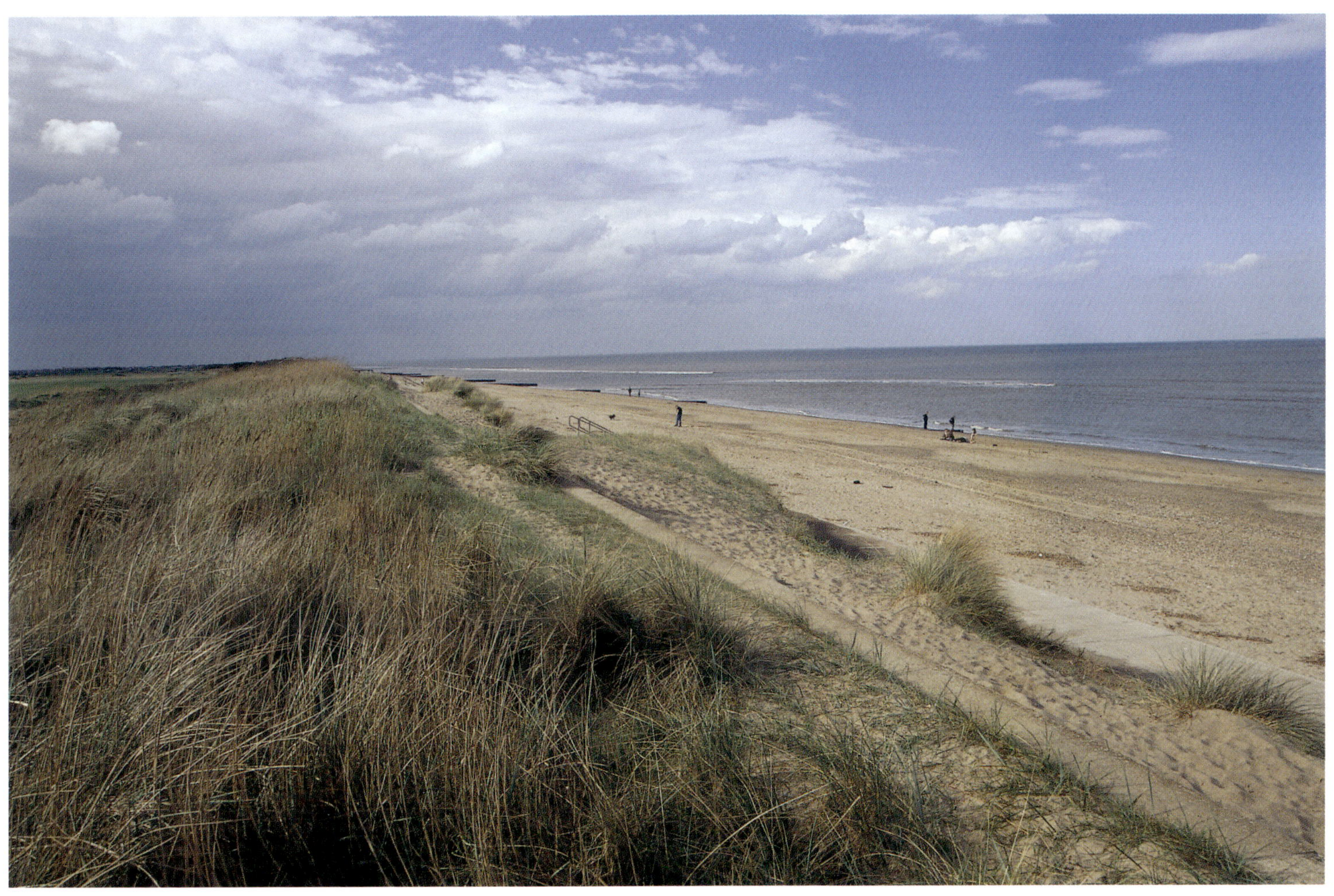

Seashore
Sand dunes line the back of the beach near Huttoft Bank.

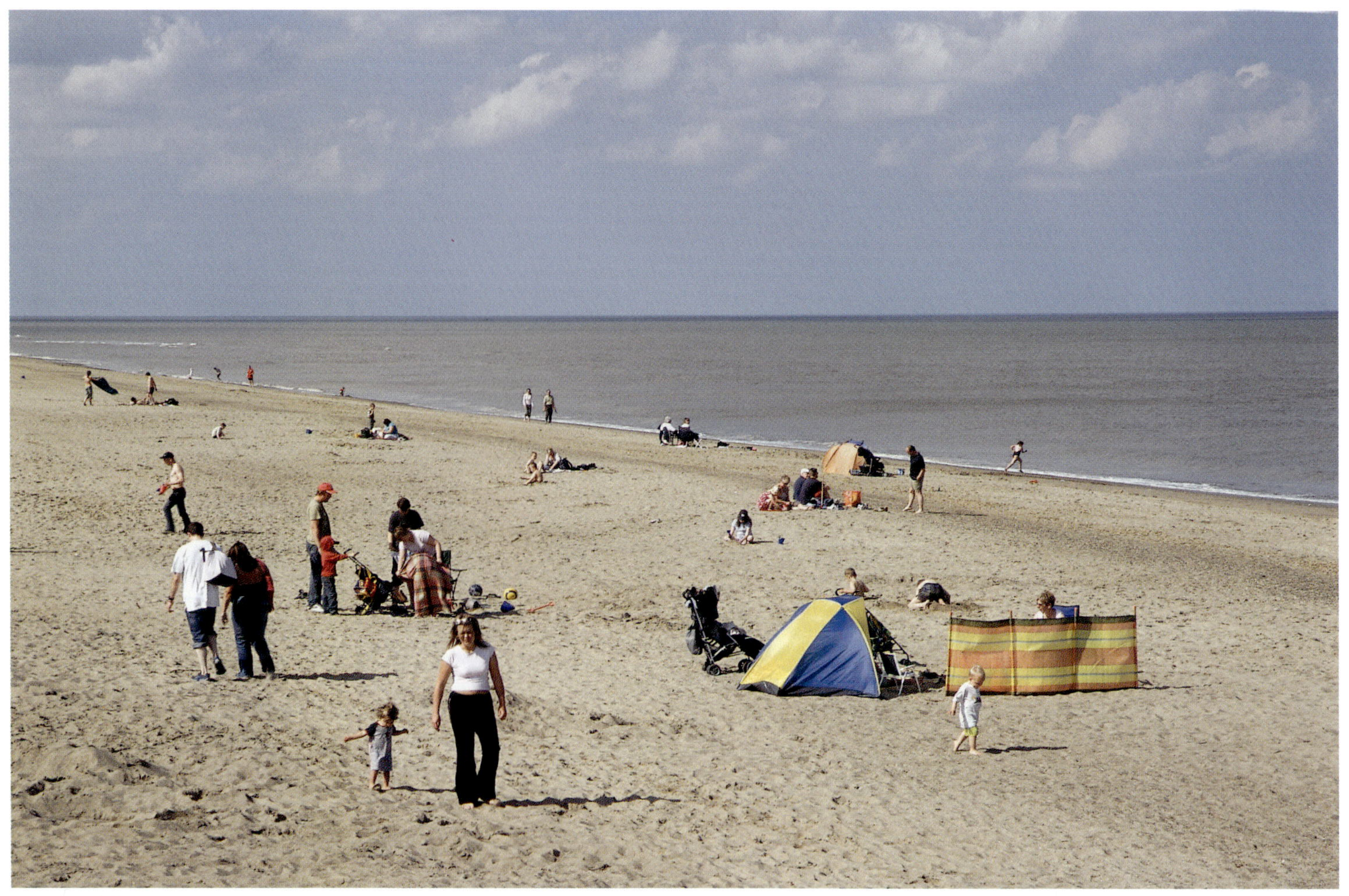

Sutton on Sea
Holidaymakers enjoy the sunshine on the sandy beach.

Opposite: The beach huts and flower beds create a splash of colour against the summer sky.

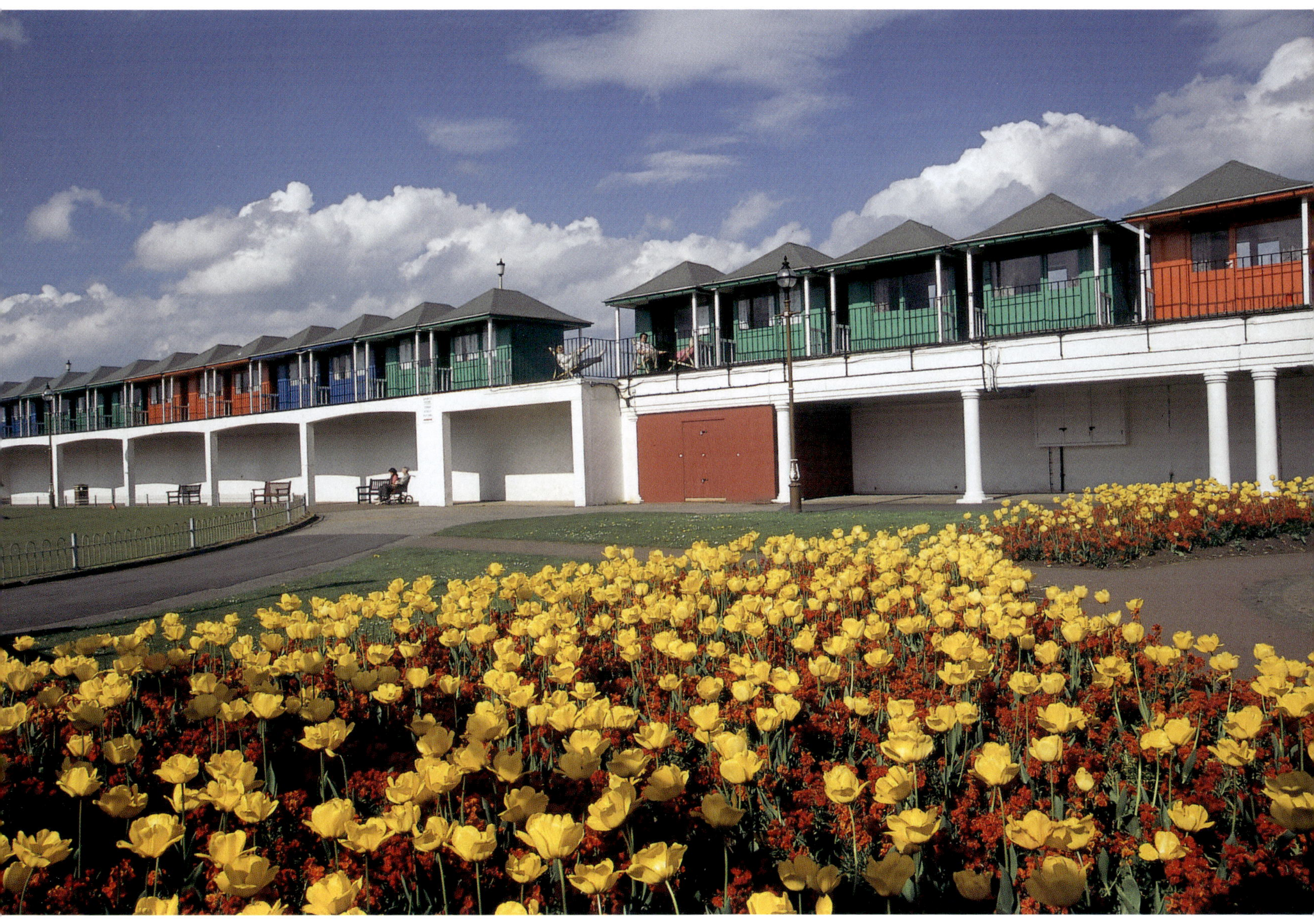

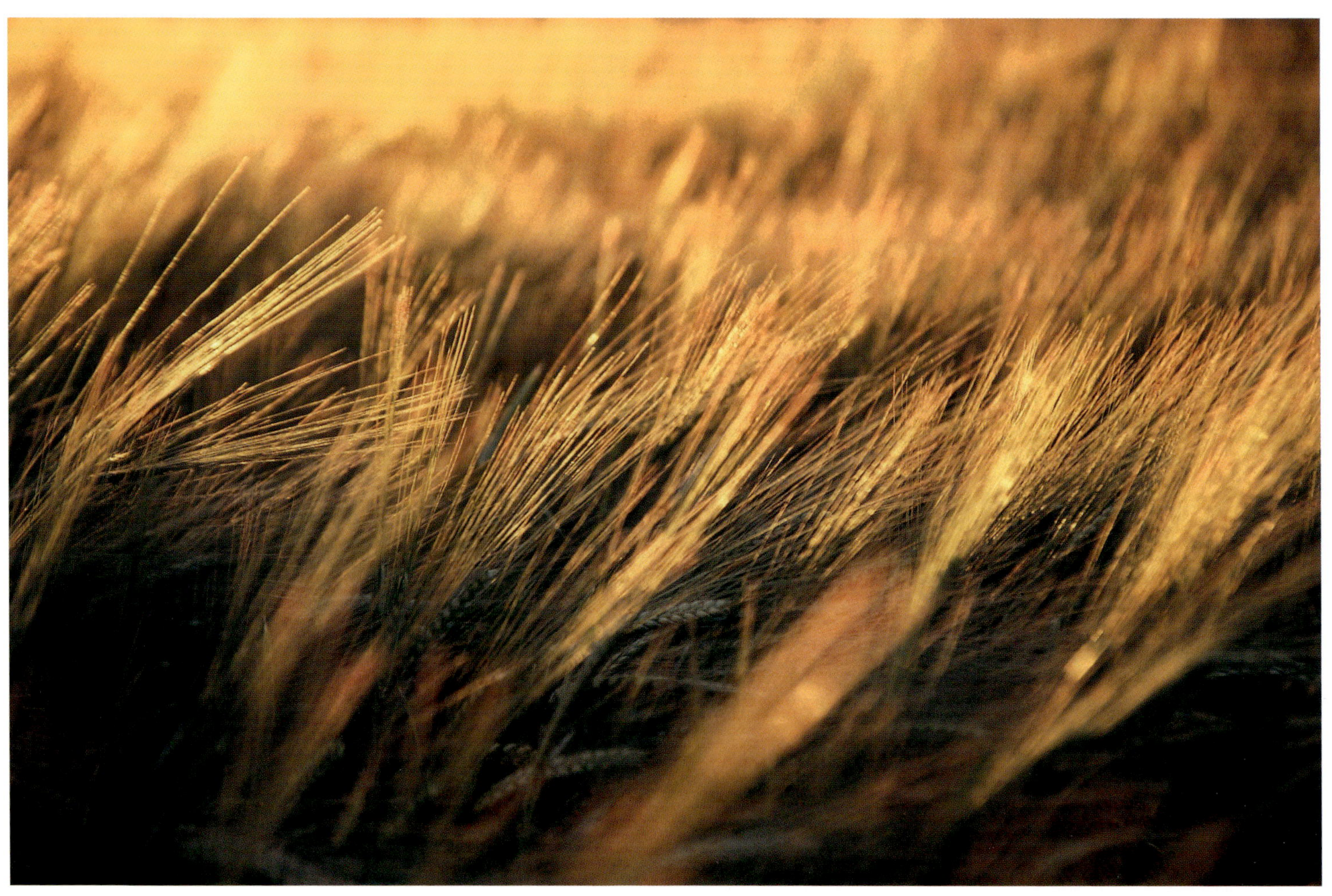

Barley awns
Late evening sunshine highlights the golden awns of ripe barley.

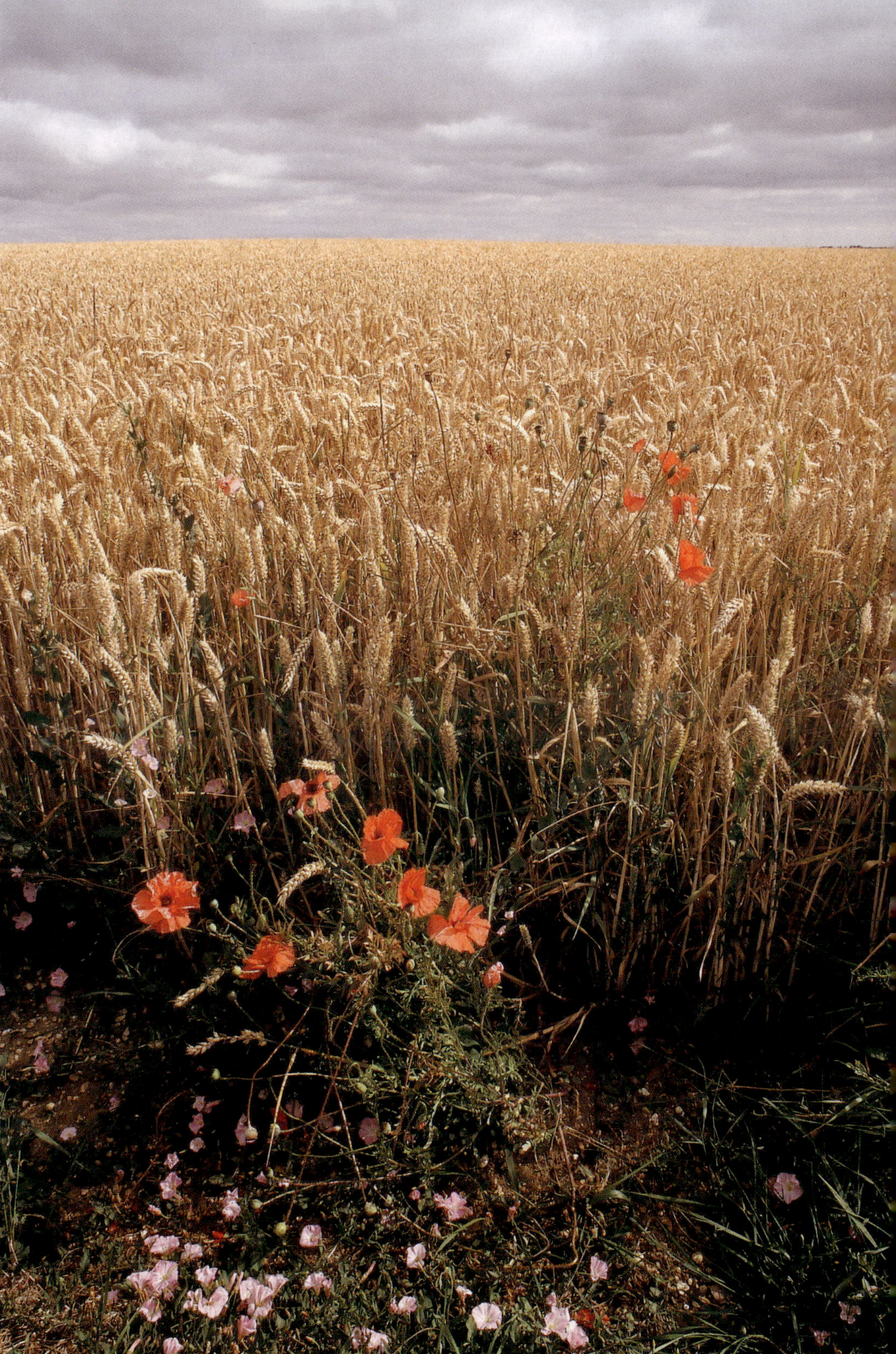

Field bindweed and poppy
Field bindweed and poppies flower on
the edge of a field of ripening wheat,
seen along the Bluestone Heath road.

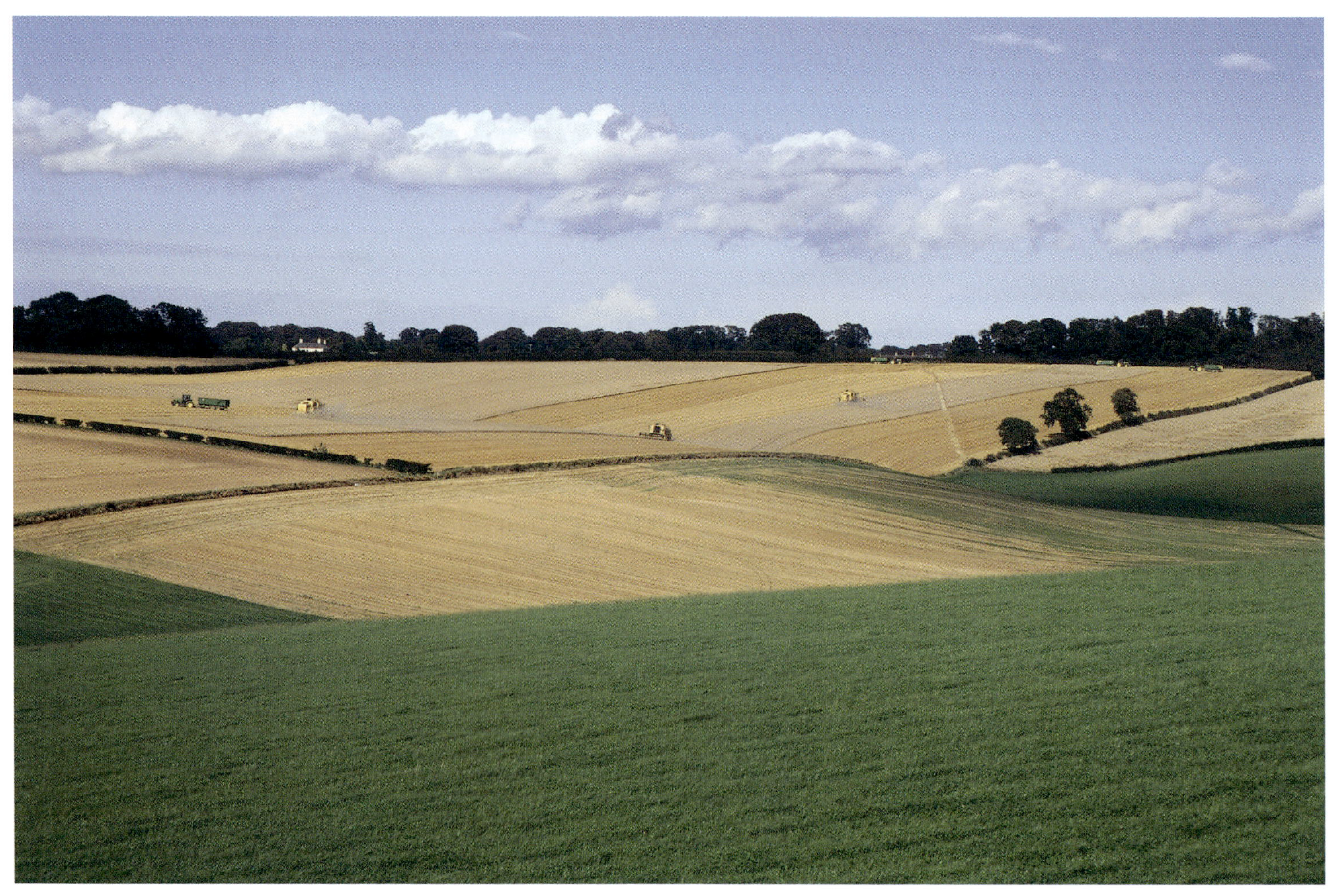

Harvest on the Wolds
It is August and the harvest is in full swing as a fleet of combine harvesters and
tractors and trailers are at work in this field of wheat near Binbrook.

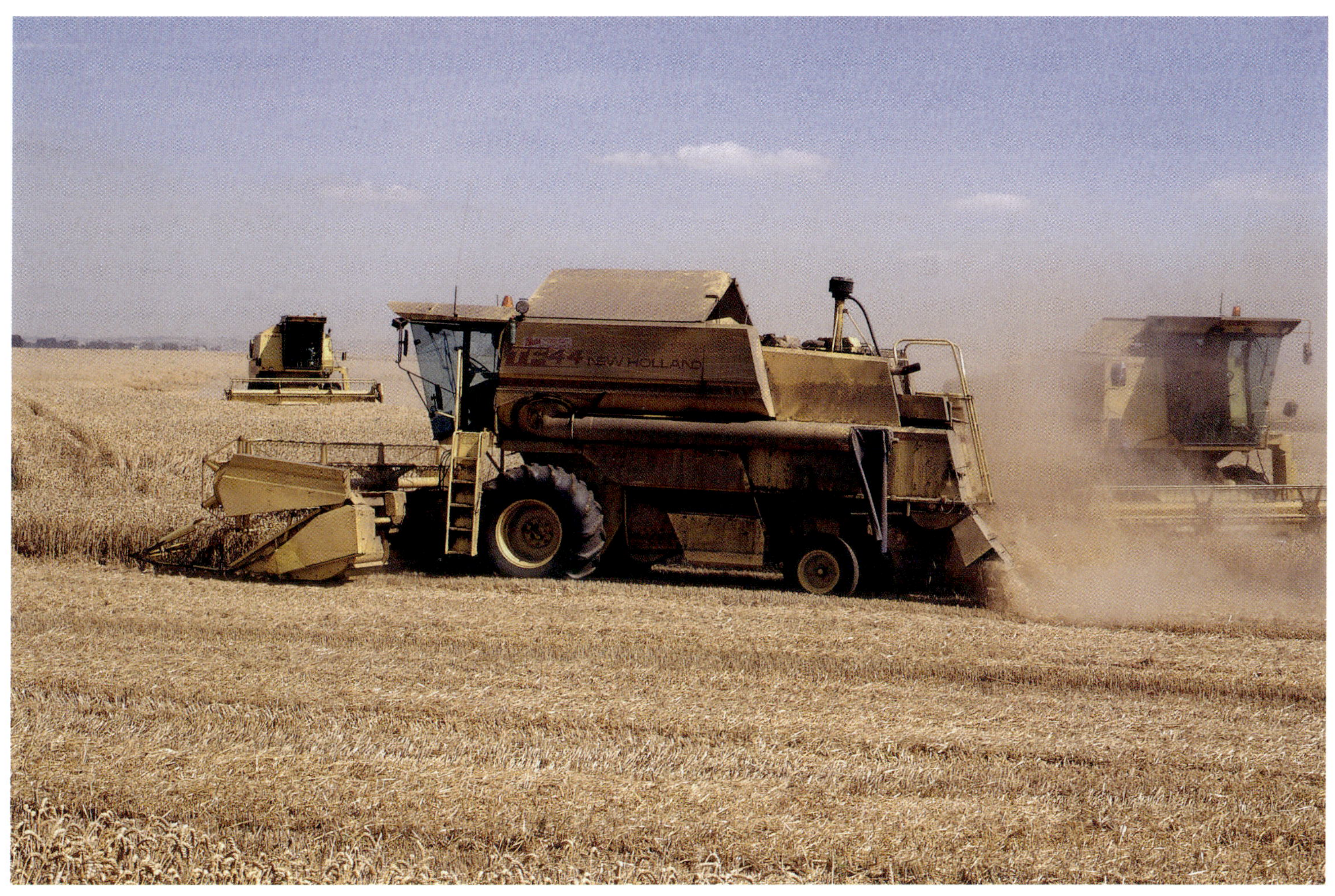

Combine harvesters
Three powerful combine harvesters cut and thresh the corn, spreading a dusty layer of chaff and chopped straw in their wake.

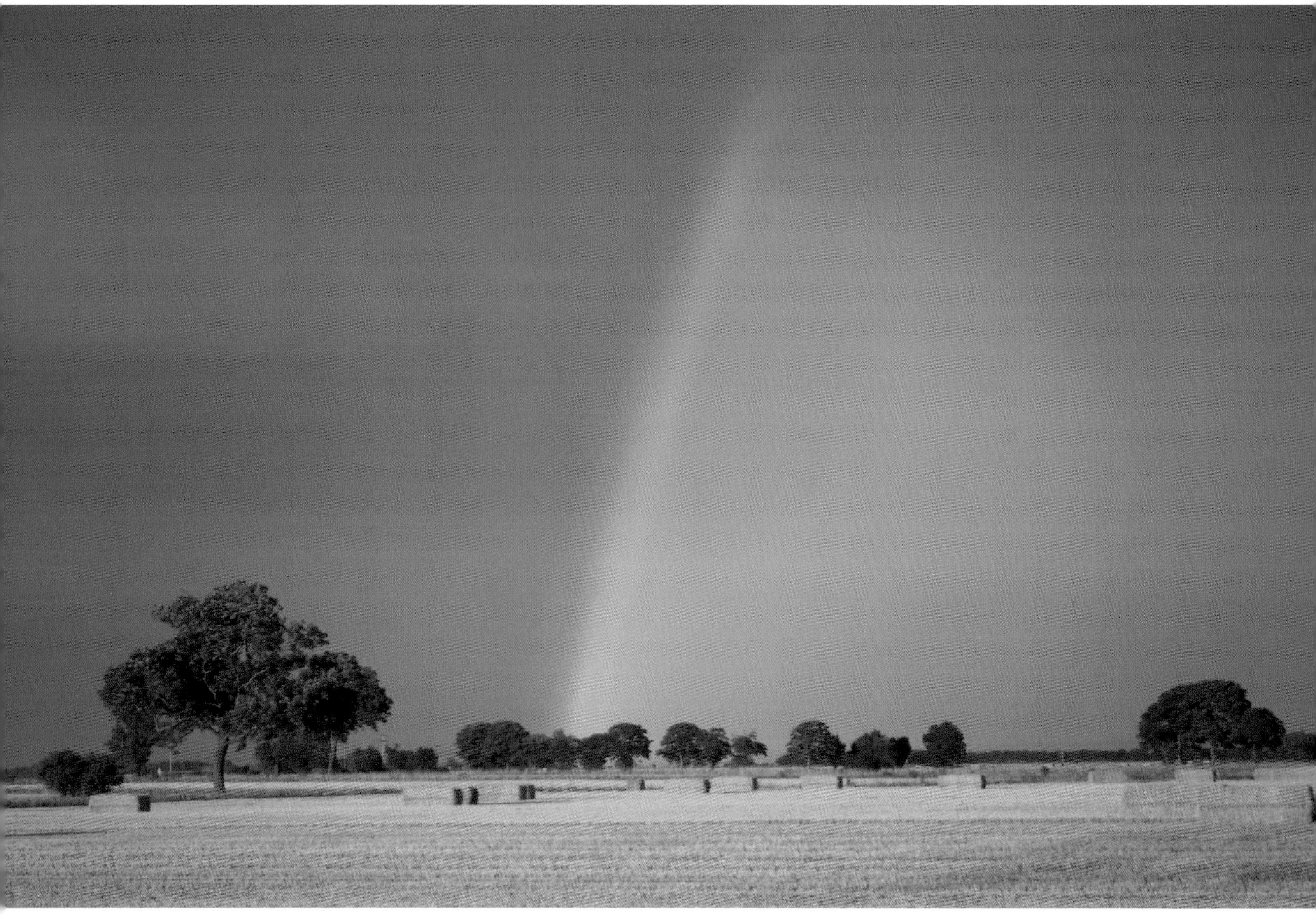

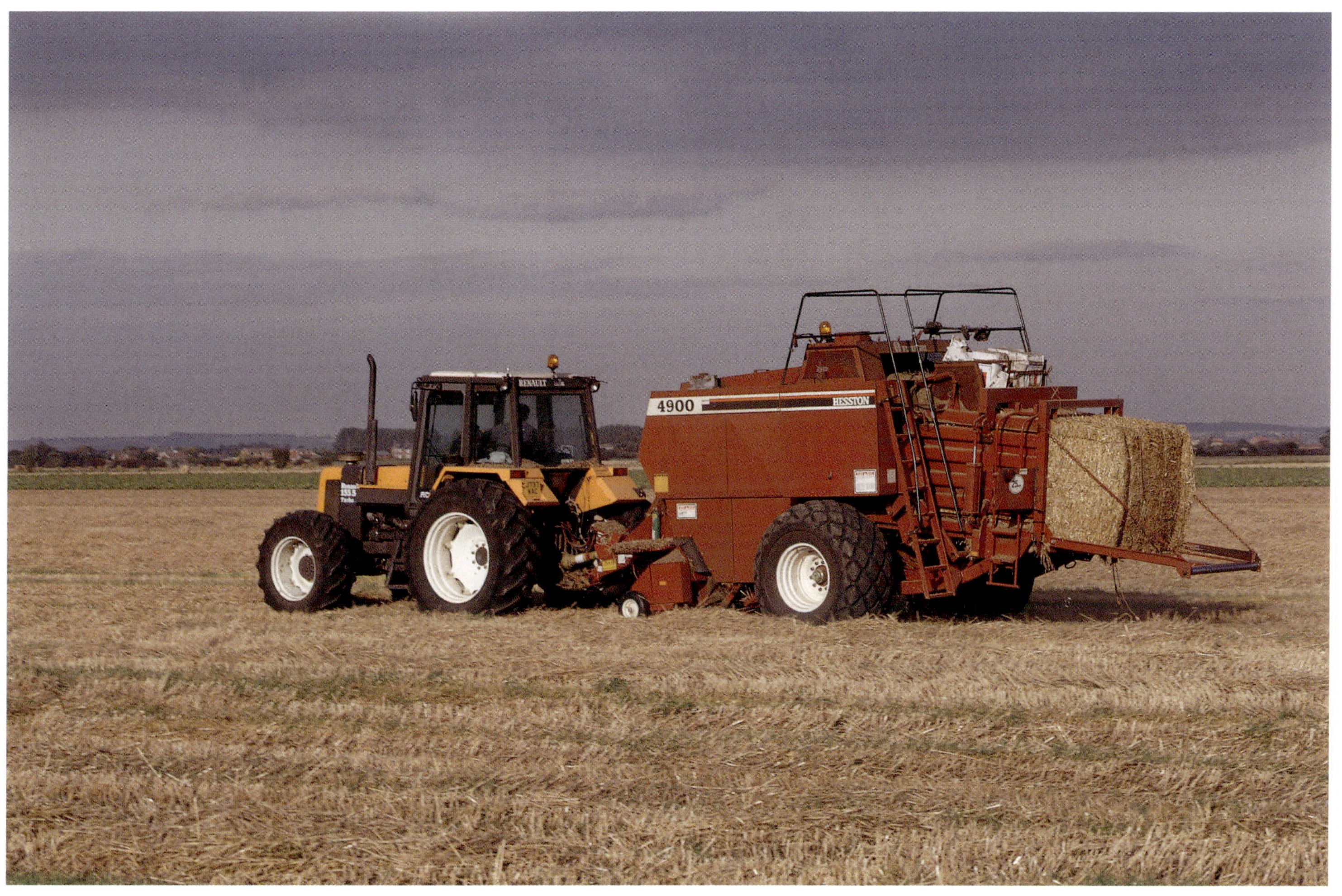

Tractor and baler
A tractor and baler at work in a field near Grayingham, baling straw as rain threatens.

Opposite: **Rainbow over cornfield**
A summer storm passes over a cornfield near Crowle.

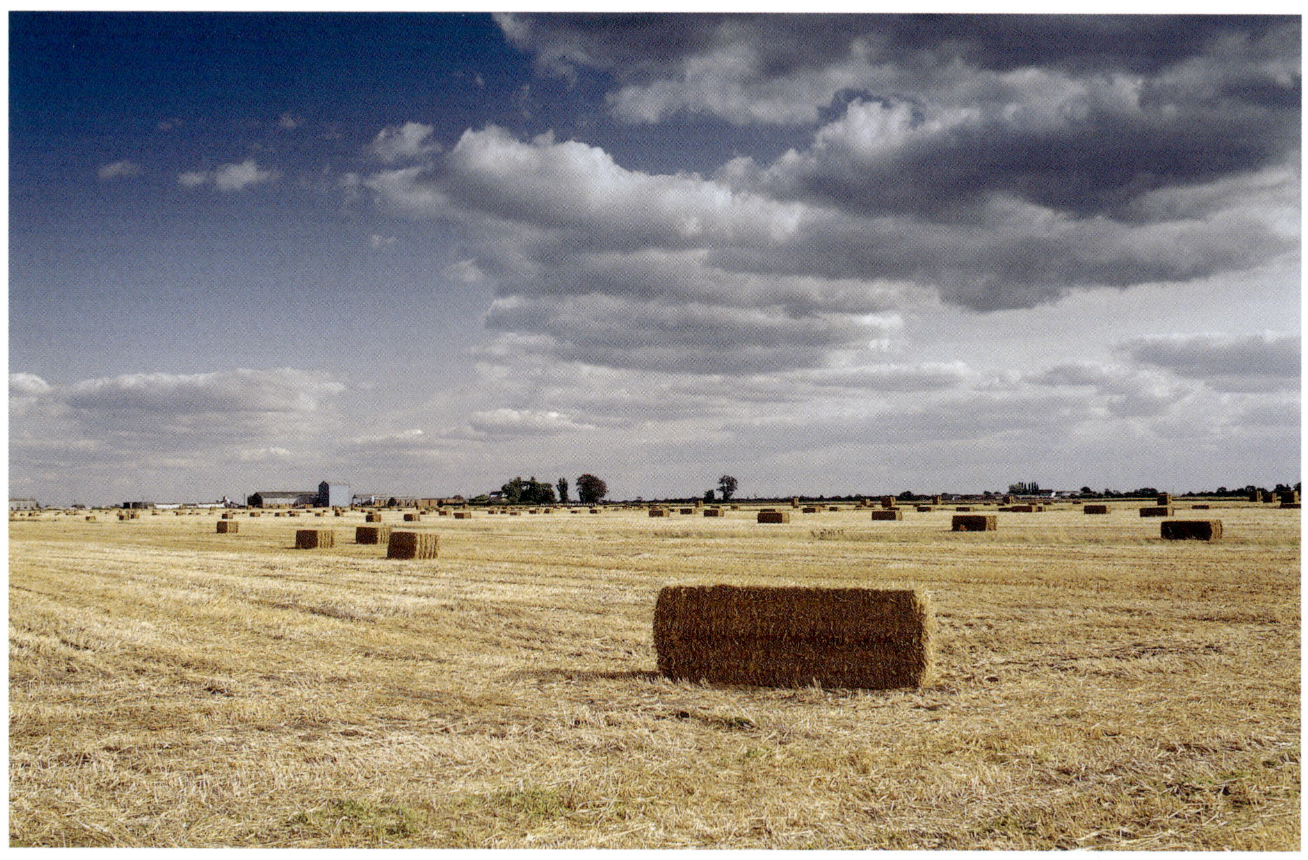

Straw bales
Large straw bales wait to be gathered-in under darkening skies near Belton, in the Isle of Axholme.

Opposite: **Storm clouds**
Turbulent cumulonimbus clouds turn the sky dark as a storm approaches Kirton in Lindsey.
Minutes later torrential rain and hail were accompanied by thunder and lightning.

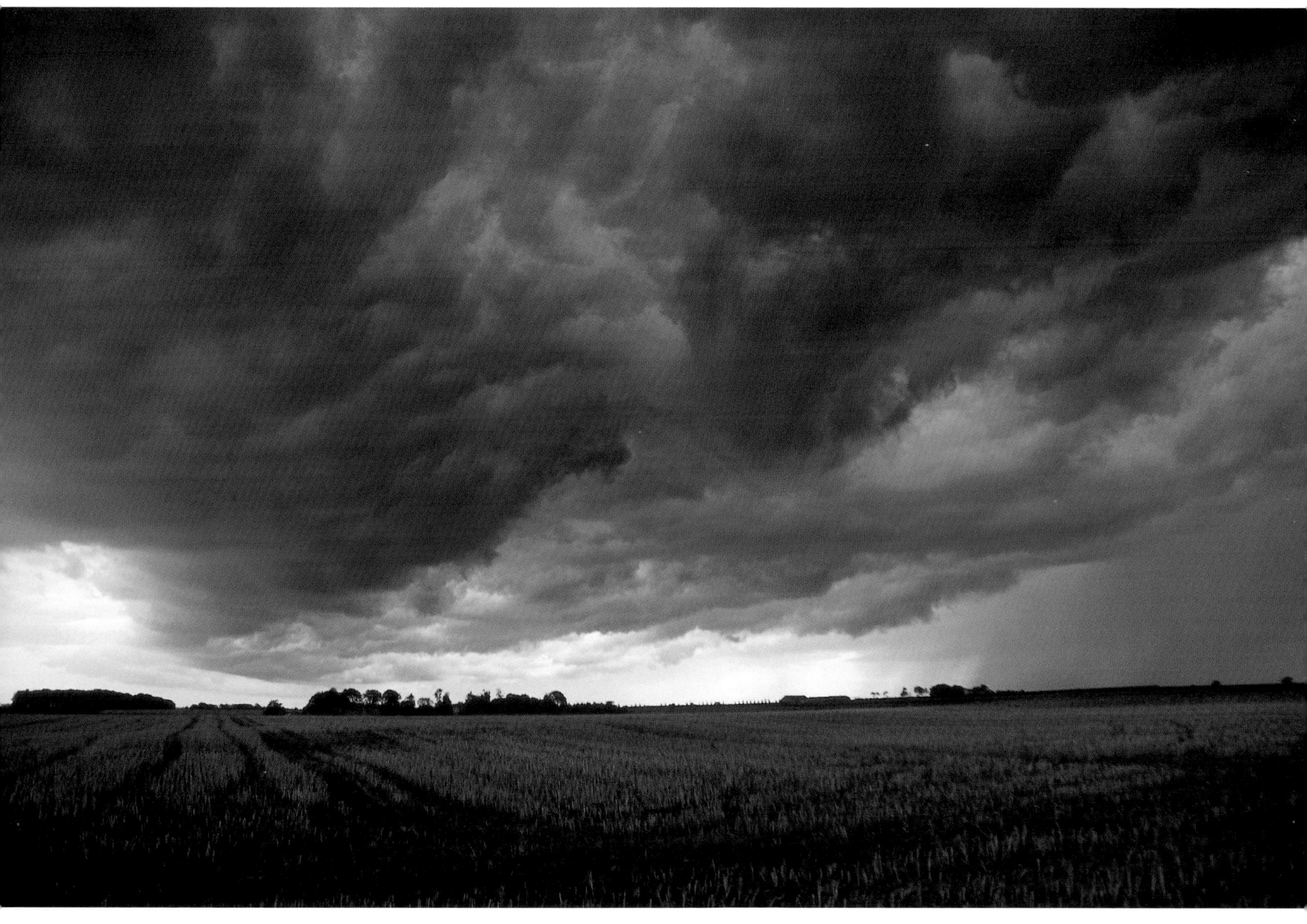

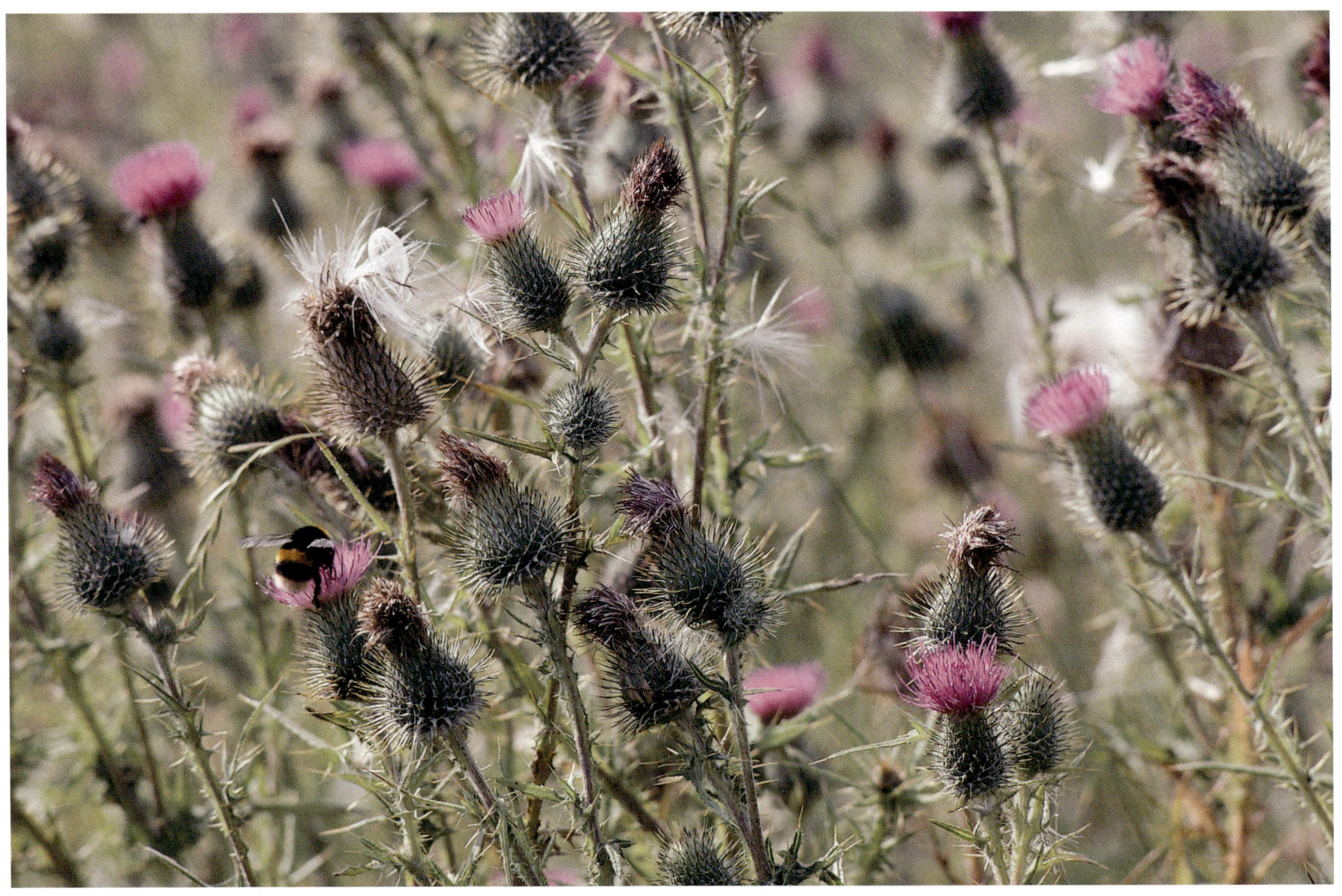

Bumble bee on thistles
A bumble bee collects pollen and nectar from the flowers of spear thistles.

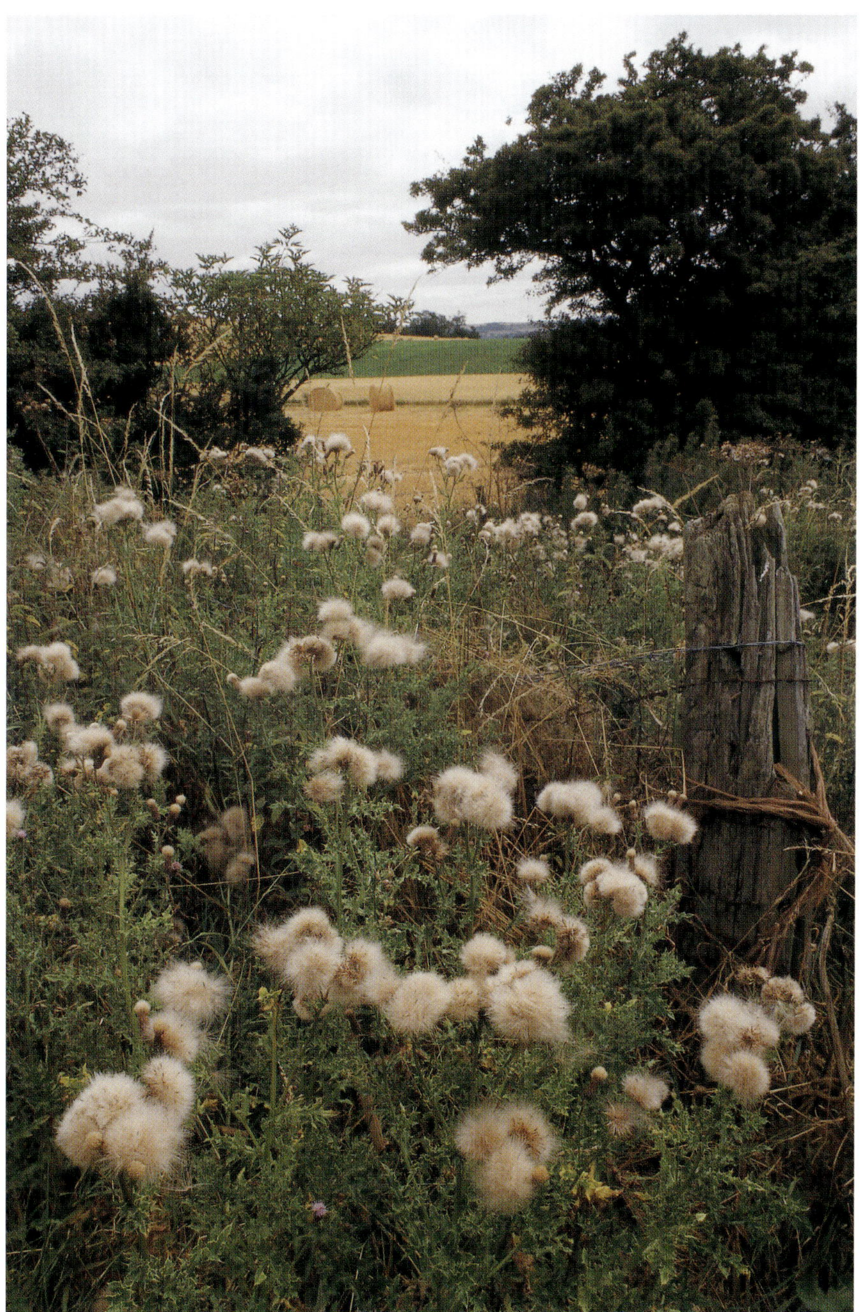

Thistle seedheads
Creeping thistles seed along the field boundary
in this late summer scene near Goulceby.

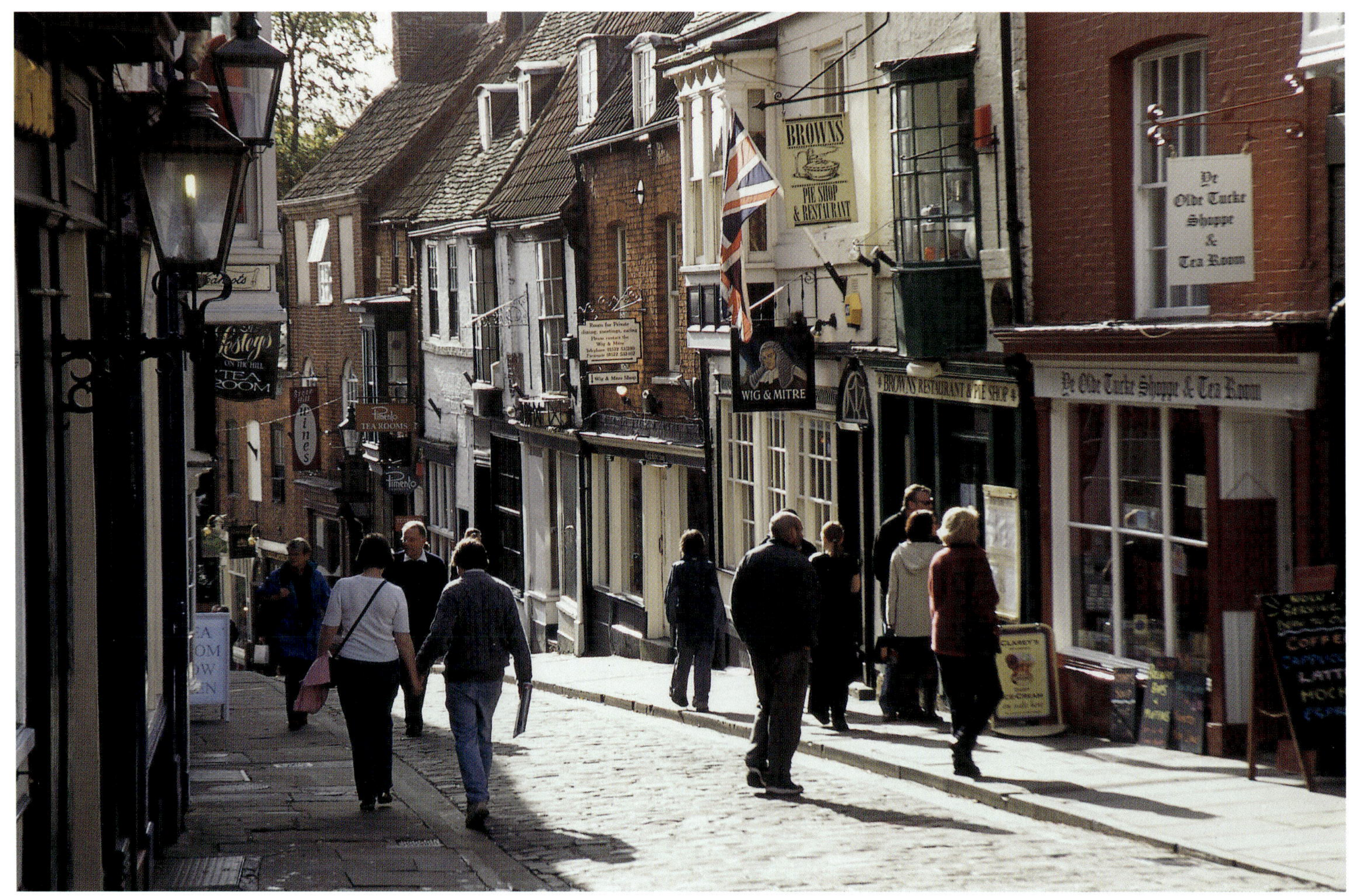

Steep Hill, Lincoln
Visitors enjoy the autumn sunshine on Lincoln's most famous street.

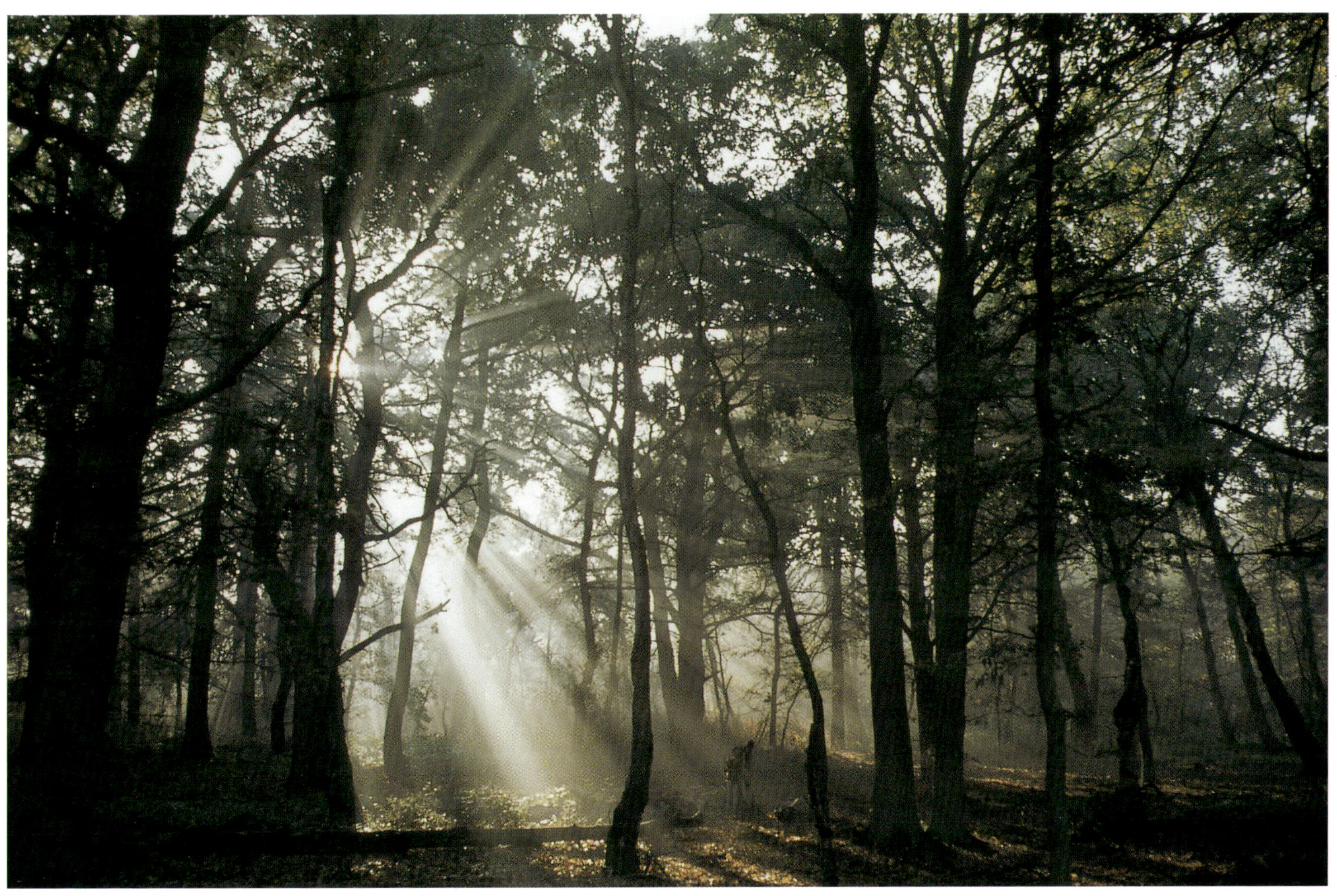

Sunburst in woodland
Early morning sunshine slants through woodland at Moor Farm Nature Reserve, near Woodhall Spa.

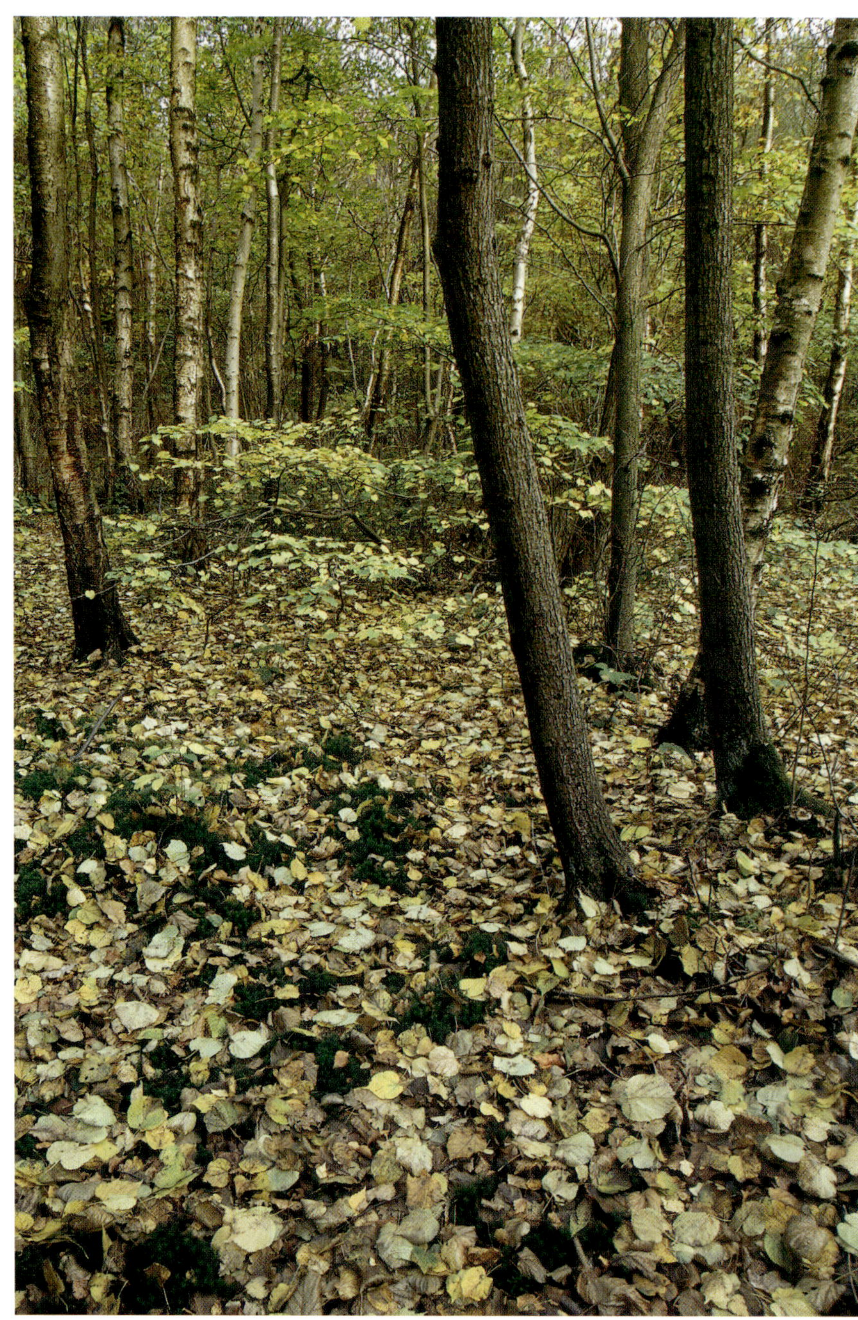

Lime leaves carpet the woodland floor
Visitors to Chamber's Farm Wood near Wragby
can enjoy walking through these ancient and
nationally-important limewoods.

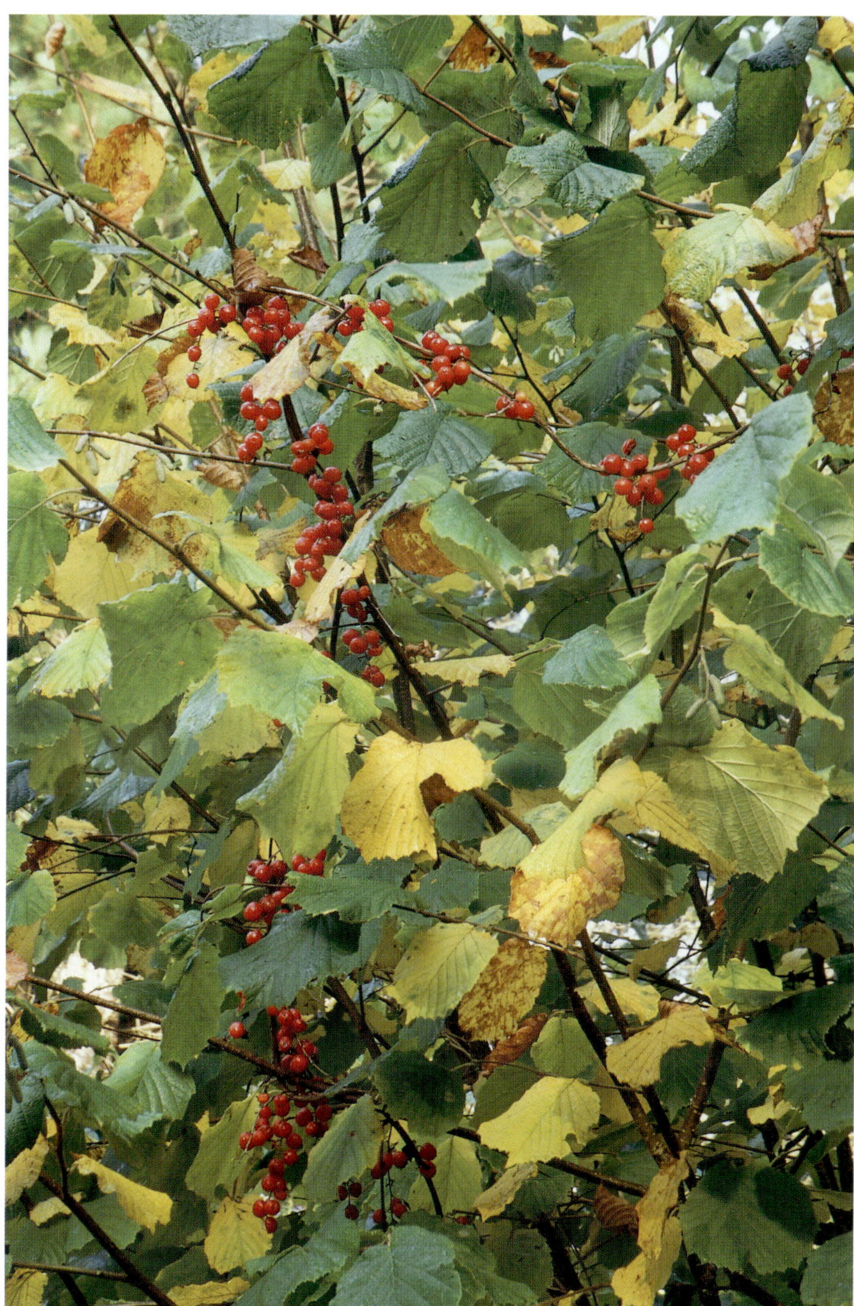

Bryony and hazel
The red berries of white bryony stand out
among the yellowing foliage of the hazel shrub.

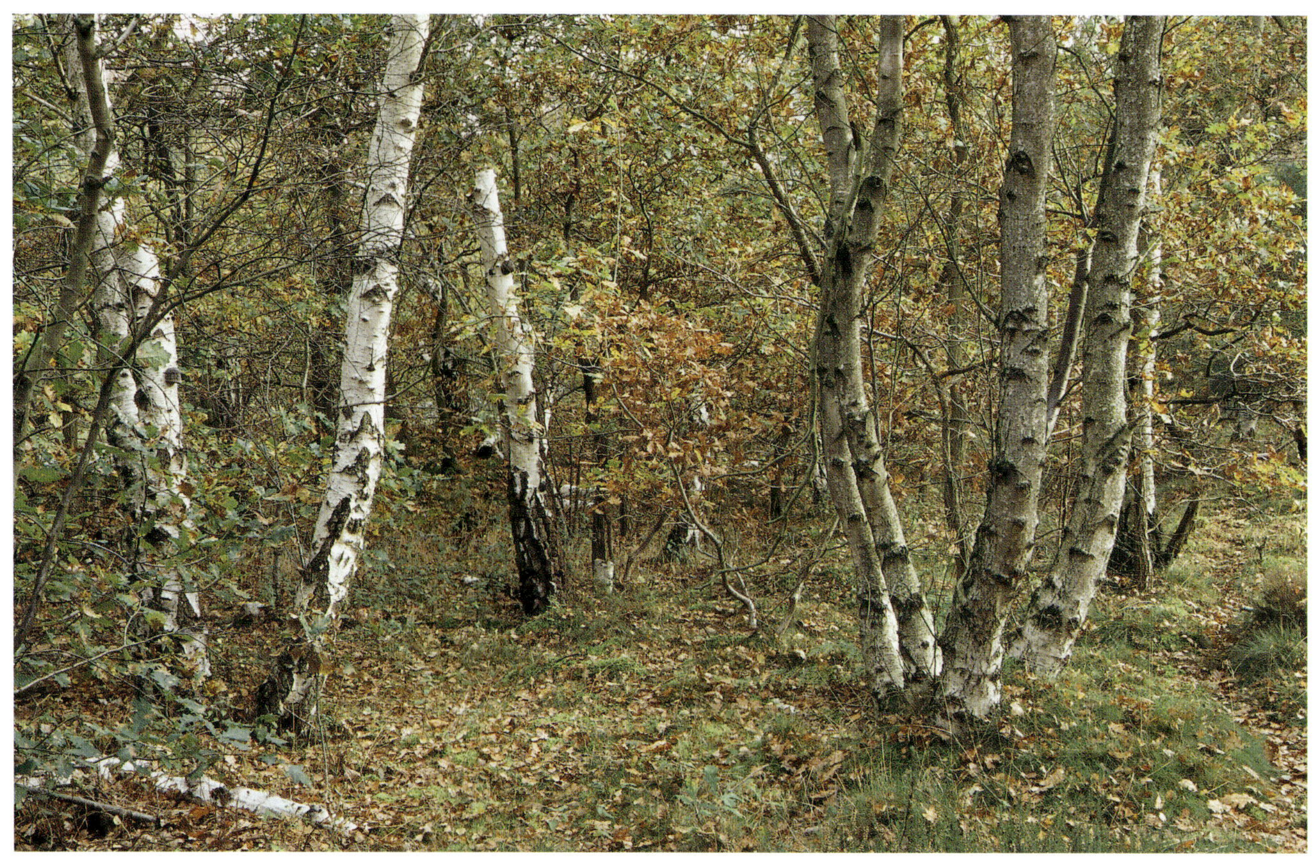

Kirby Moor
An autumn scene of silver birch and fallen leaves in woodland near Woodhall Spa.

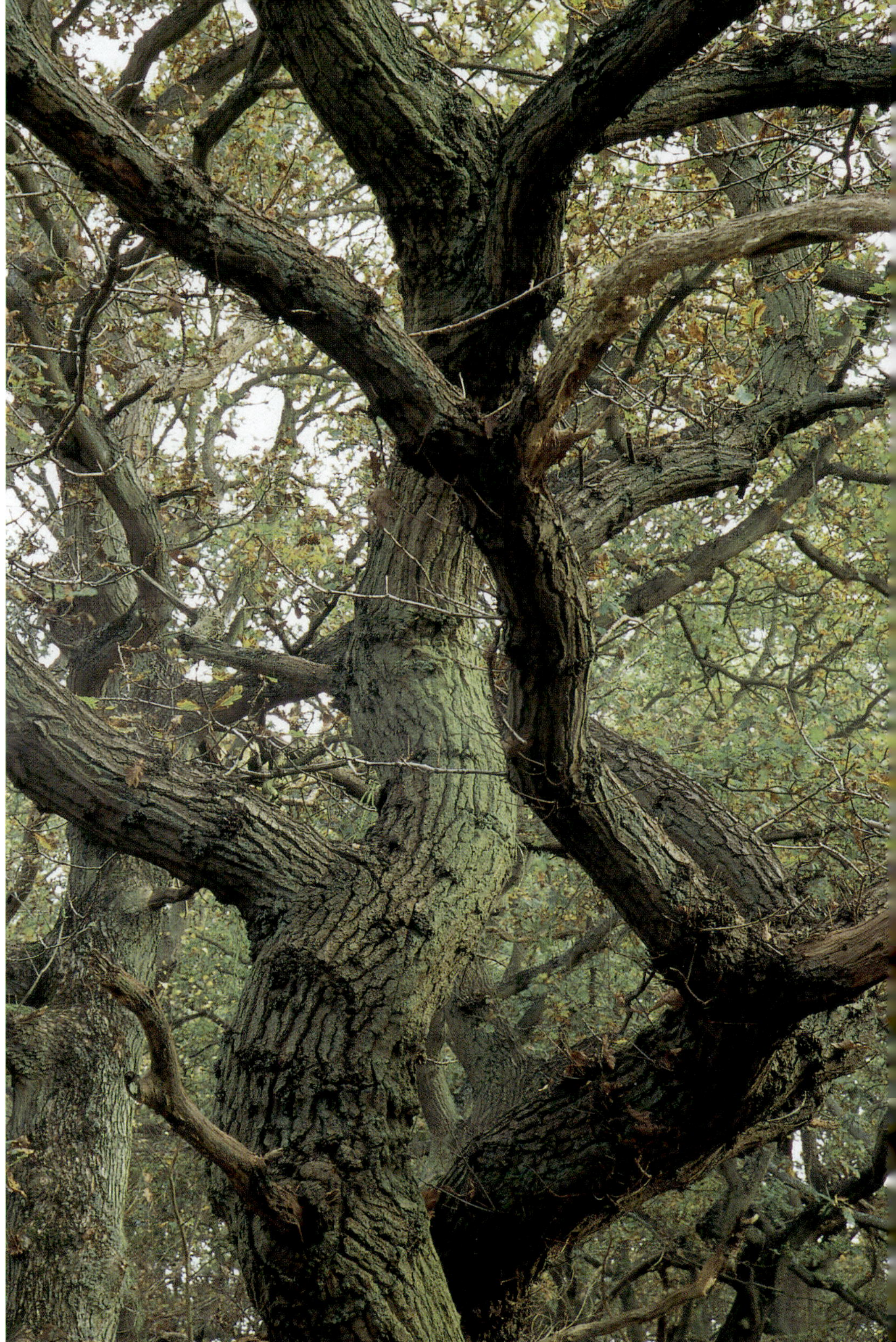

Oak tree
The knarled and twisted branches of this
oak tree are revealed as the leaves fall.

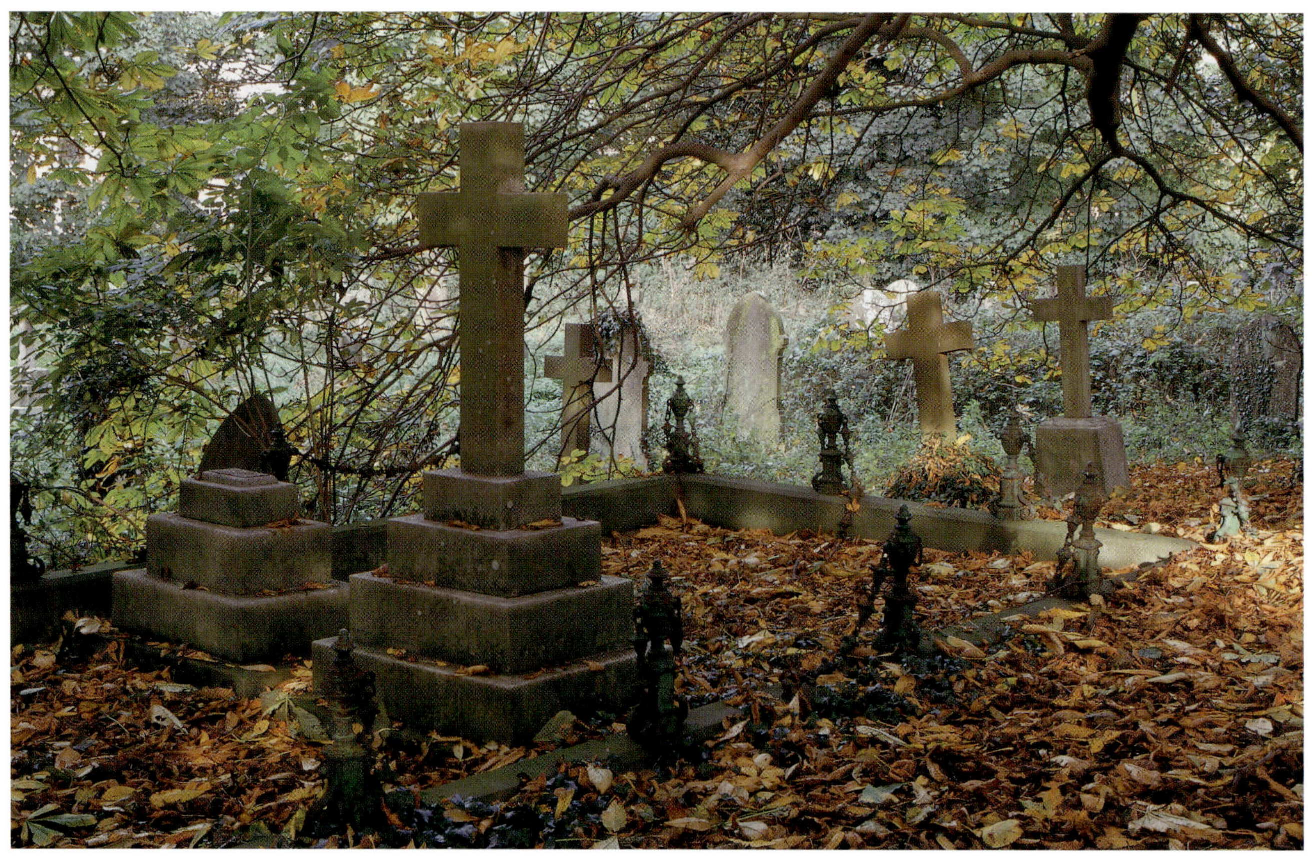

Gravestones at Owston Ferry
Dappled autumn light catches the gravestones in Owston Ferry churchyard.

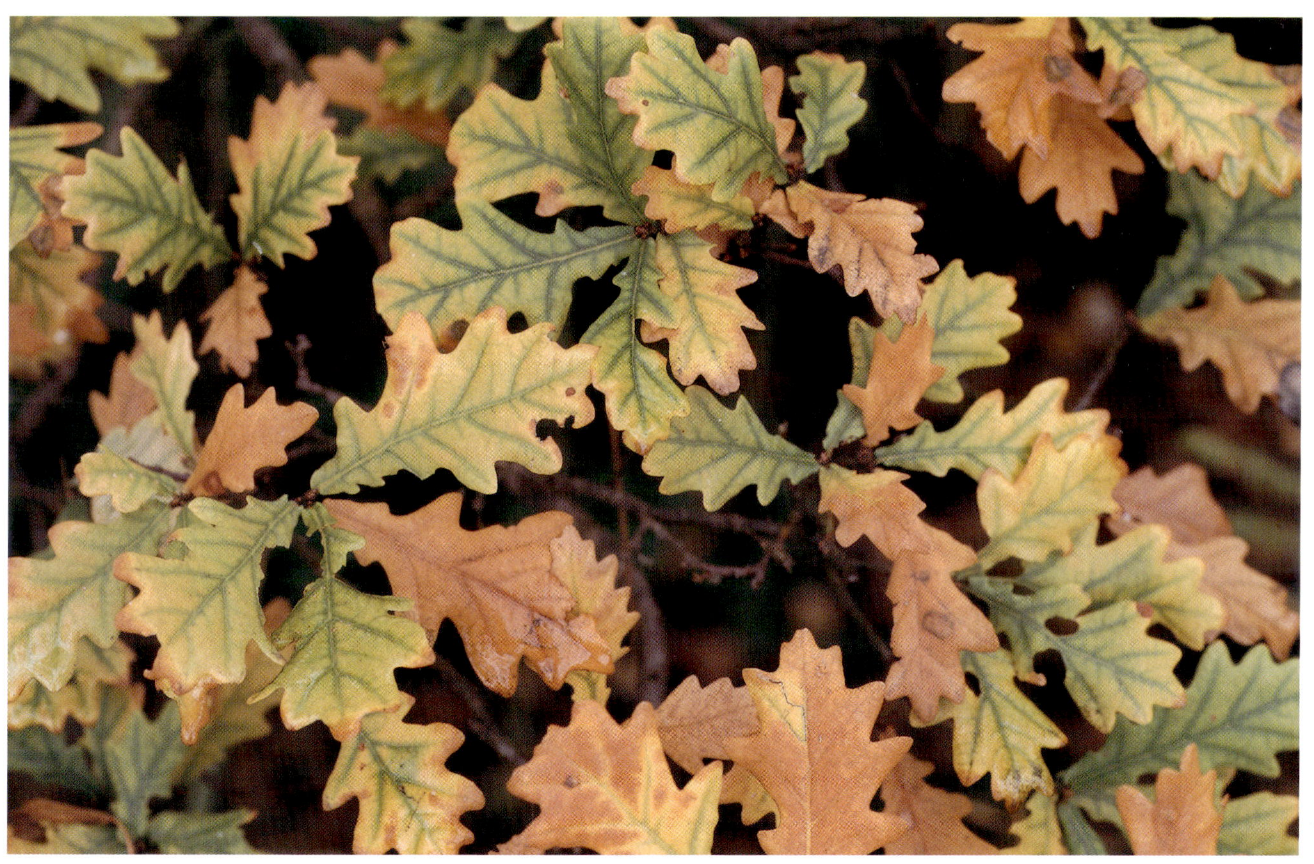

Oak leaves
Oak leaves reveal a range of colours as autumn changes them from green to yellow and brown.

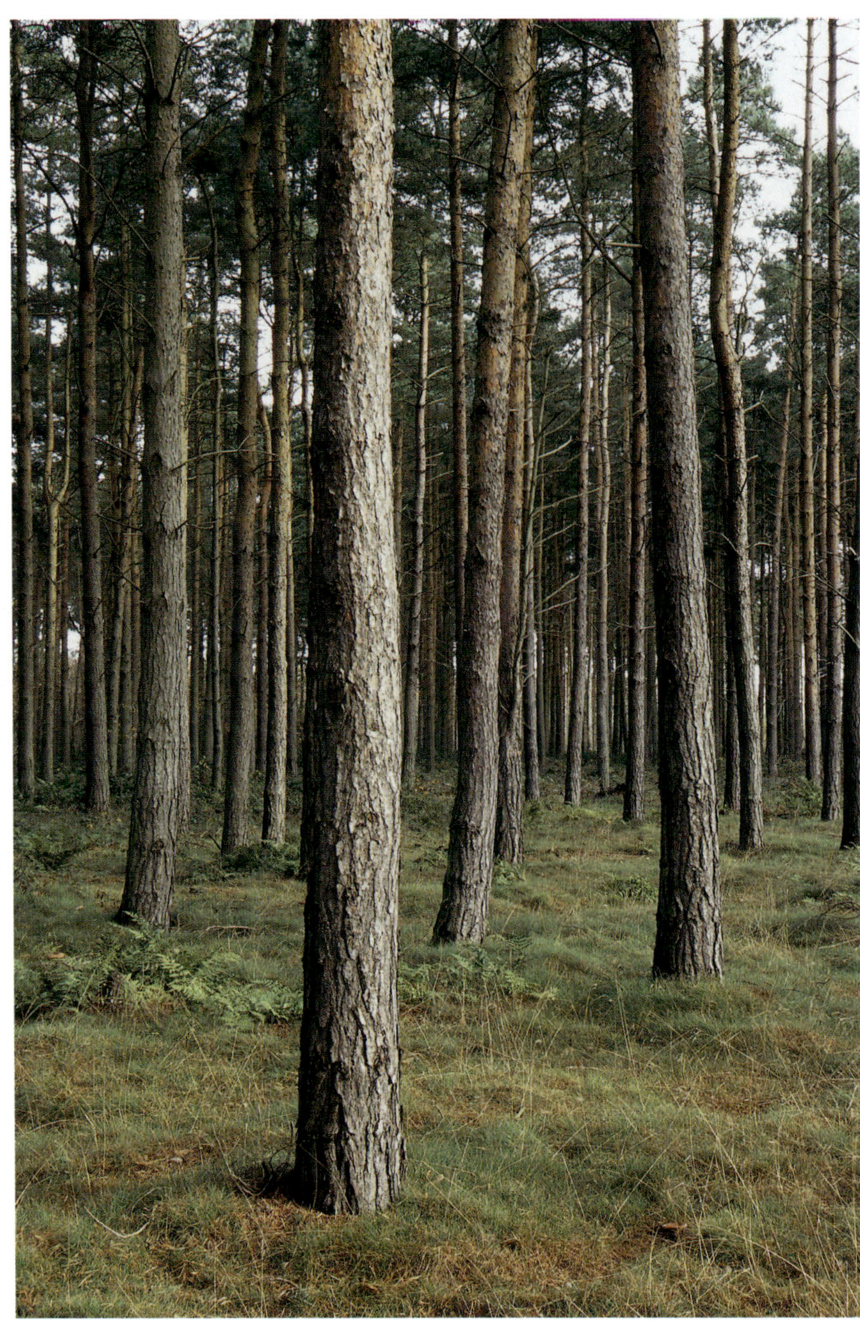

Left and opposite: **Ostler's Plantation
near Woodhall Spa**
Scots pine trees, planted close together, grow
tall and straight as they search for light.

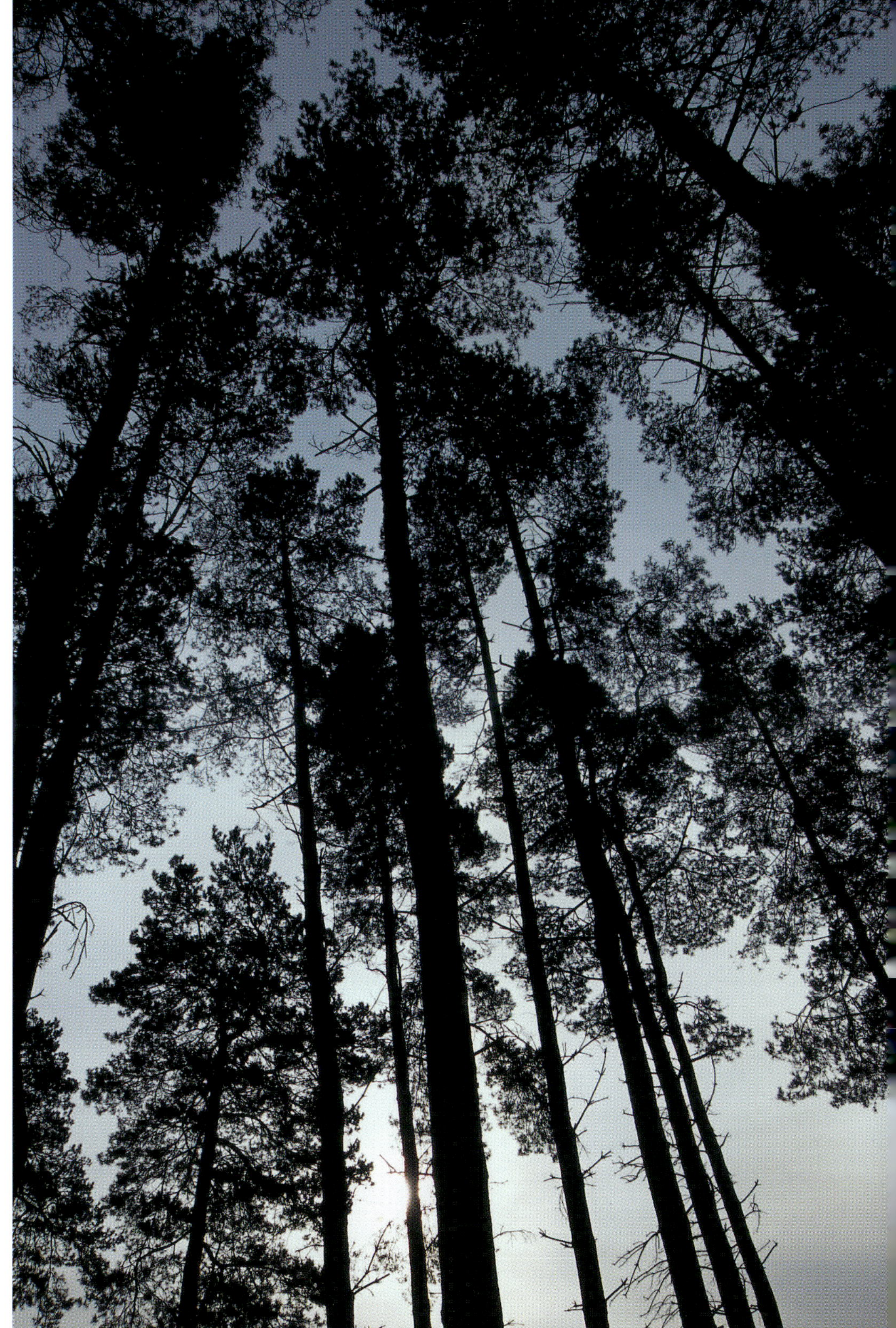

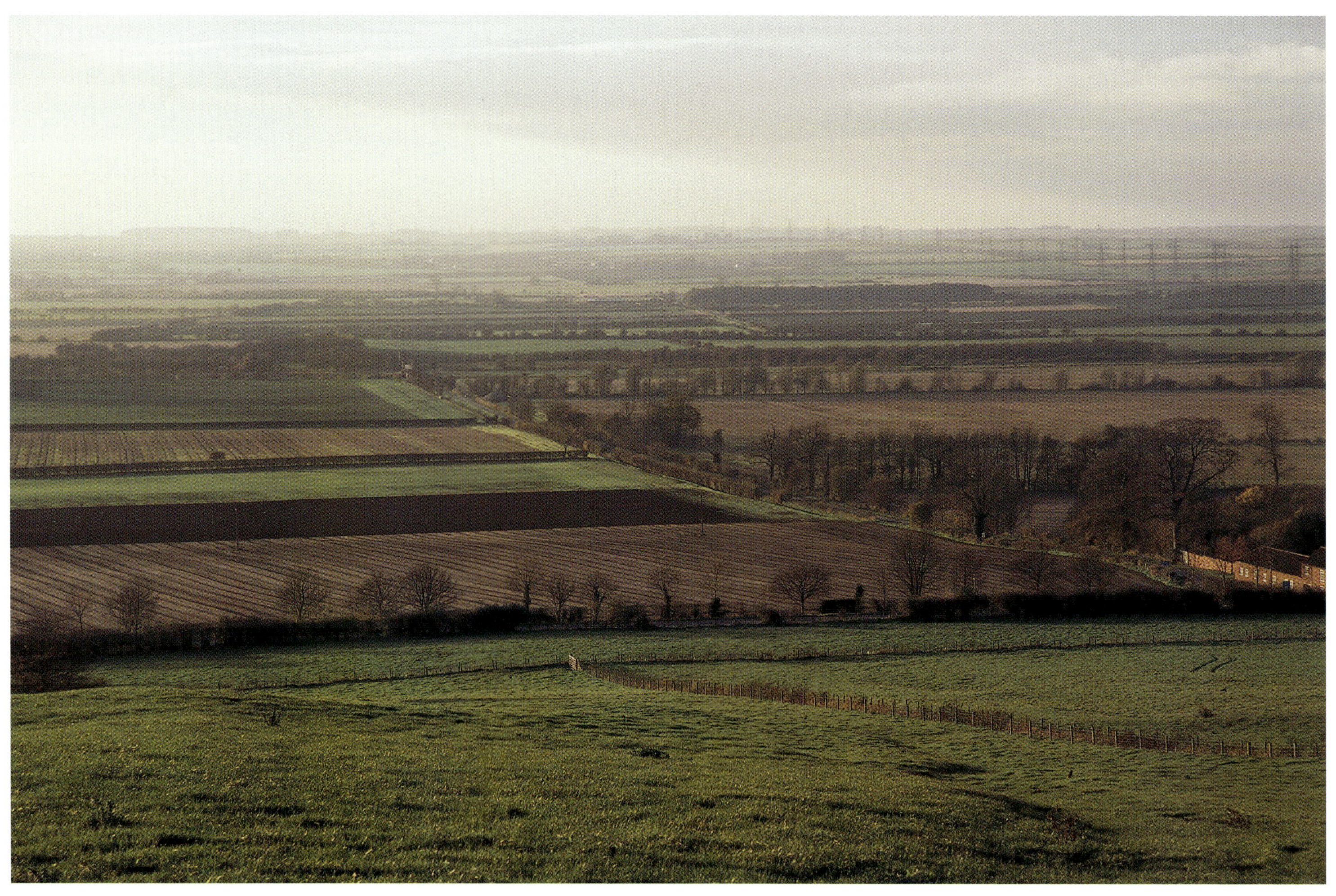

Ancholme valley
Warm autumn sunlight highlights the pattern of rich fertile farmland in the Ancholme valley.

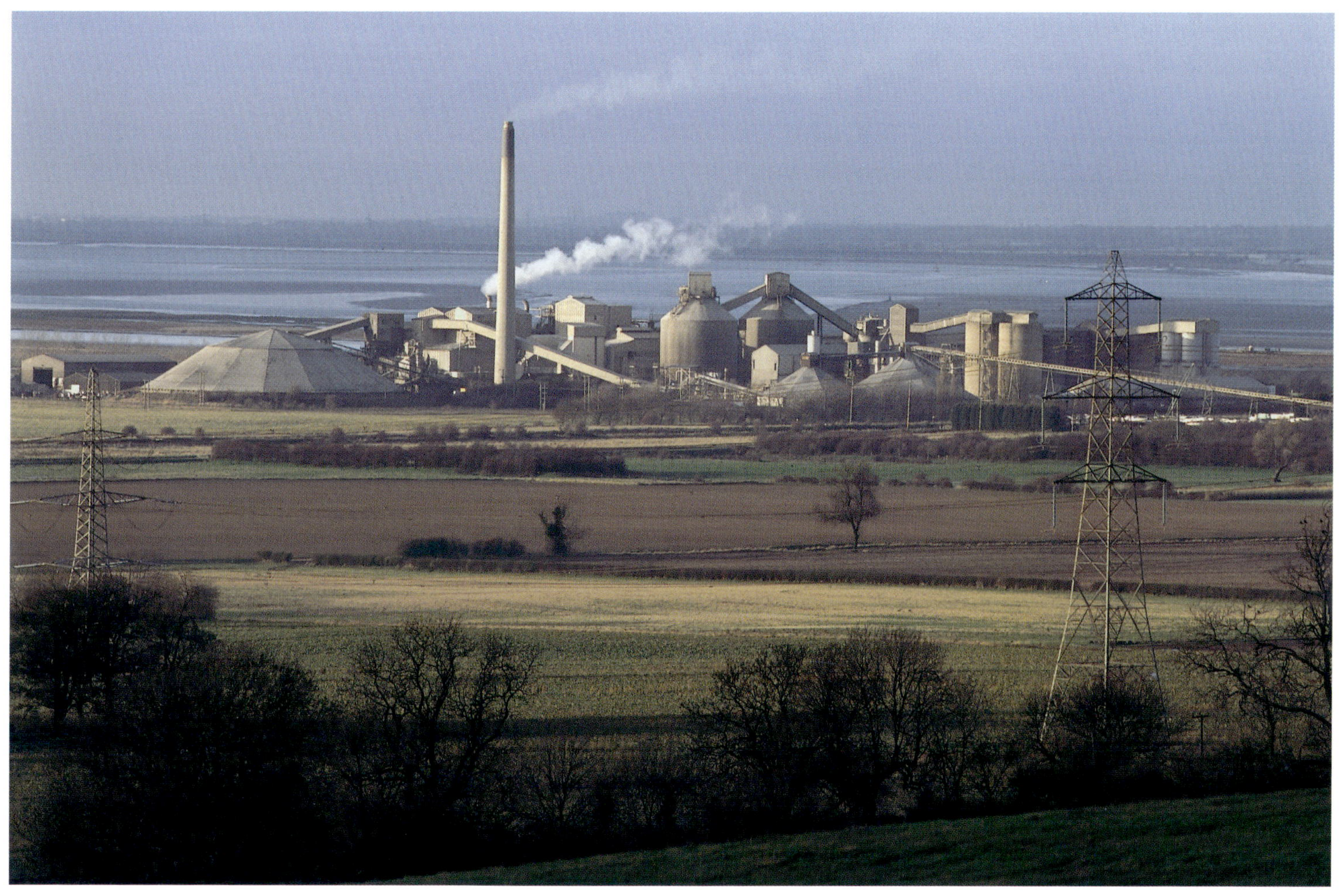

Cement works at Ferriby Sluice
A view from the Wold edge near Horkstow, looking over the cement works at Ferriby Sluice to the Humber estuary beyond.

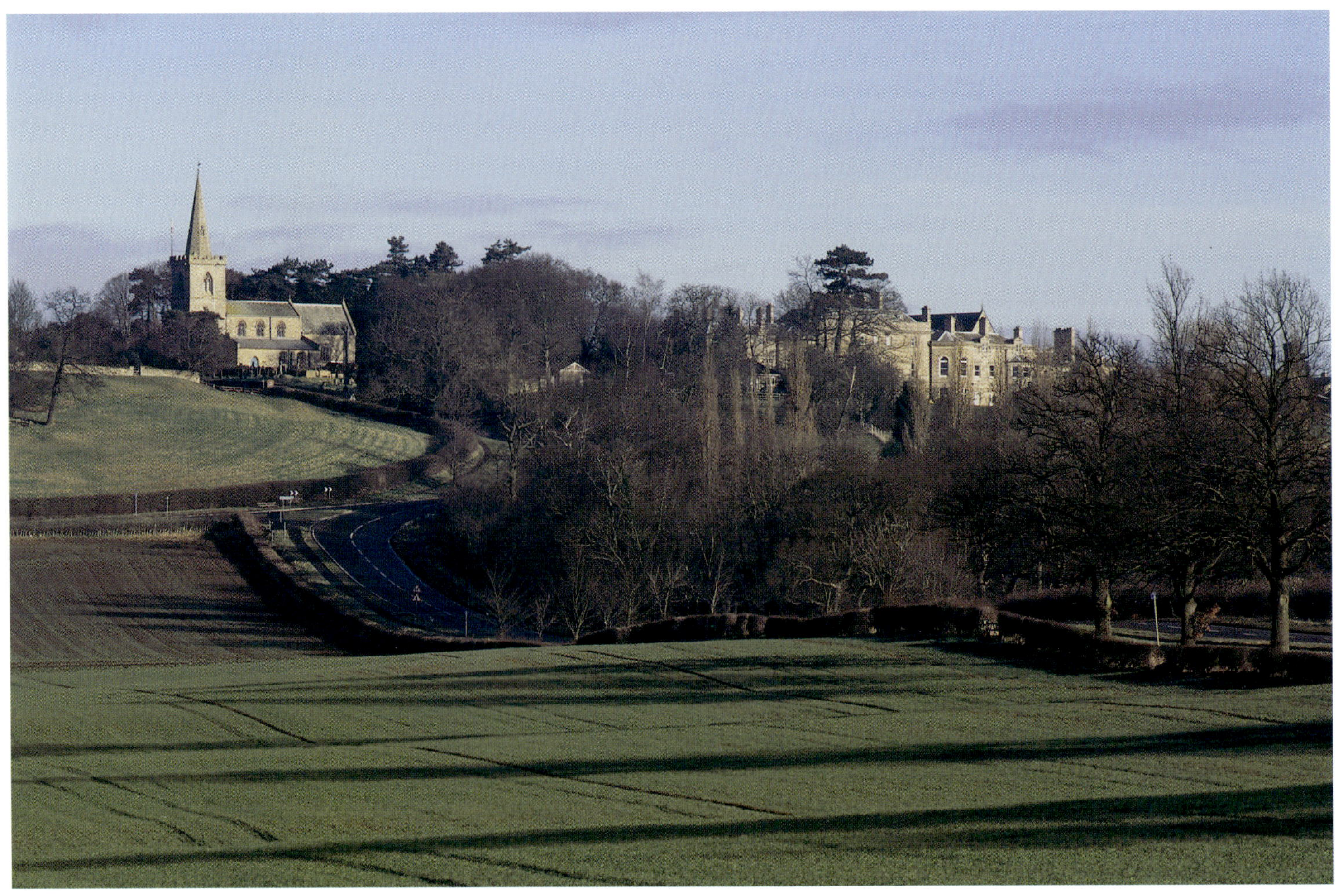

Wellingore
Looking north towards the village of Wellingore as early morning sunlight highlights
the limestone masonry of the church and hall, and spreads long shadows across the field.

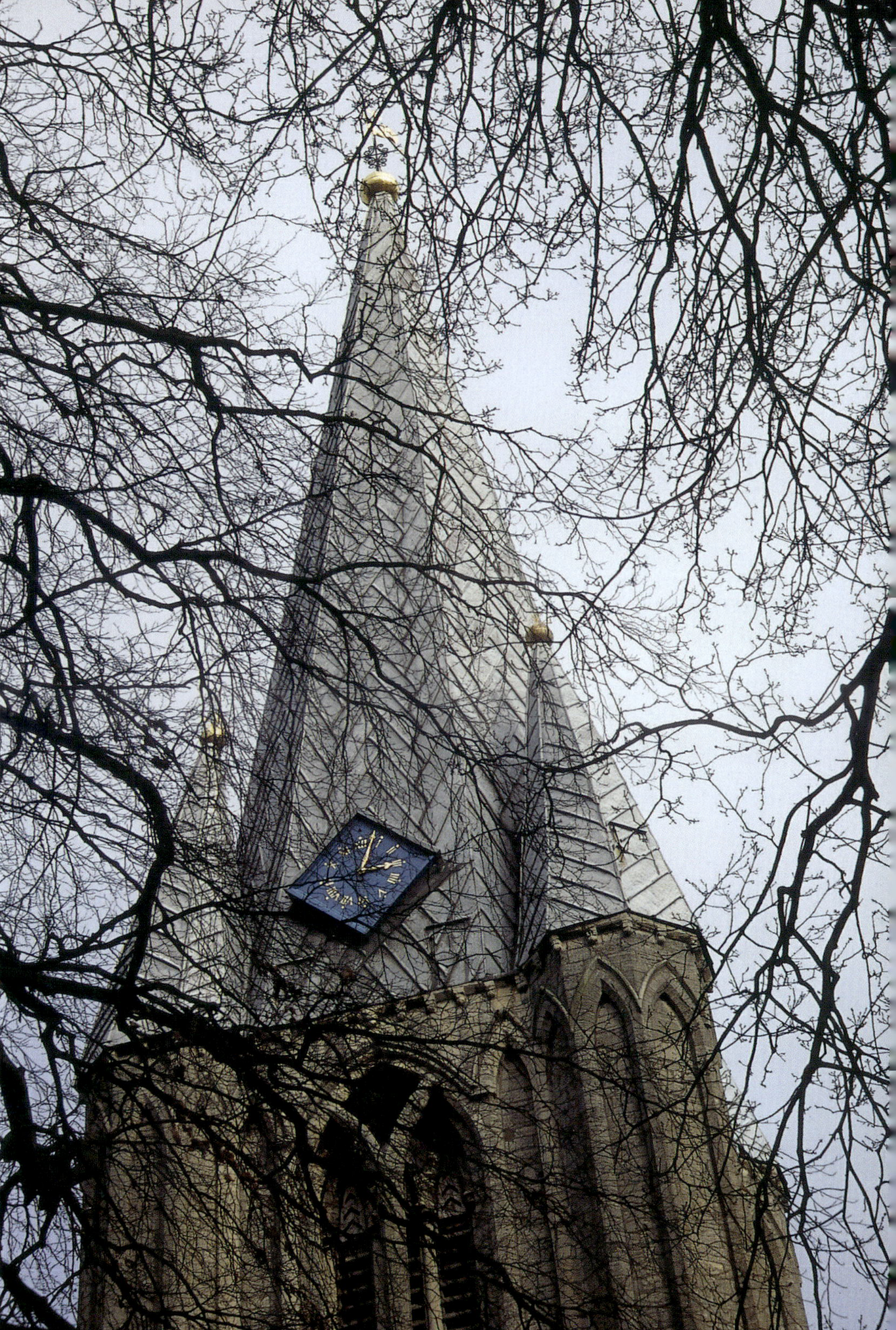

The church spire at Long Sutton
The leaded spire of St Mary's church at
Long Sutton is seen through a pattern
of lime branches in this winter scene.

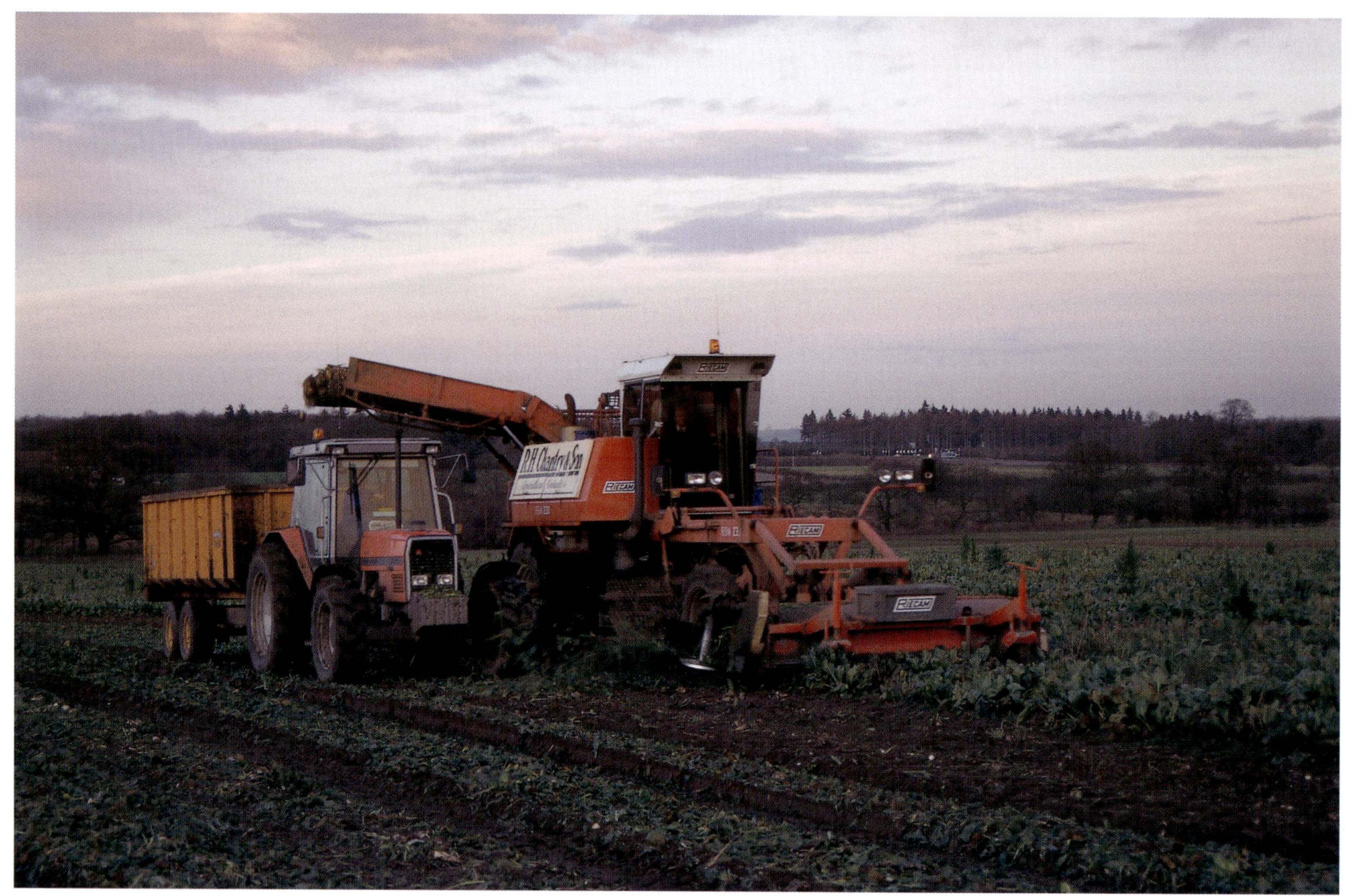

Harvesting sugar beet
The late afternoon sunlight is tinged with pink as sugar beet harvesting continues near Scawby.

Opposite: **Sunset near Sutterton Dowdyke**
The winter sun sets beyond the polythene-covered field. Perforated polythene and fleece is increasingly used to protect early vegetable crops, and from a distance can be mistaken for open water.

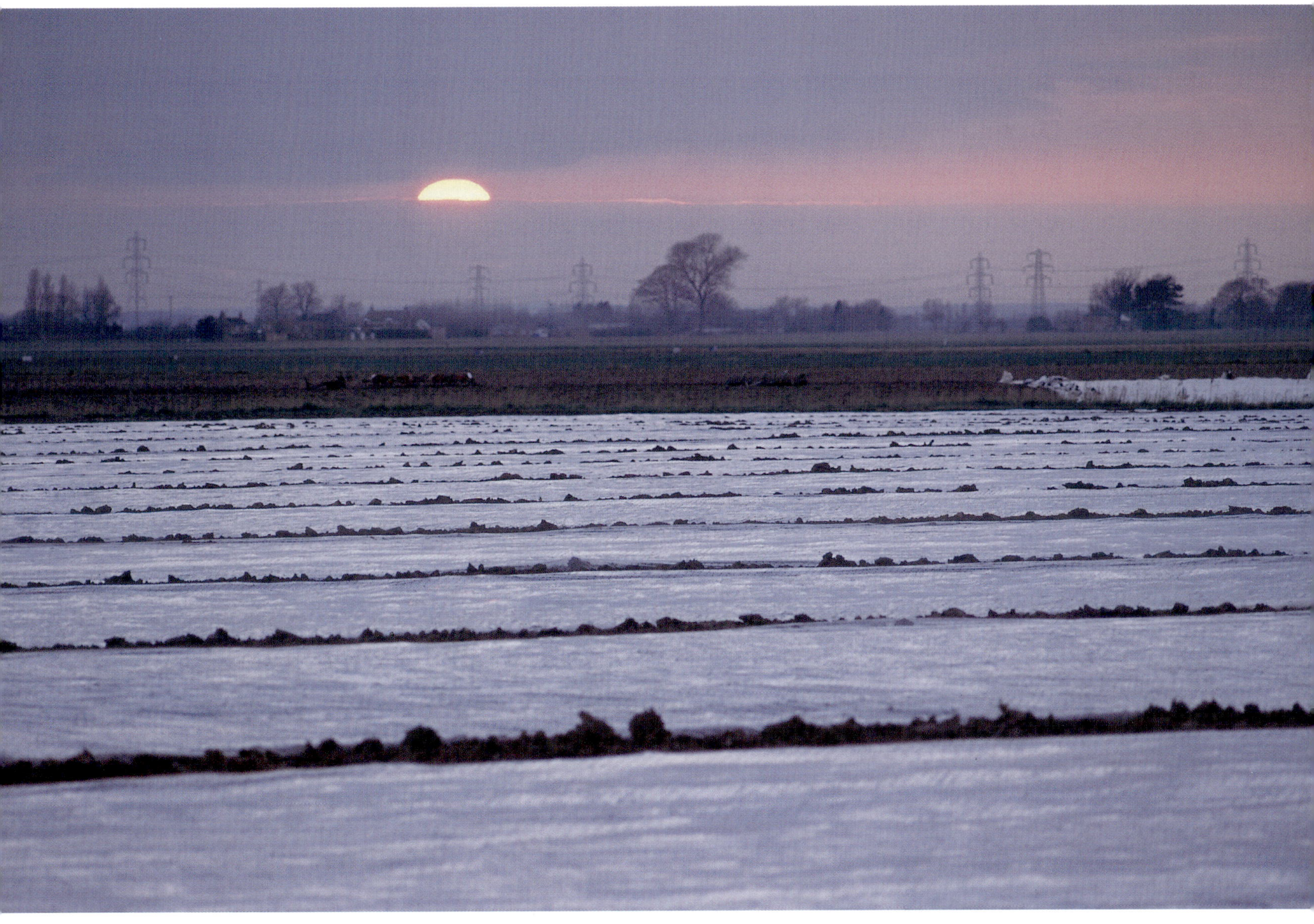

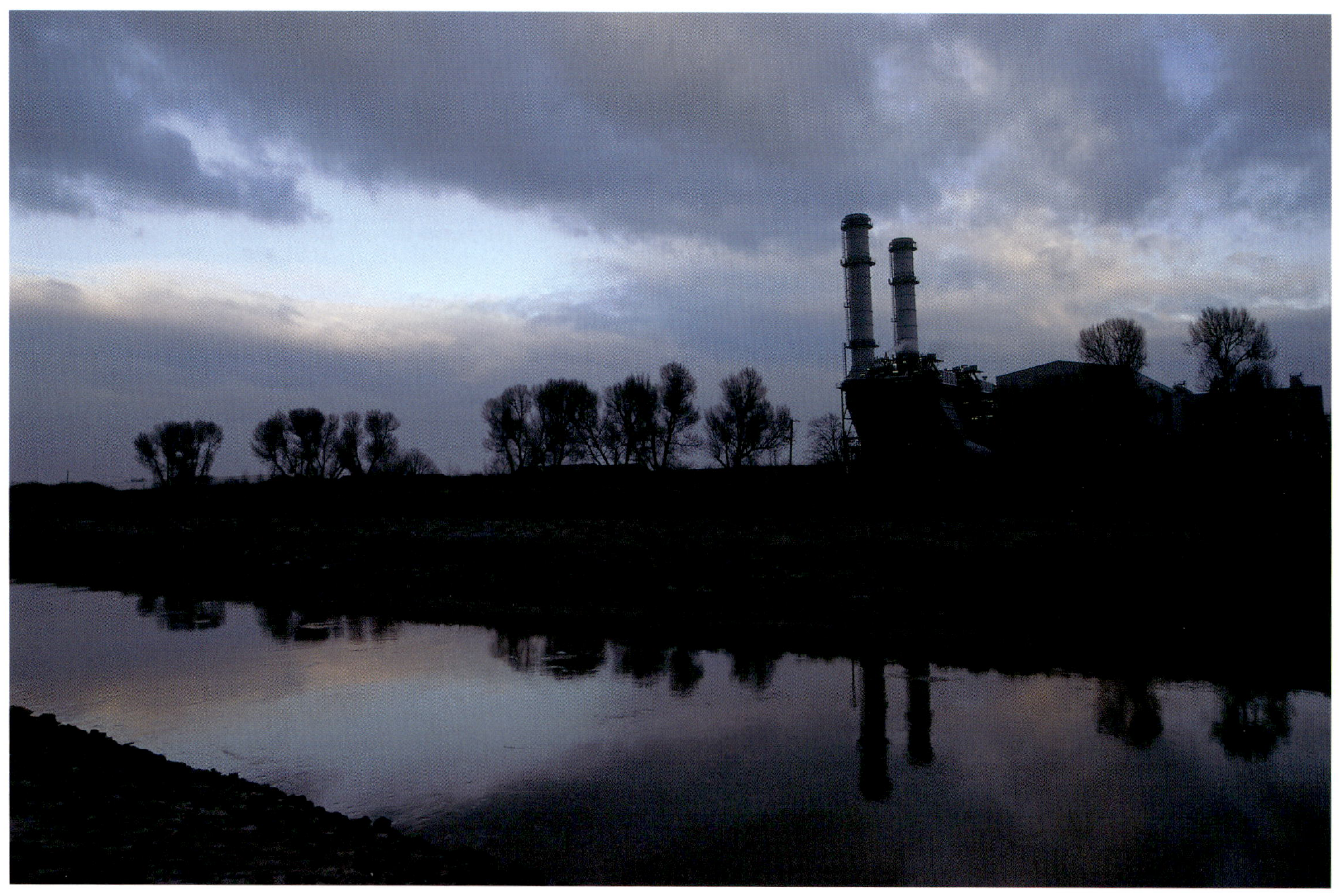

The power station at Sutton Bridge
The silhouette of the power station is reflected in the River Nene in late evening light.

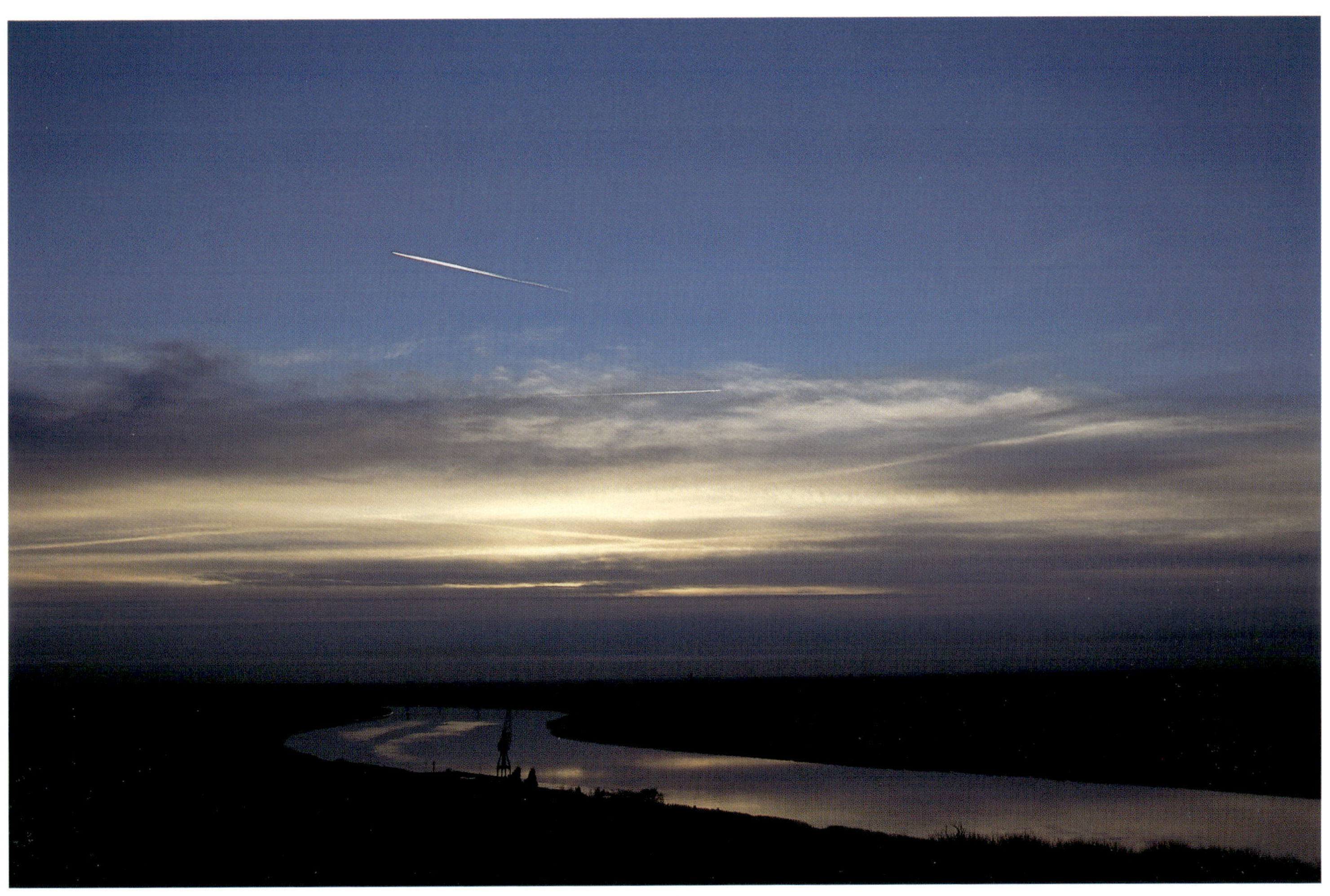

Aeroplane trails
The sun has sunk below the horizon but it still lights the vapour trails of aircraft
as they cross the sky over the River Trent at Burton Stather.

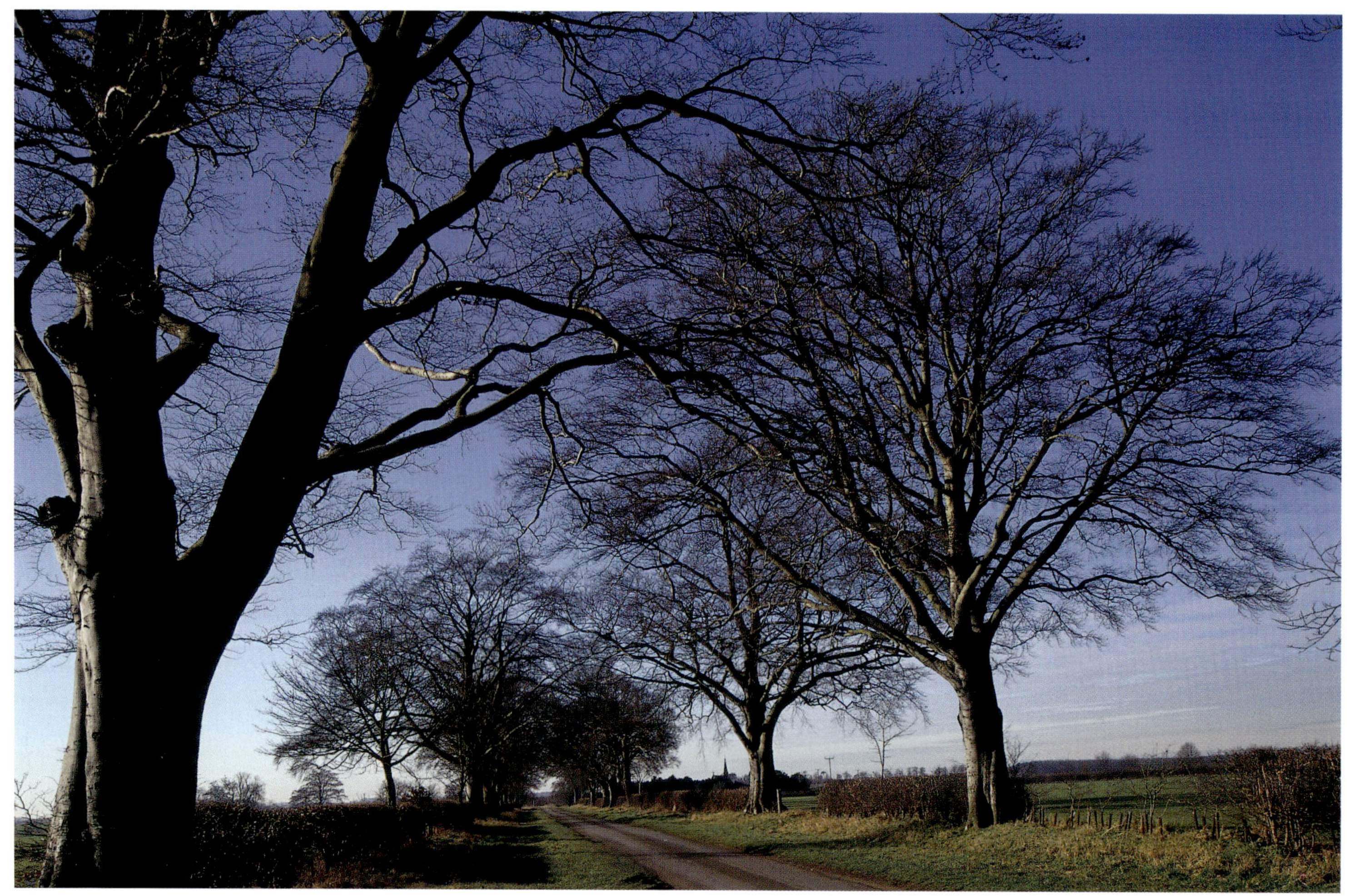

Beech trees
Silhouettes of beech trees line this country lane on Wellingore Heath.

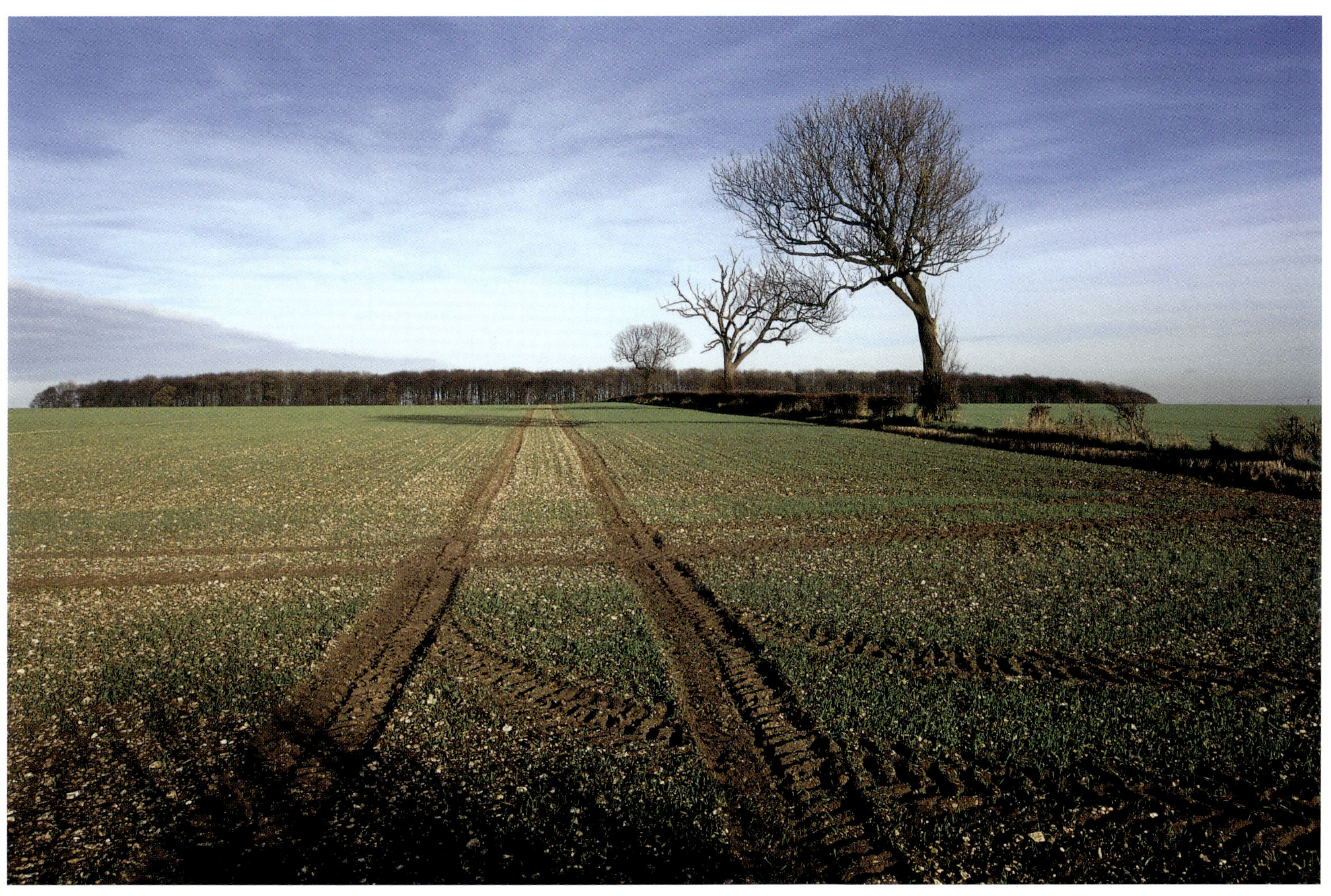

Tramlines in winter corn
Tractor wheelings stand out in this field of winter corn on Saxby Wold.

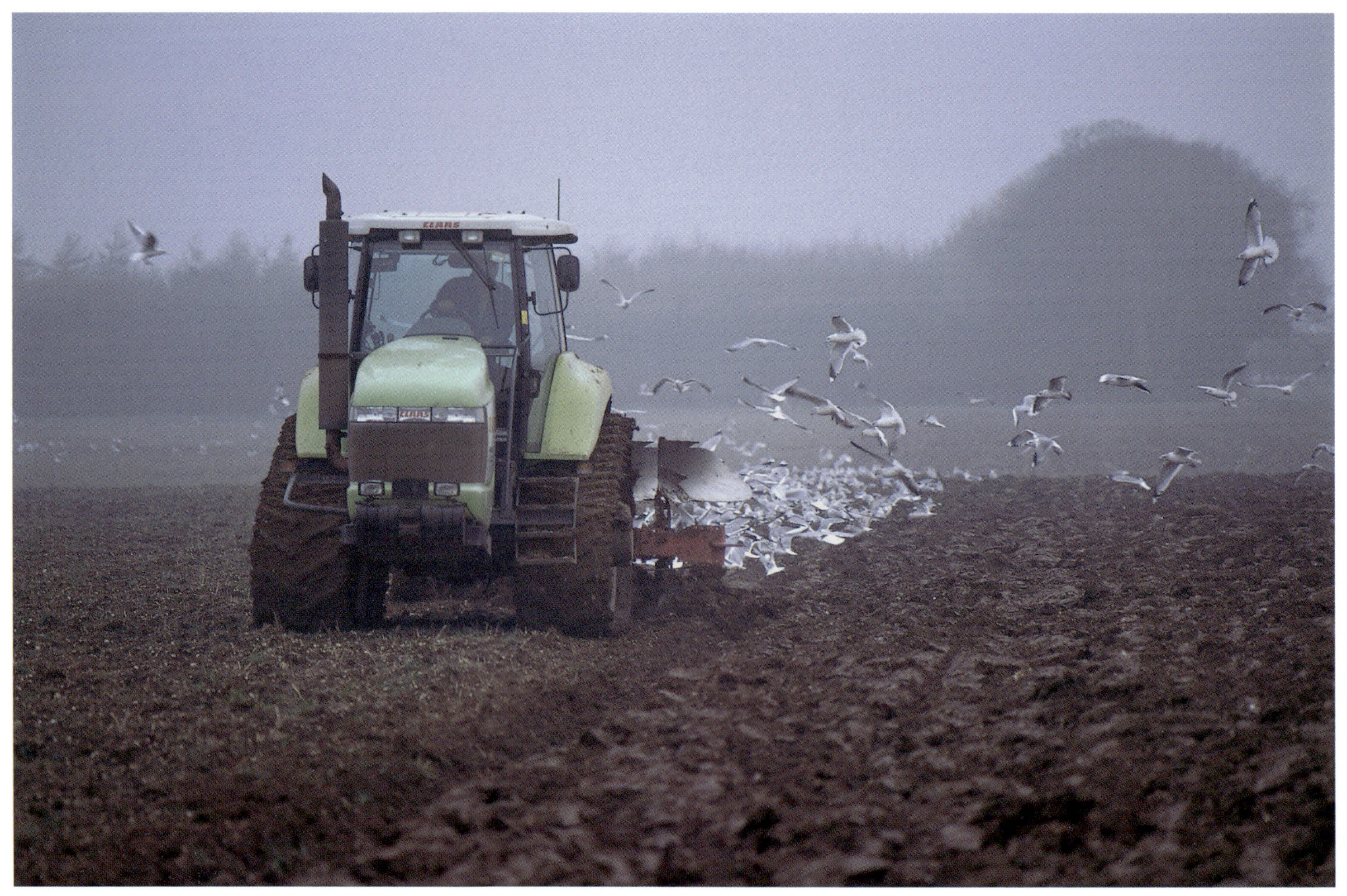

Winter ploughing near Donington on Bain
Common gulls follow the plough, on a dank, foggy day on the Wolds.

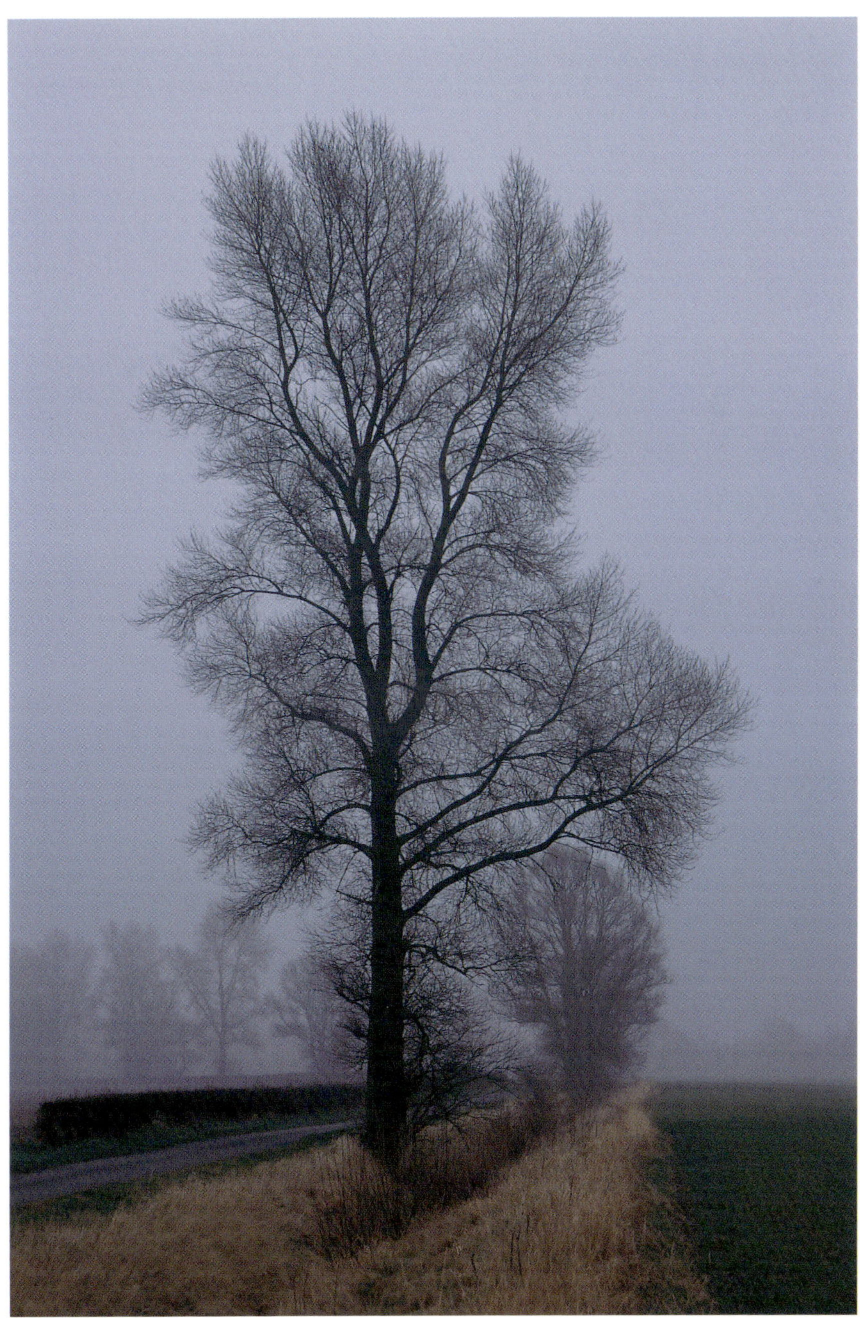

Poplar tree
The outline of a white poplar looms out
of the mist along a country lane near
Holbeach St Matthew.

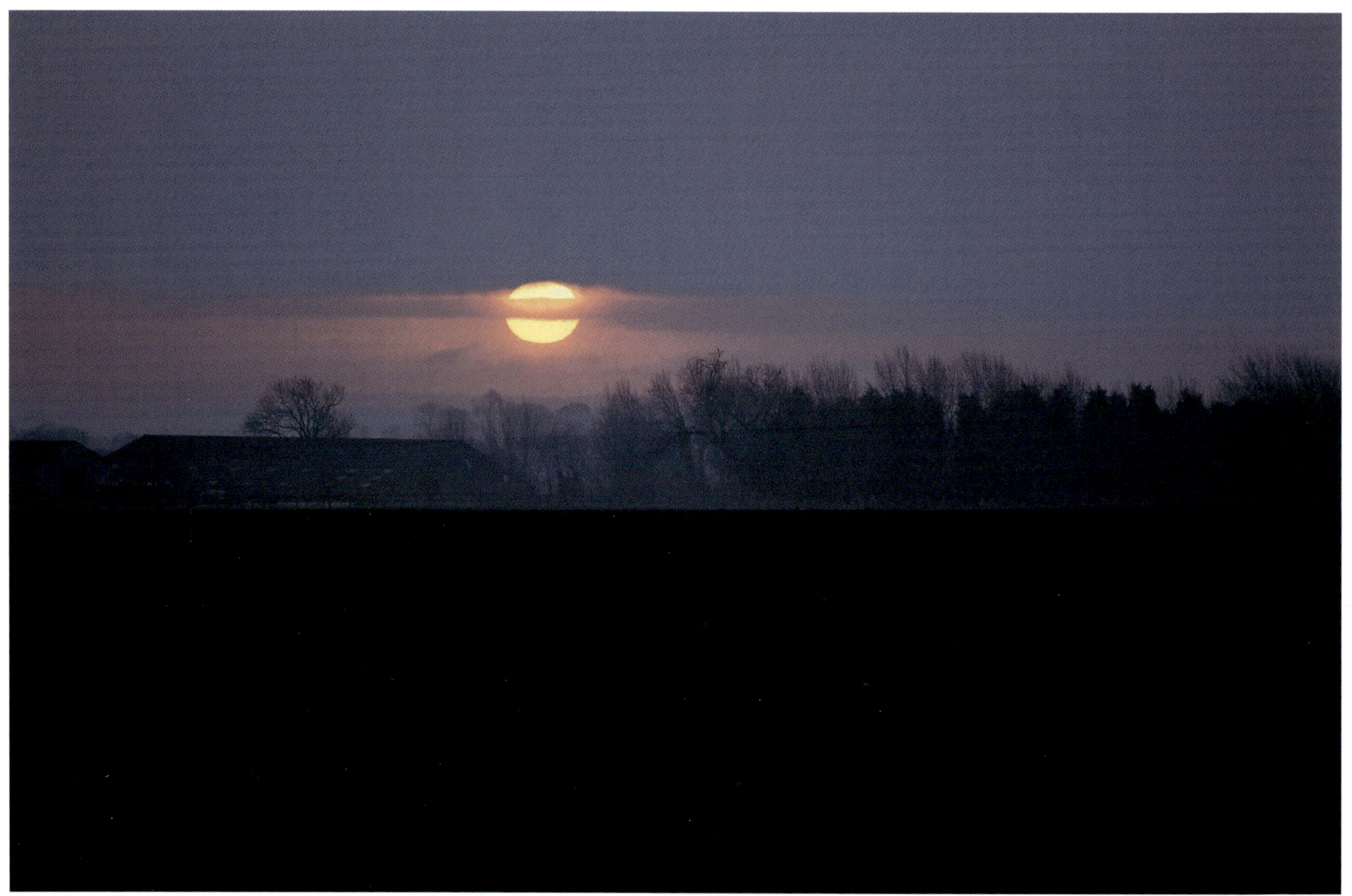

Dawn
It is November and the sun rises on a cold morning over farm buildings near Welton.

Opposite: **Dusk**
Daylight hours are short and the sun sets in late afternoon behind a small copse of trees near Frampton.

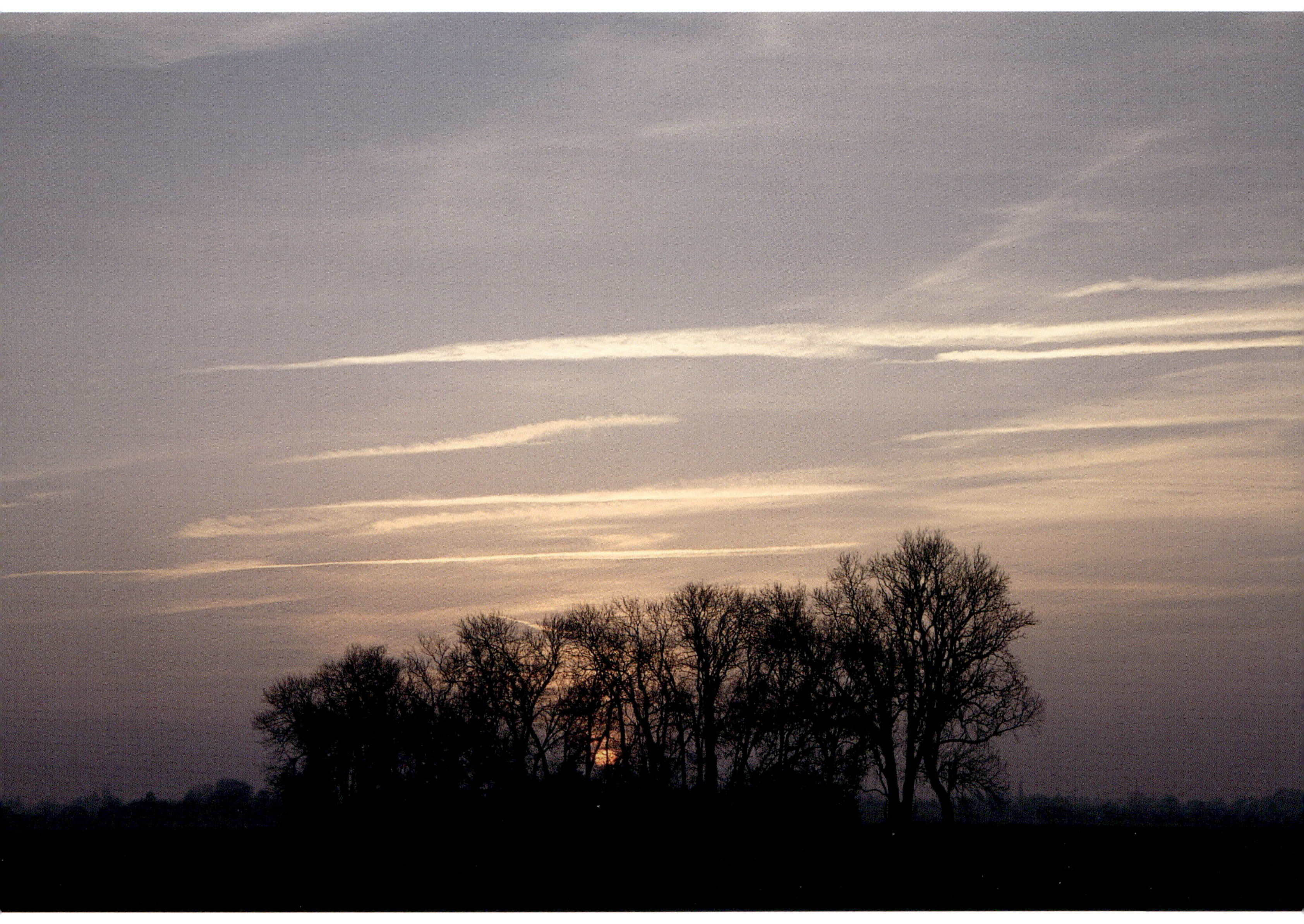

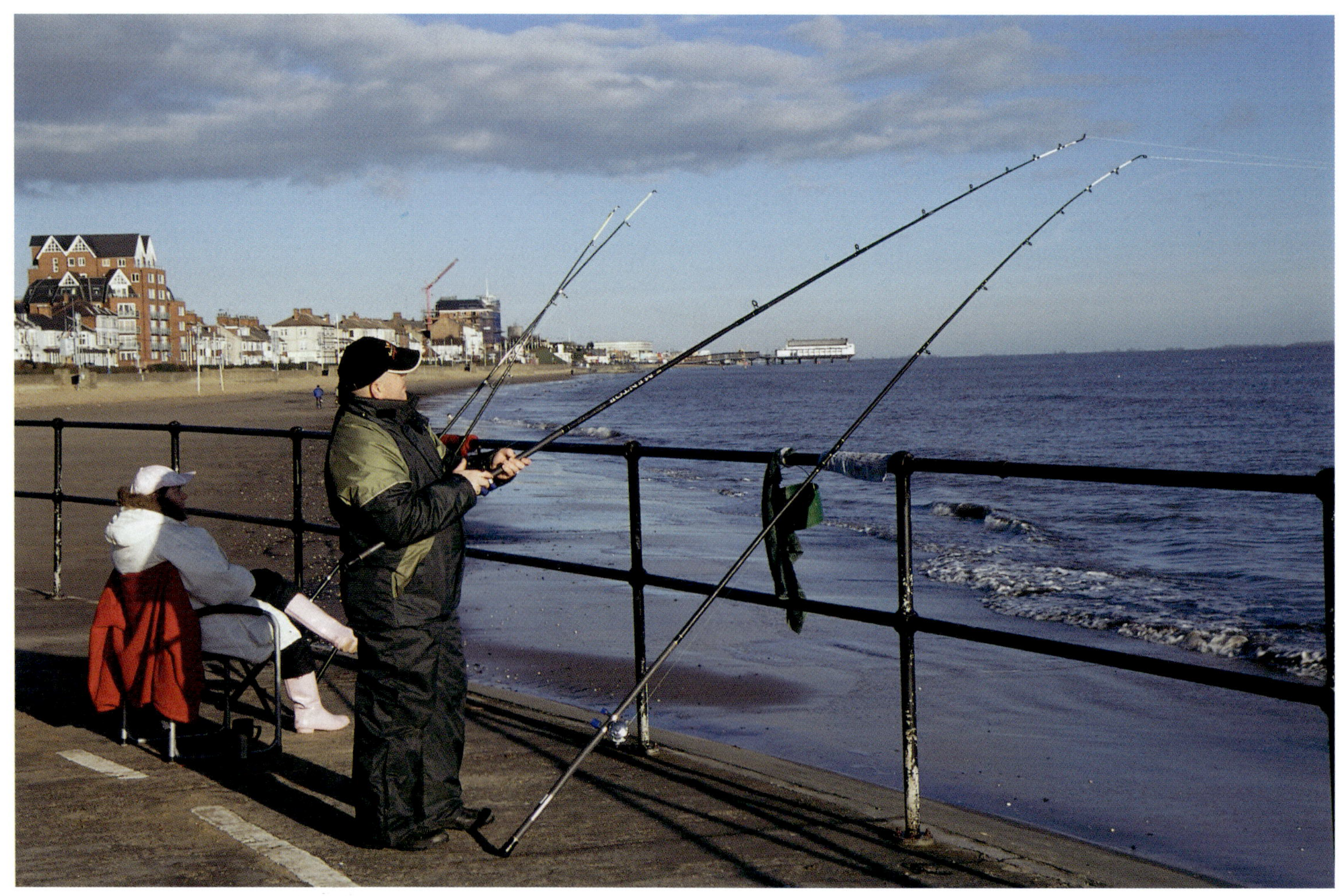

Fishing at Cleethorpes
Enjoying the early morning sunshine, a lone fisherman tries his luck from the seafront at Cleethorpes.

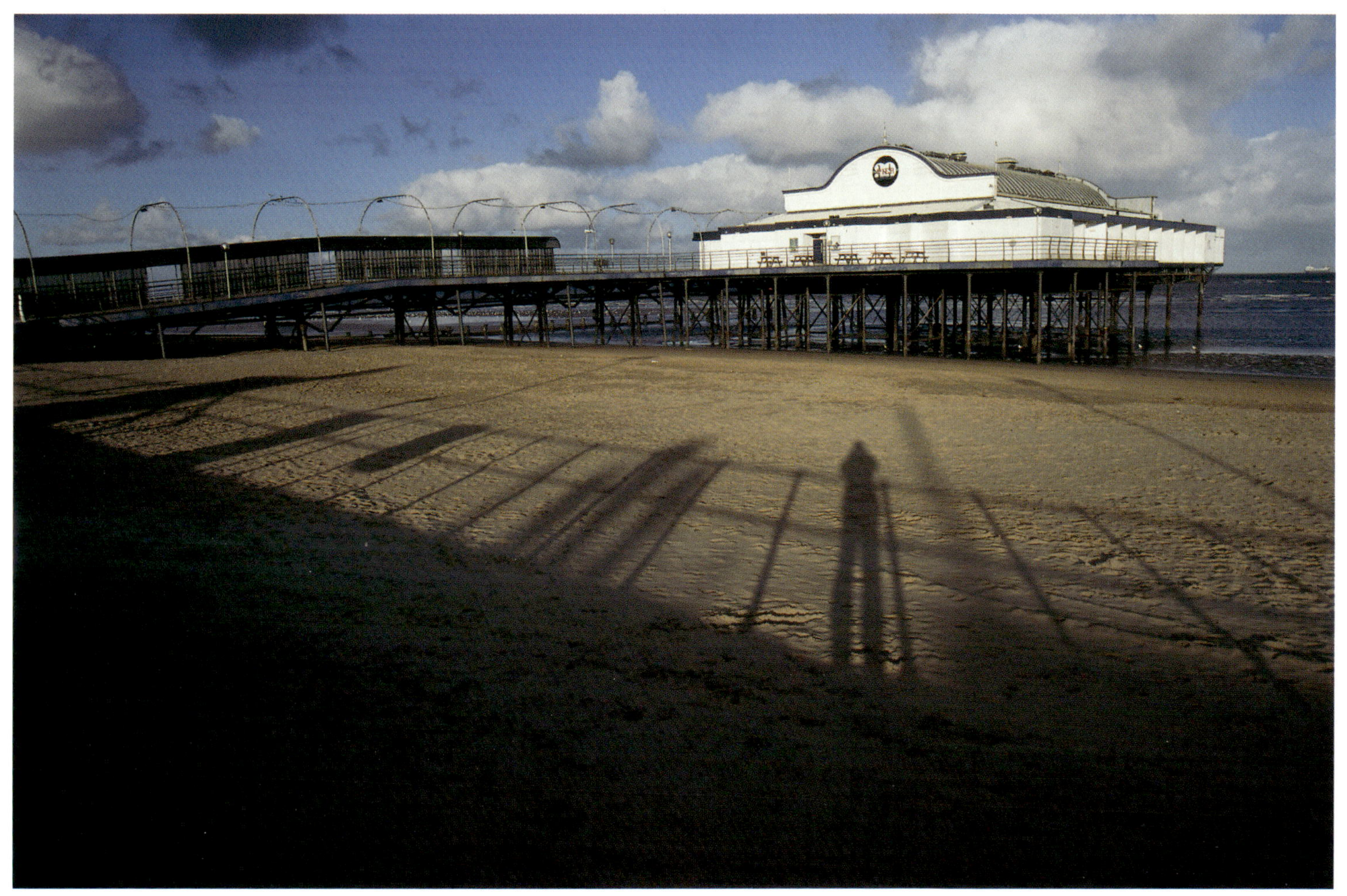

The pier at Cleethorpes
The low winter sunshine casts long shadows across the beach in front of the pier, witnessed only by the photographer.

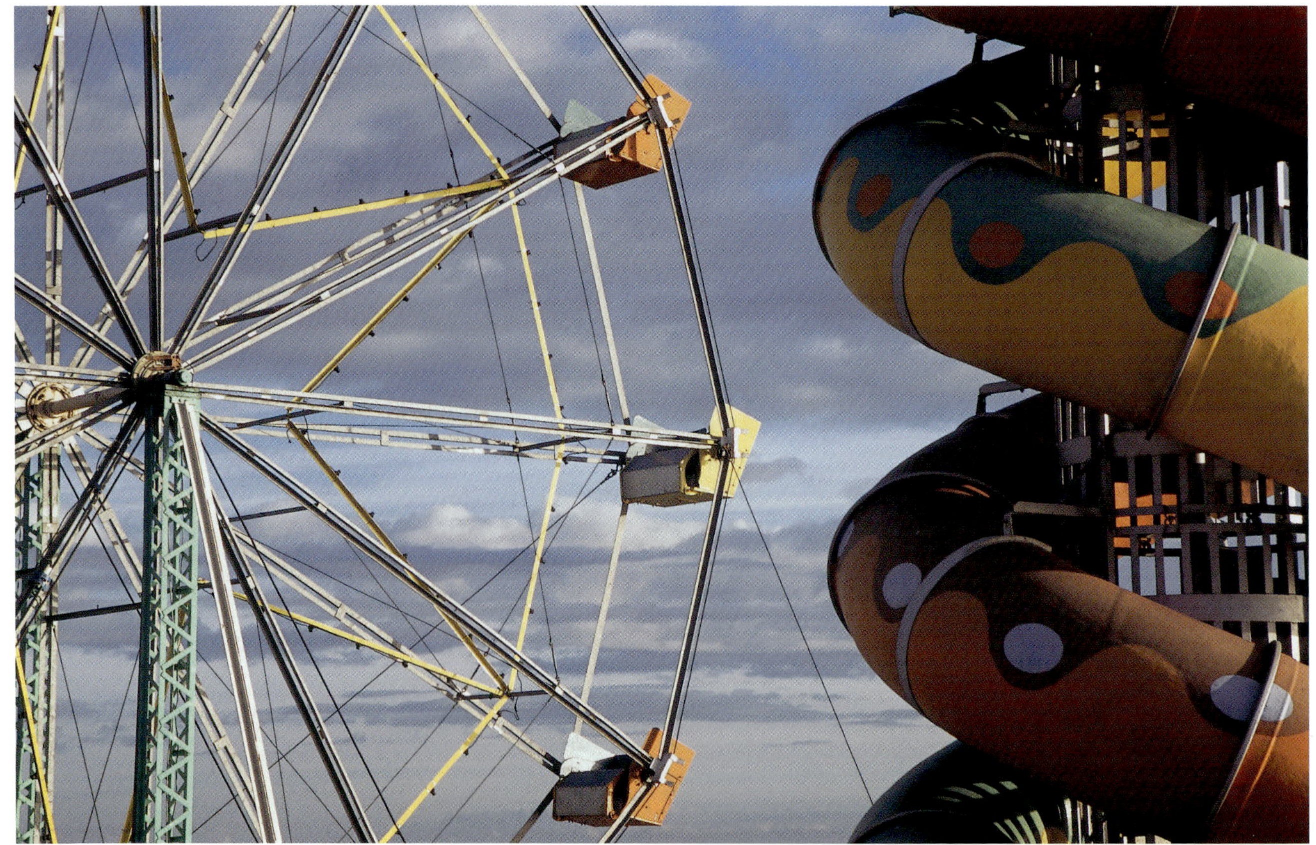

Amusements at Cleethorpes
The big wheel and helter-skelter lie closed and silent during the winter months.

Opposite: **High tide at Cleethorpes**
Seen through the spokes of the big wheel, ships on the horizon queue up
to enter the Humber estuary on the high tide.

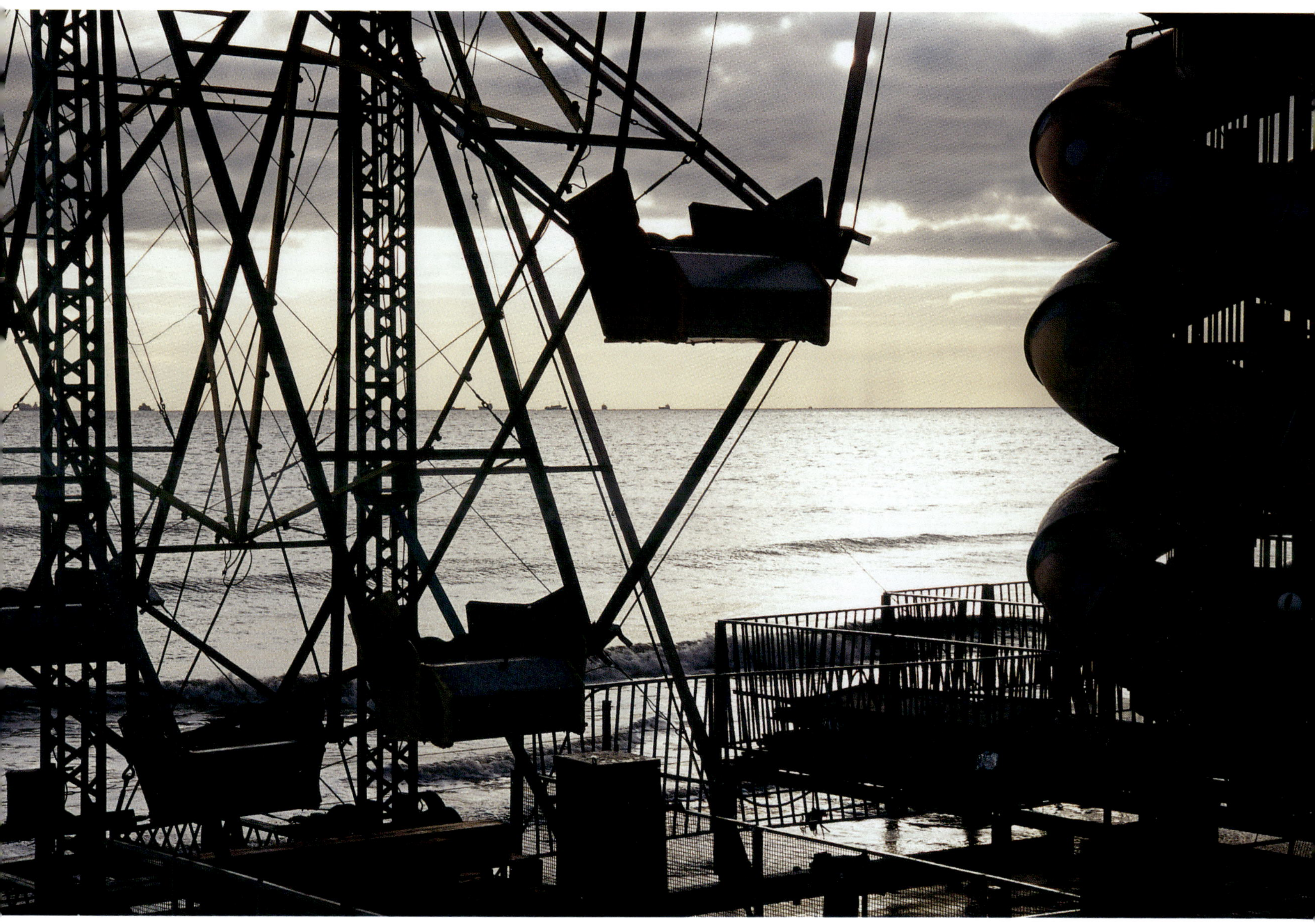

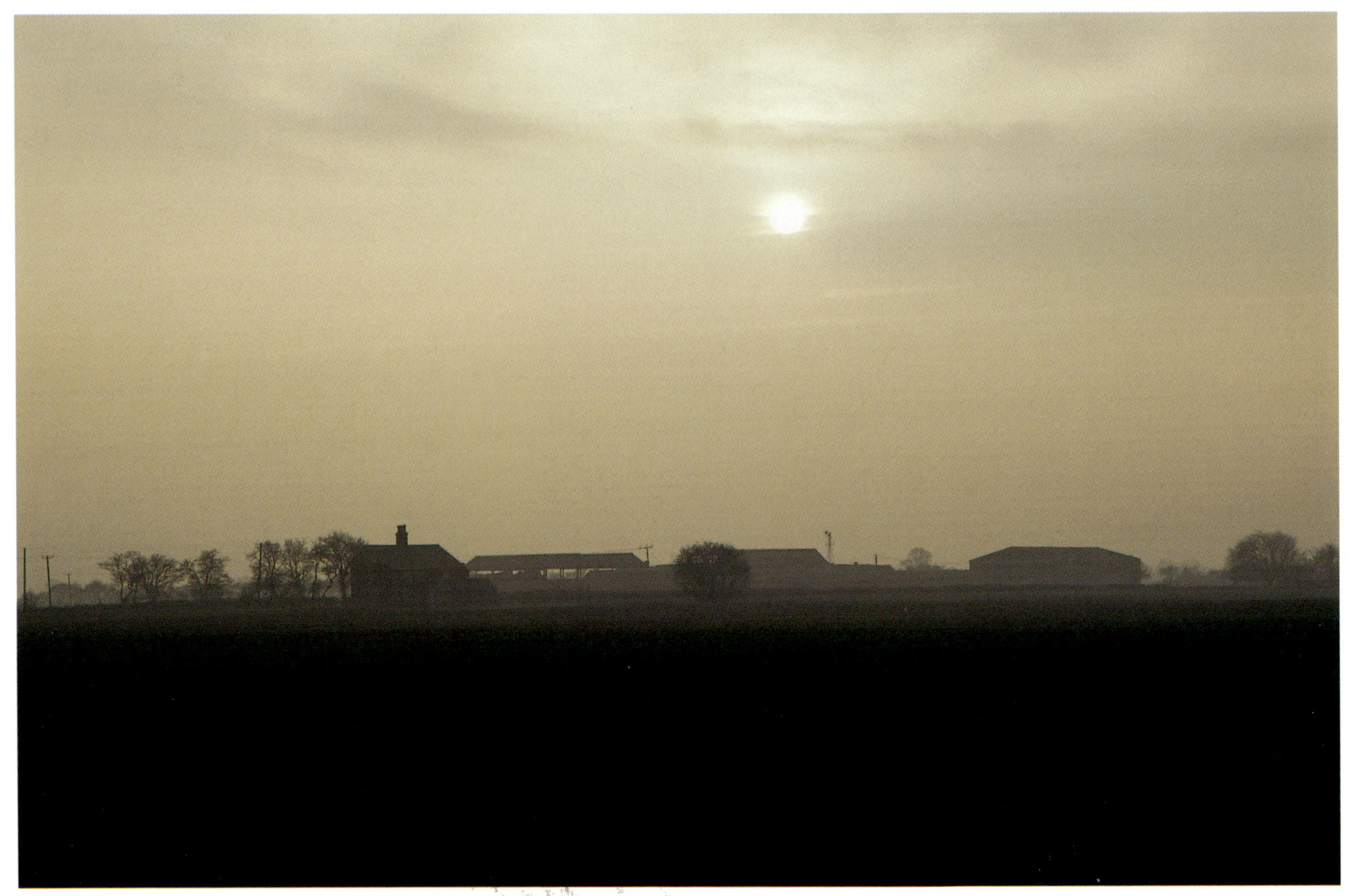

Riggalls Farm
A weak winter sun casts a yellow glow on Riggalls Farm, in the fenland west of Frithville.

Opposite: **Lombardy poplars**
The skeletal outline of a windbreak of Lombardy poplars was photographed on Fleet Fen.

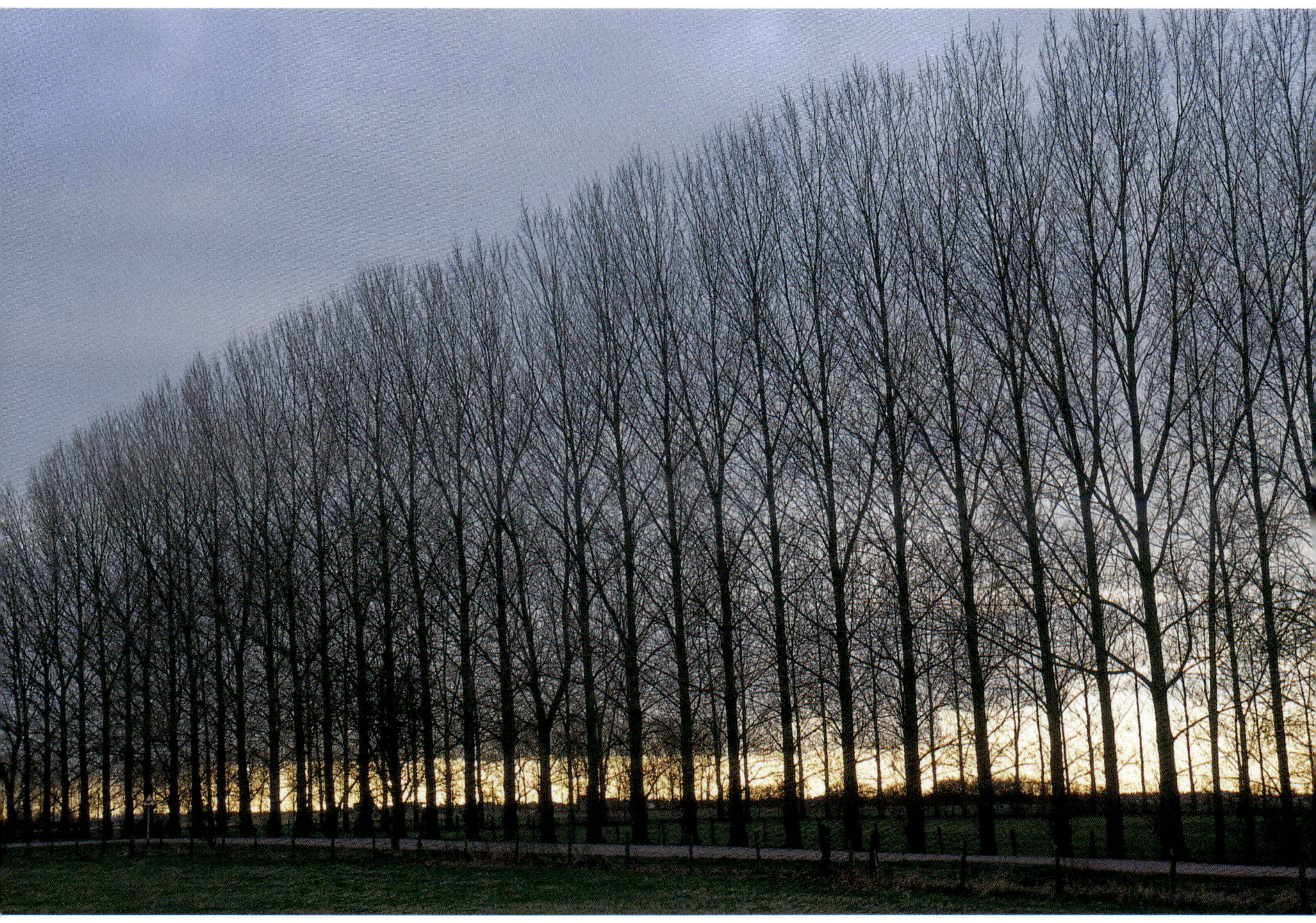

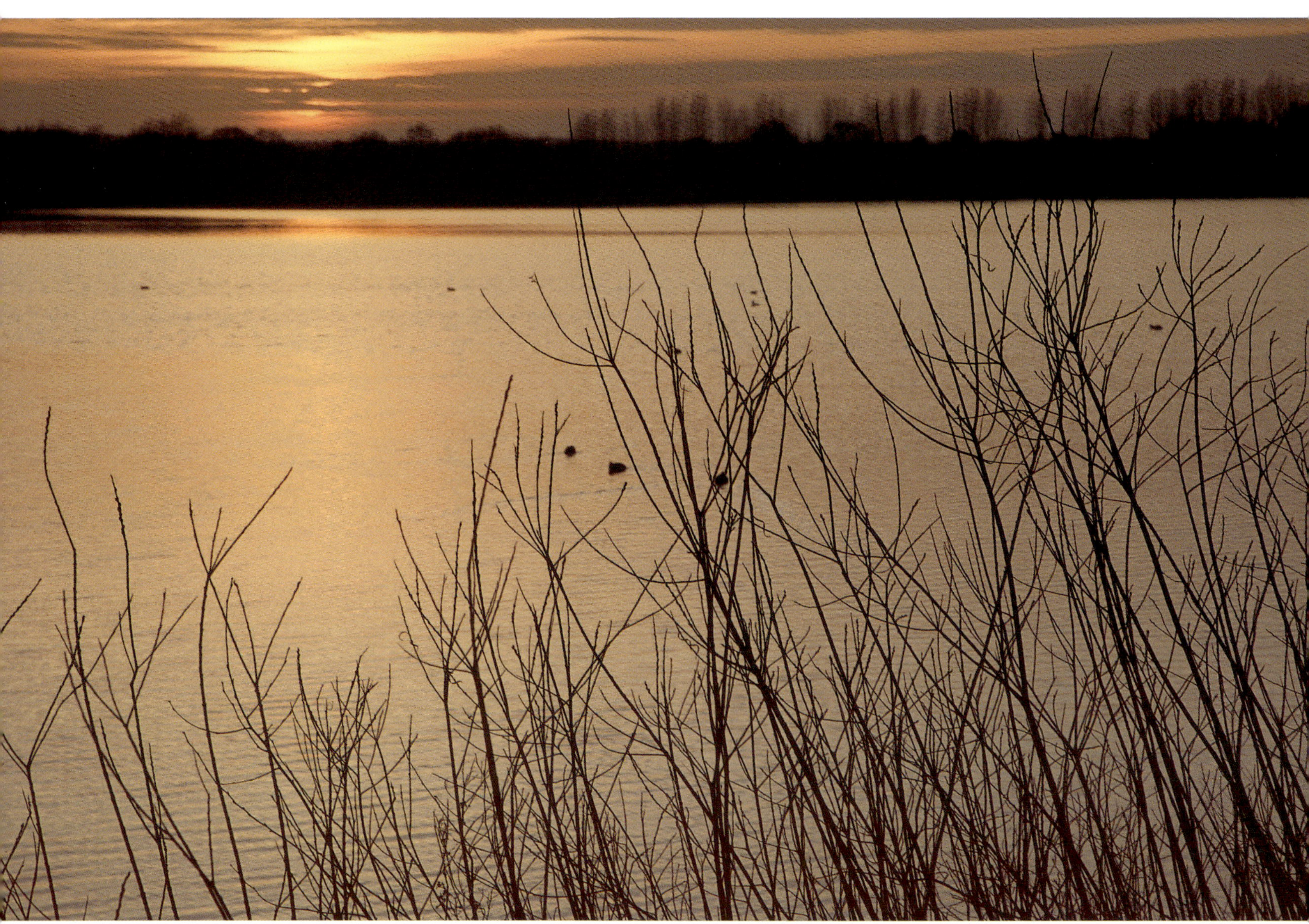

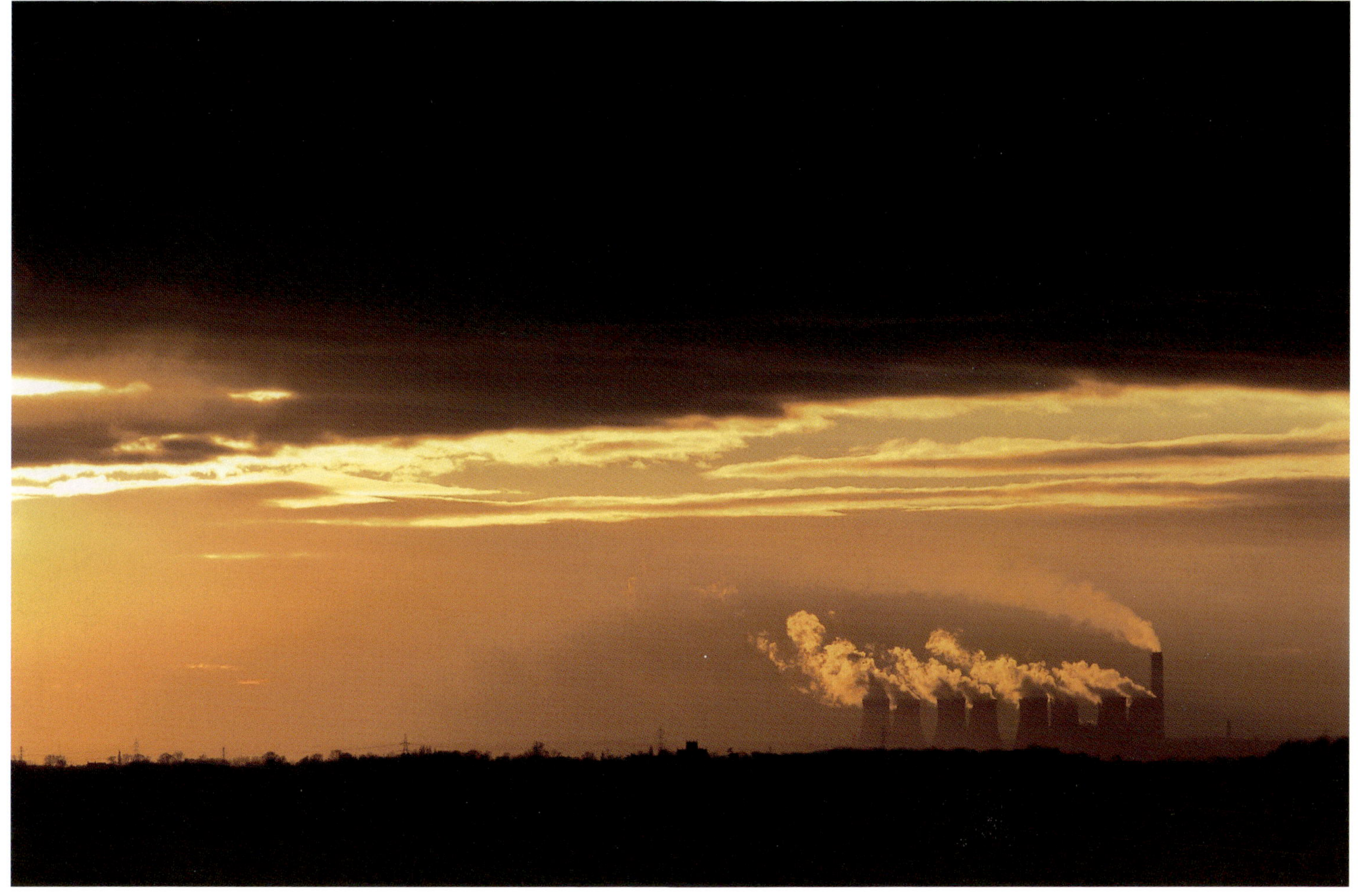

Sunset over the Trent Vale
The setting sun highlights the steam rising from the cooling towers of Cottam power station, which lies
on the west bank of the River Trent. The outline of Stow church is visible on the skyline.

Opposite: **Sunset over Whisby Pits**
Willows fringe one of the lakes at Whisby Nature Park.

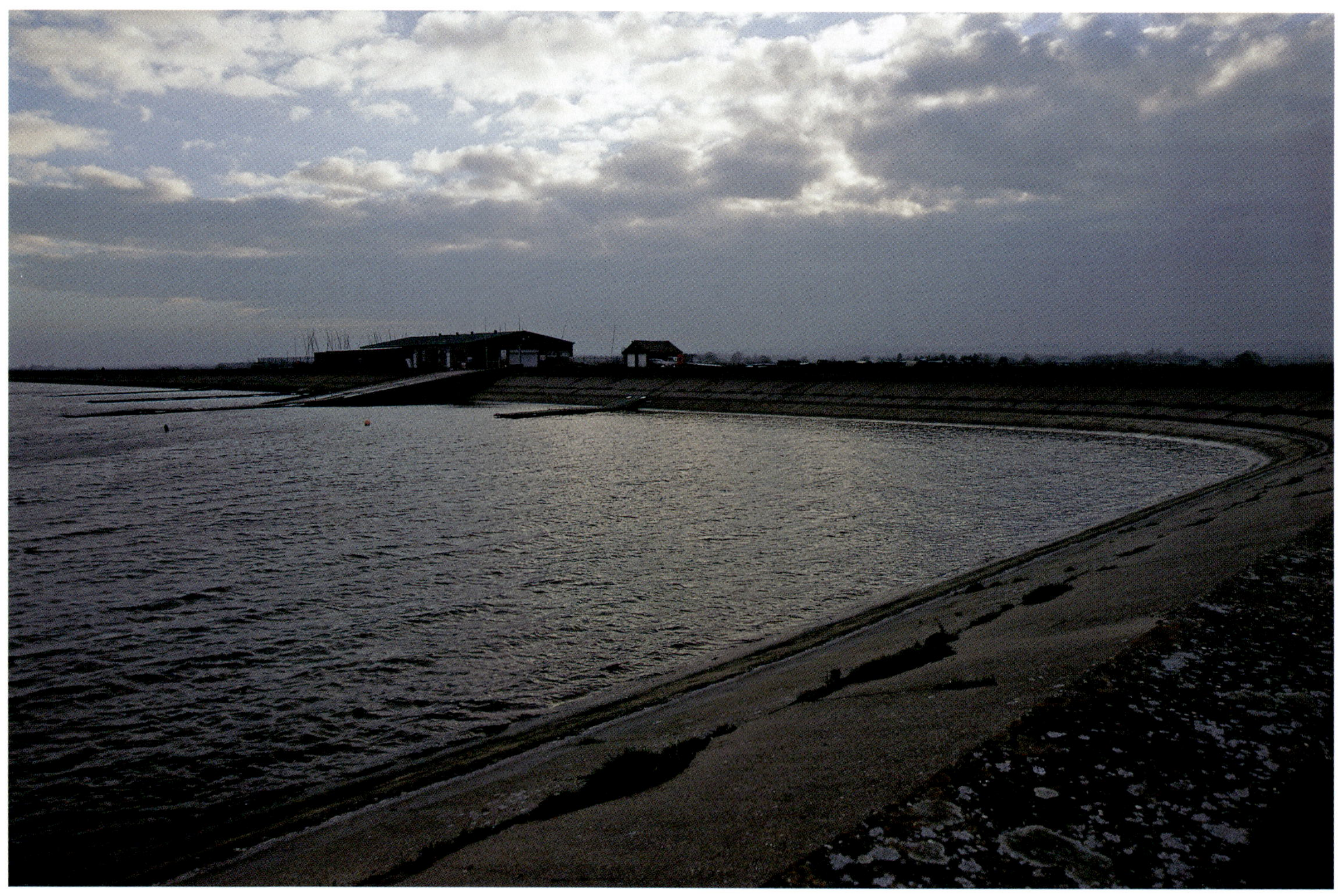

Covenham Reservoir
Evening light fades as rain clouds approach the reservoir at Covenham.

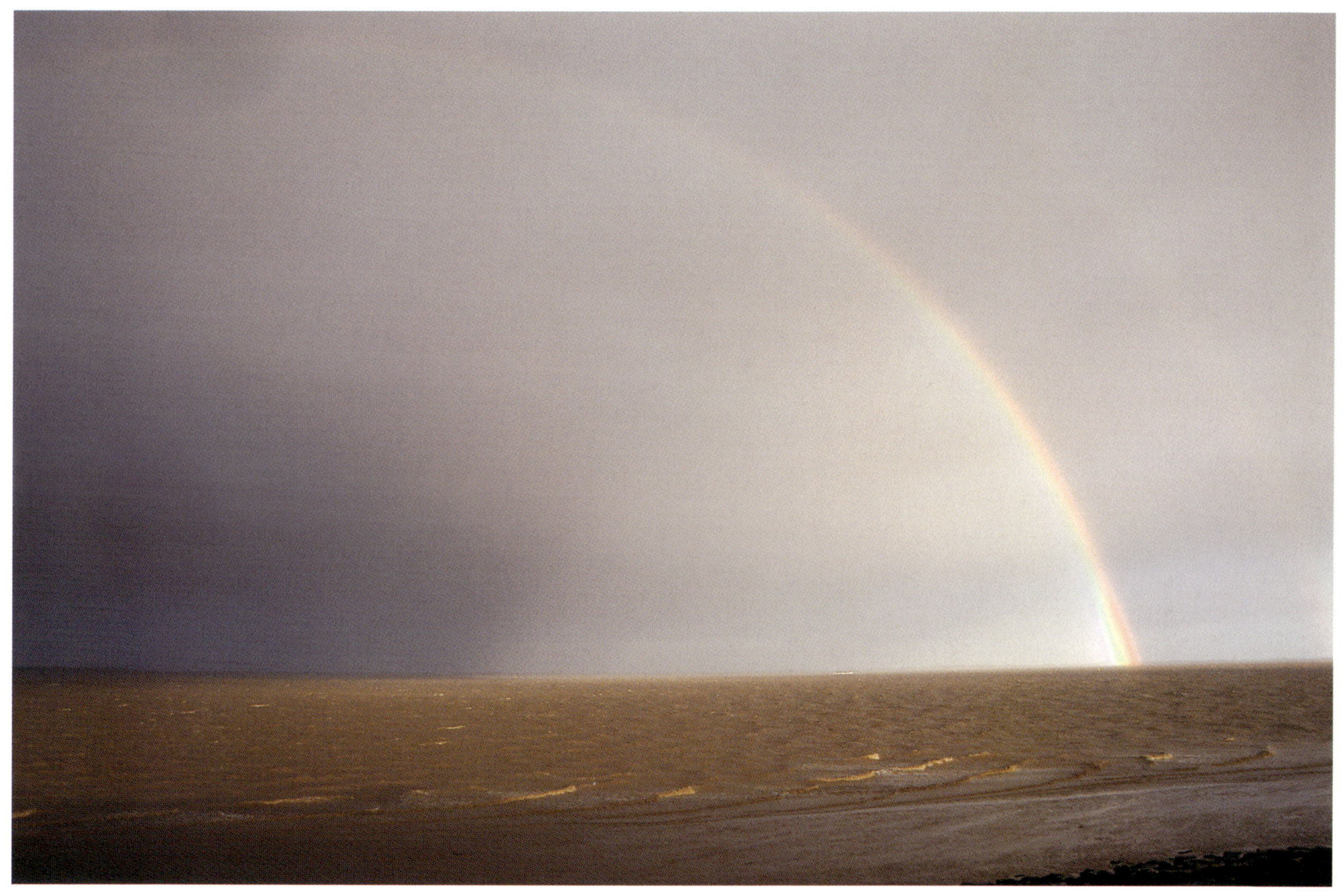

Rainbow over the Humber estuary
A double rainbow arcs over the Humber estuary near East Halton as the sky darkens and a violent storm approaches.

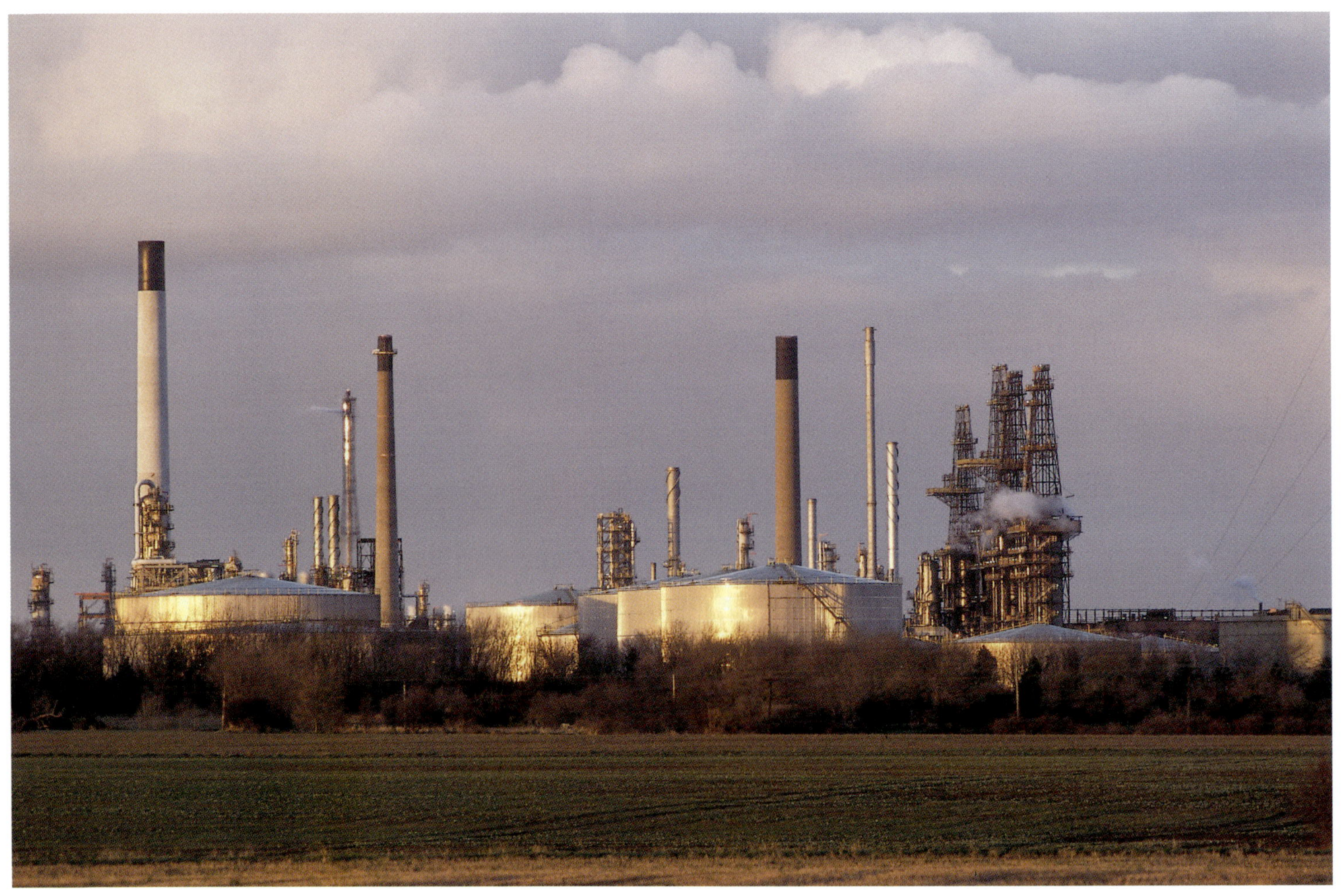

Oil refinery
Warm evening light highlights the oil refinery at South Killingholme.

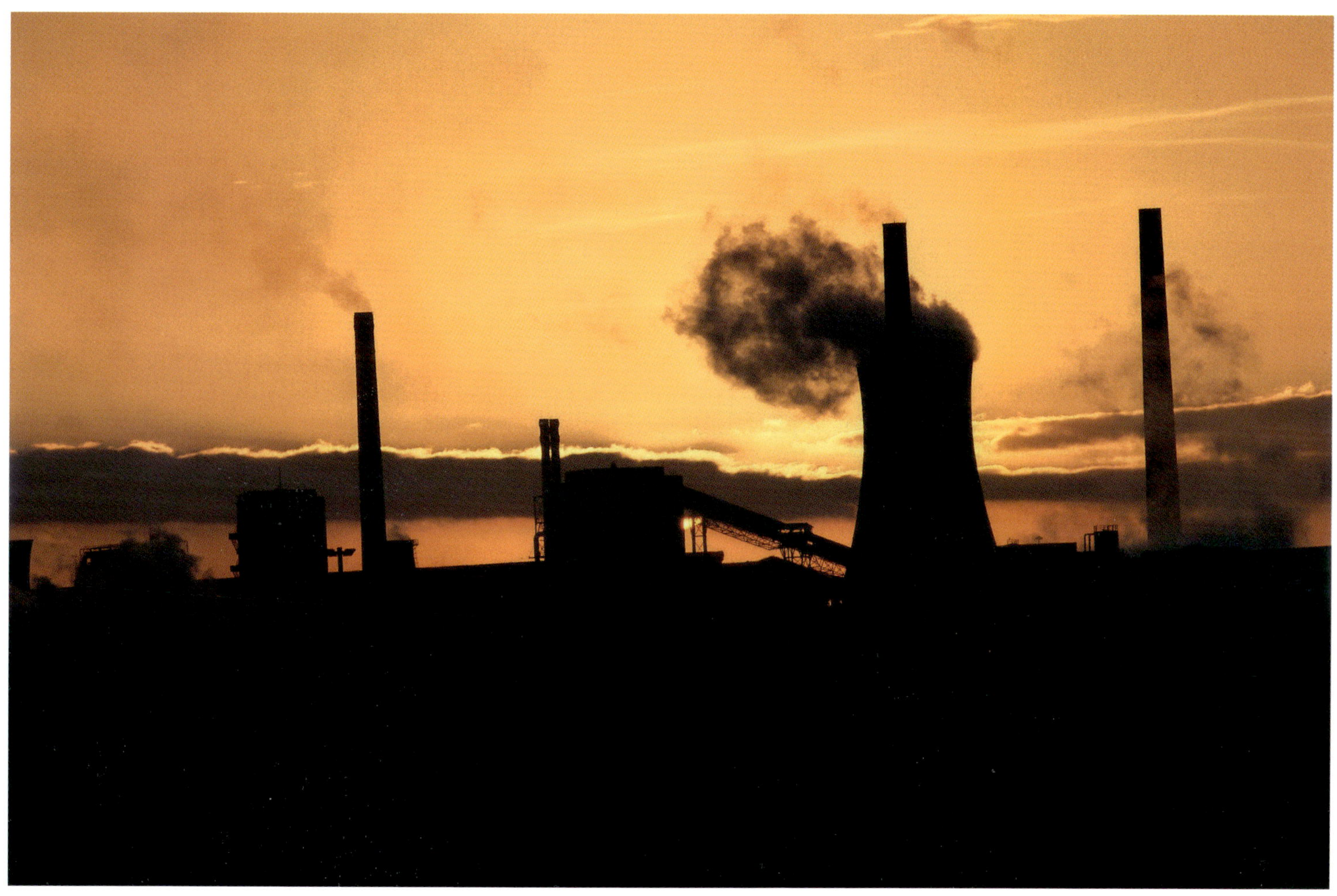

Steel works
The orange glow of a rich winter sunset silhouettes the steel works at Scunthorpe.

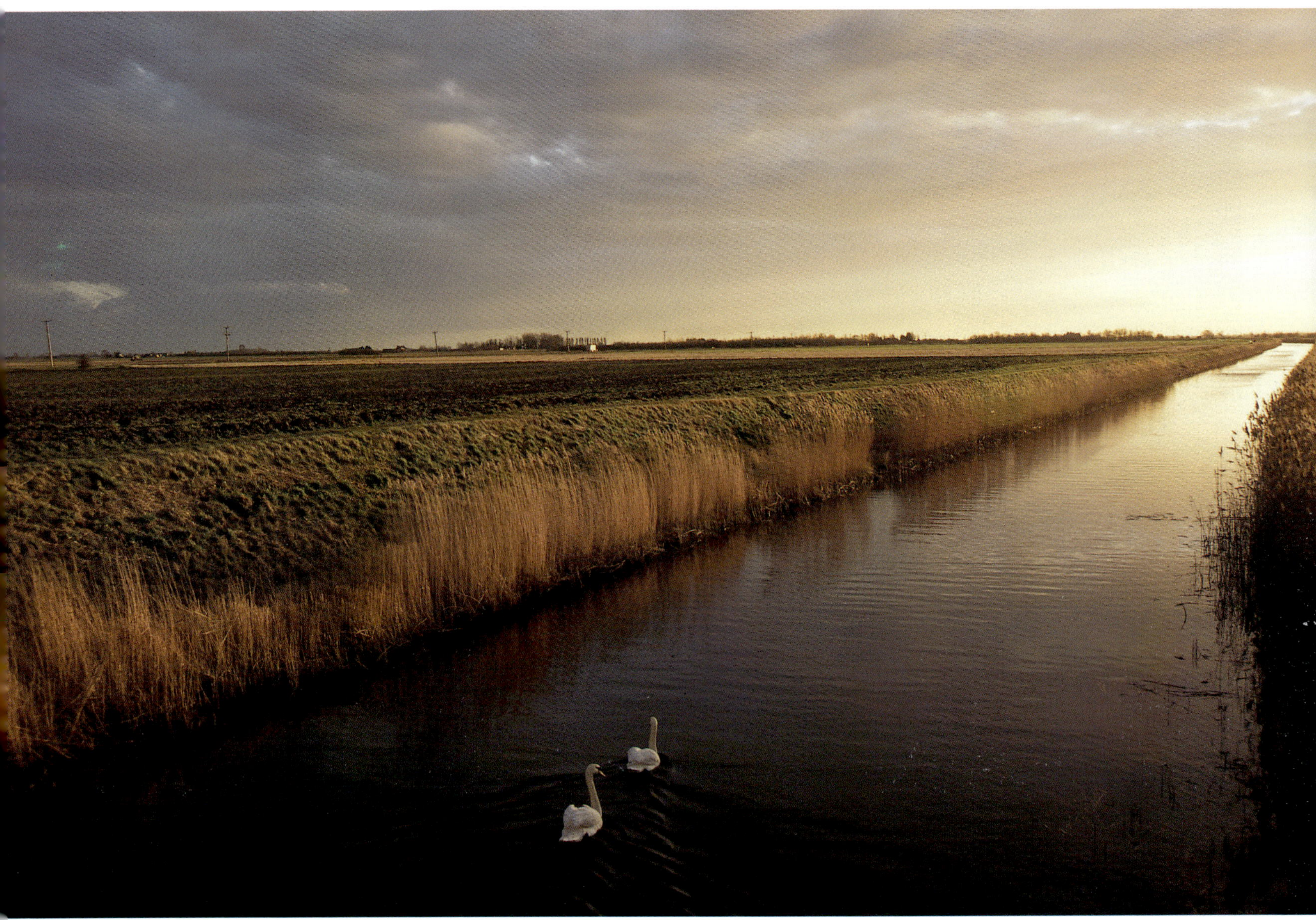

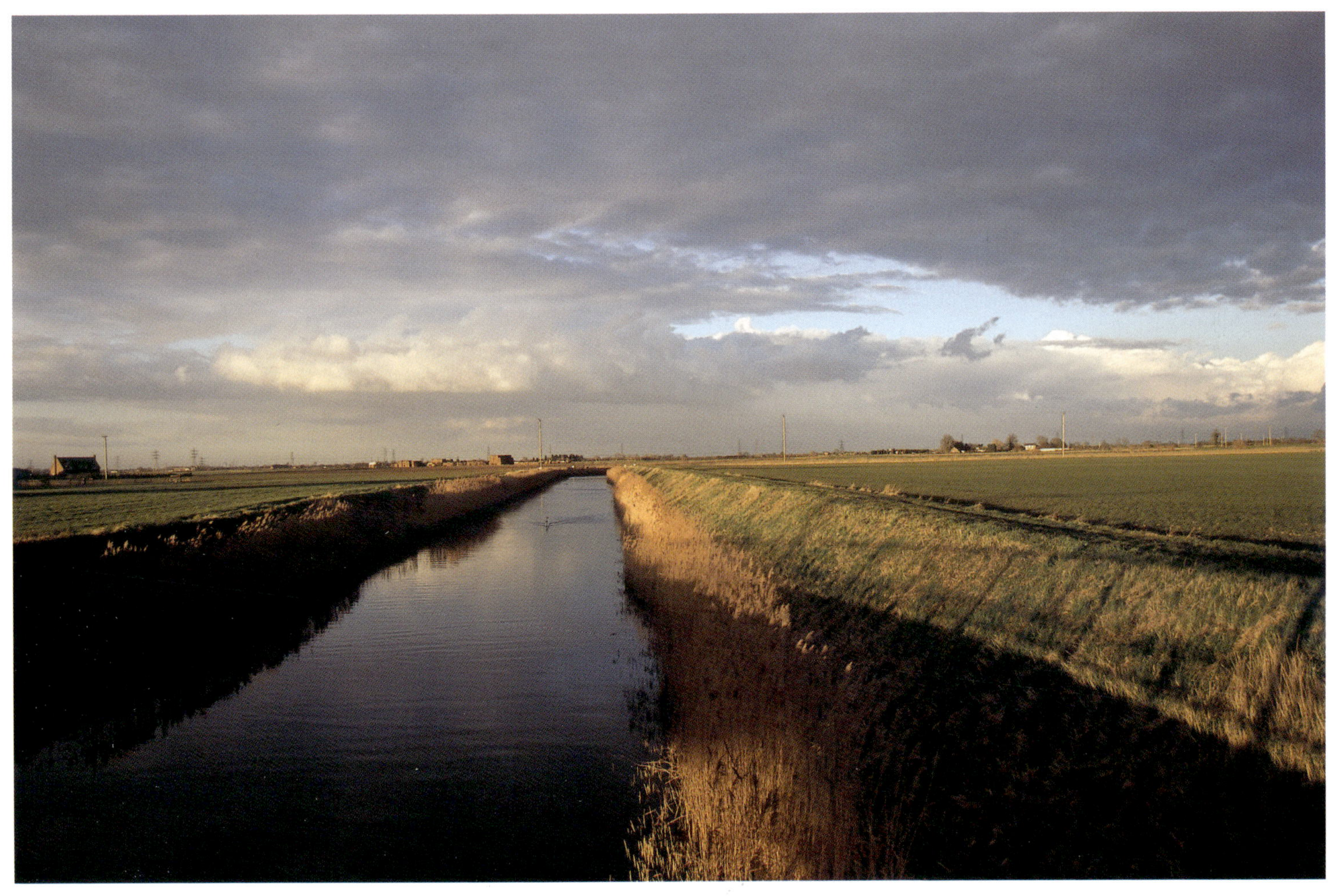

South Holland Main Drain
The view looking northeast from Bell's Bridge. This waterway is one of the main drains in the fenland south of Holbeach.

Opposite: Looking southwest from Bell's Bridge, a pair of mute swans drift lazily
along the still waters of the South Holland Main Drain.

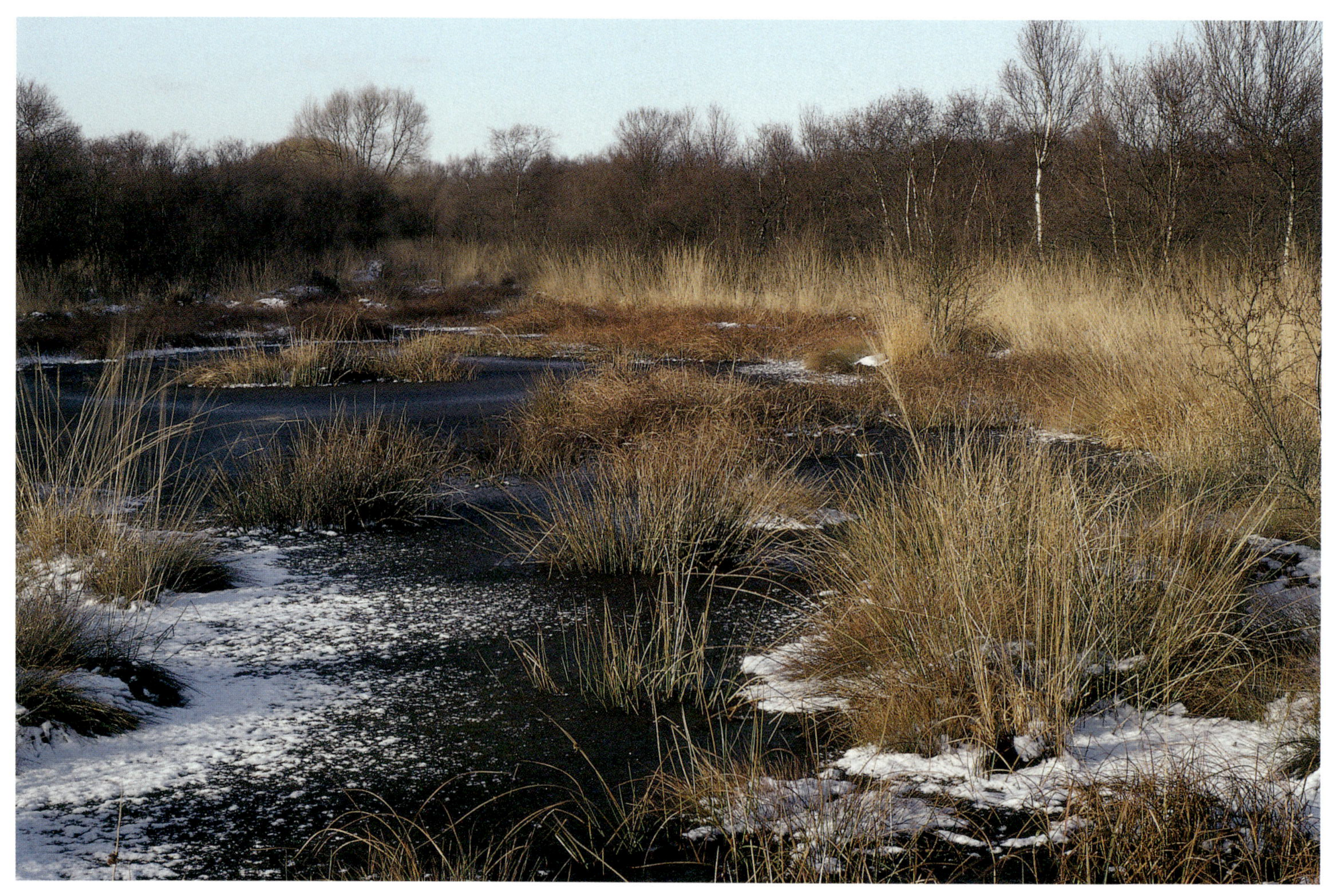

Crowle Moors Nature Reserve
A light dusting of snow covers the frozen surface of the old peat cuttings.

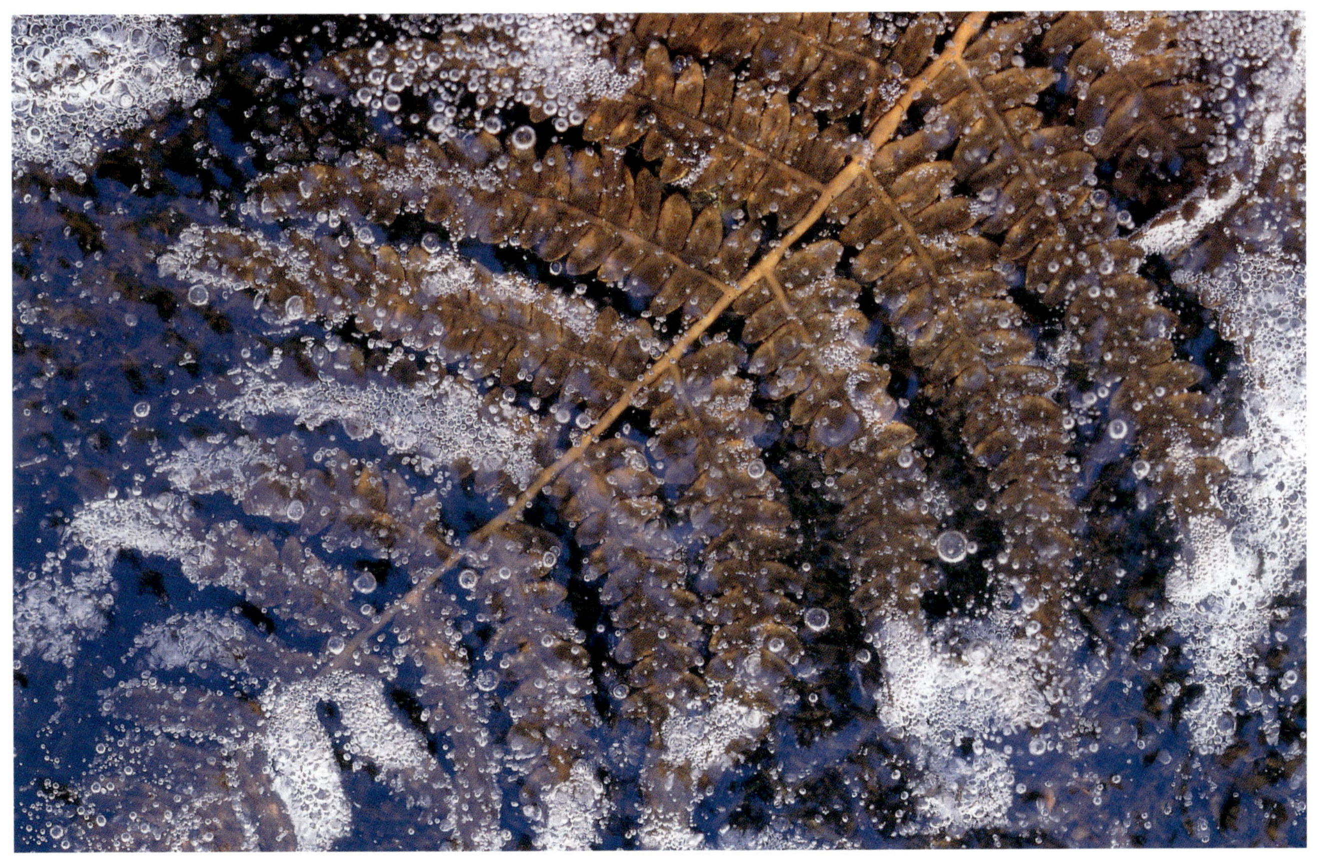

Bracken frond in ice
A bracken frond lies frozen in ice on Crowle Moors.

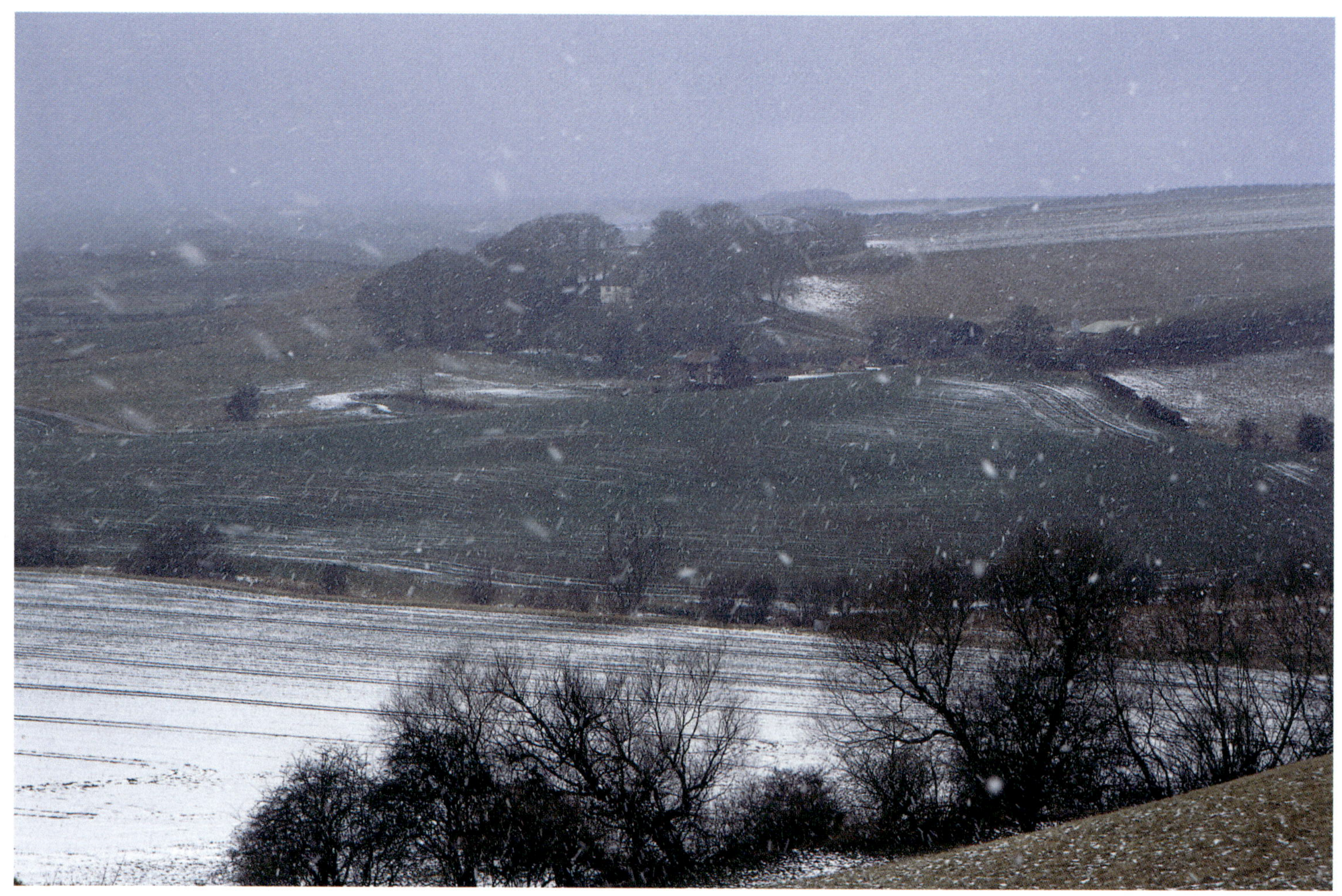

Above and opposite: **Snowfall at Scamblesby Thorpe**
A snow shower passes over the Wolds…

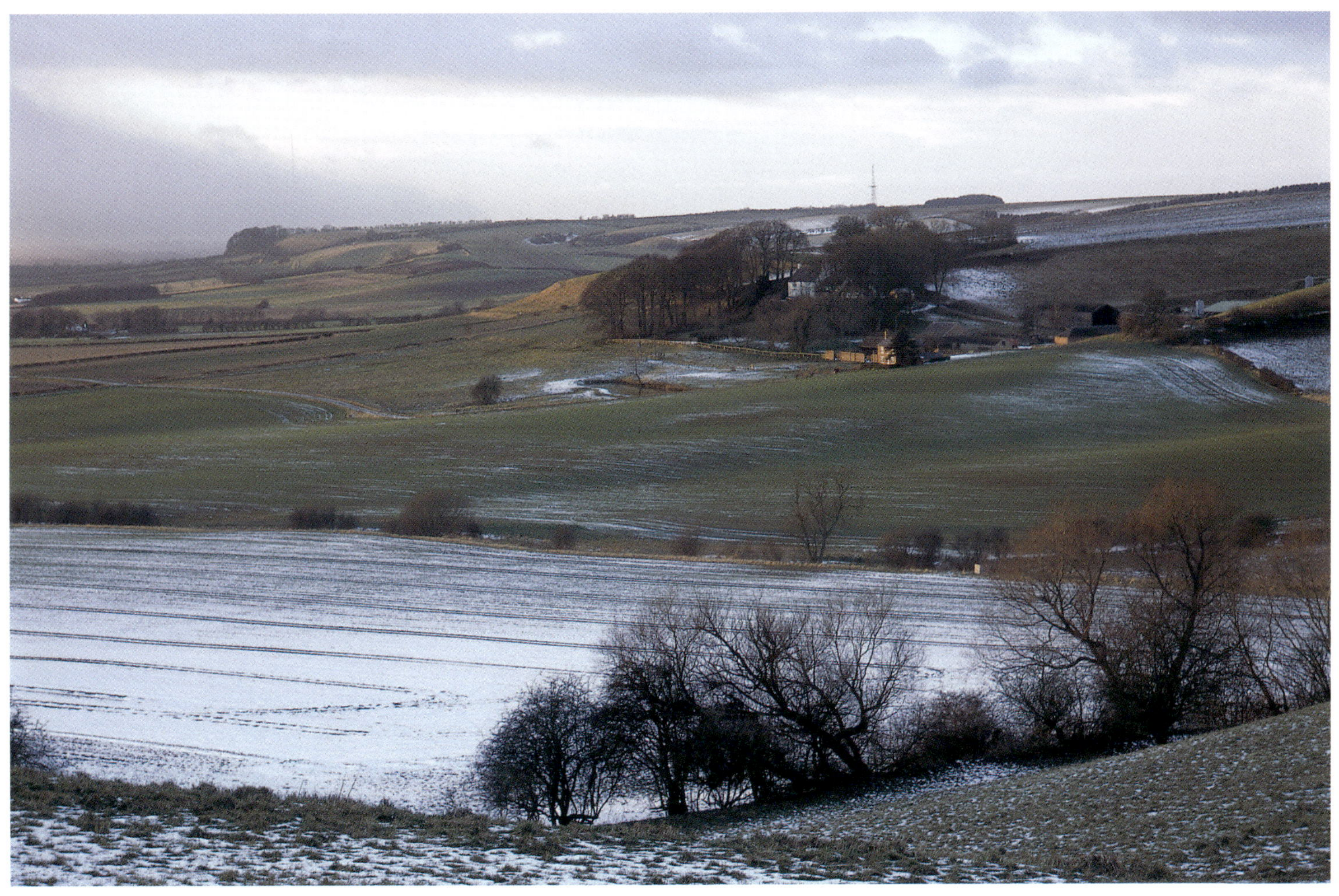

…and minutes later the snow has stopped falling and the evening light reveals the view towards Scamblesby Thorpe.

Overleaf: **View towards Tetford**
A winter scene looking southeast from the viewpoint on the Bluestone Heath road.

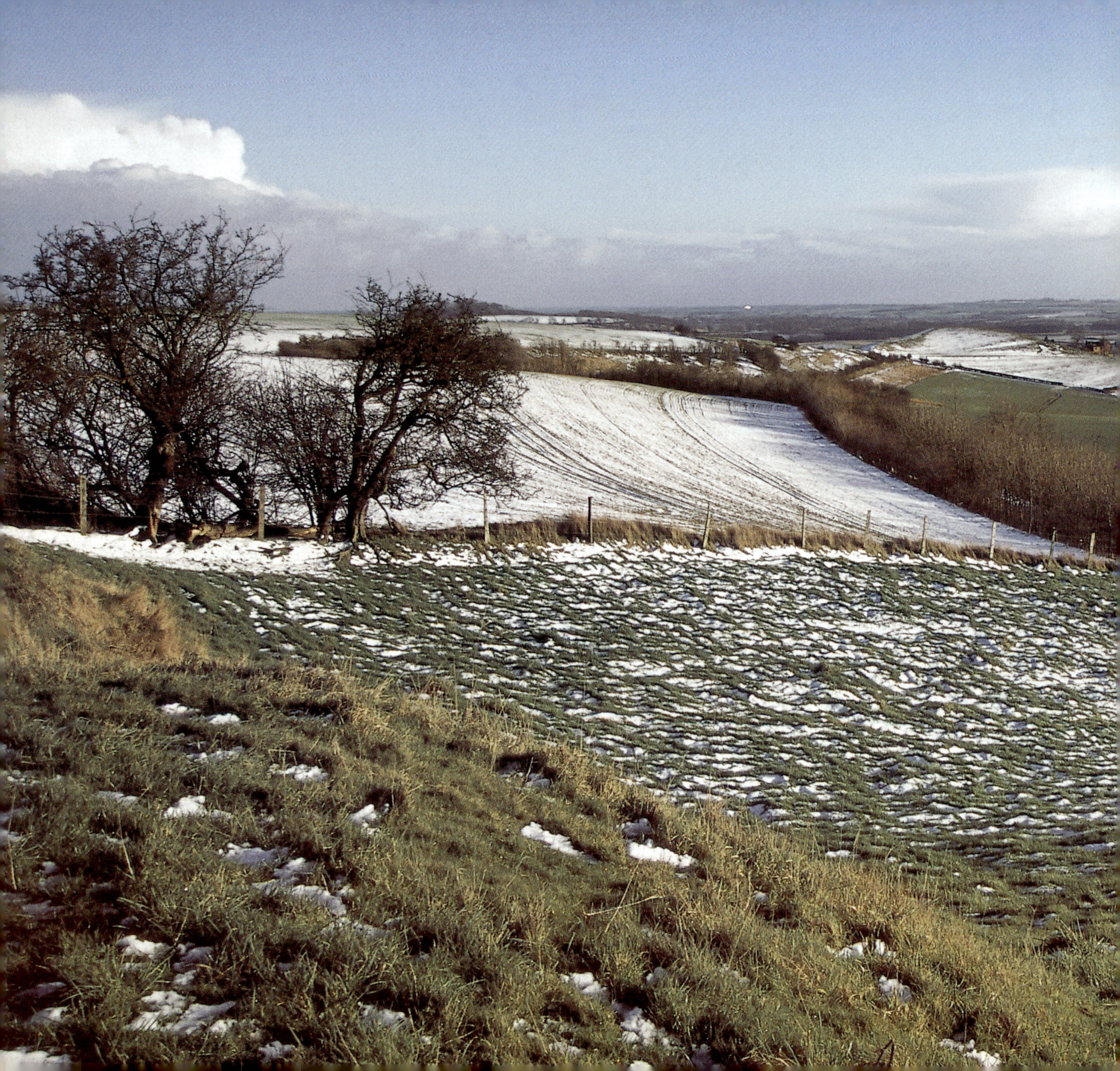

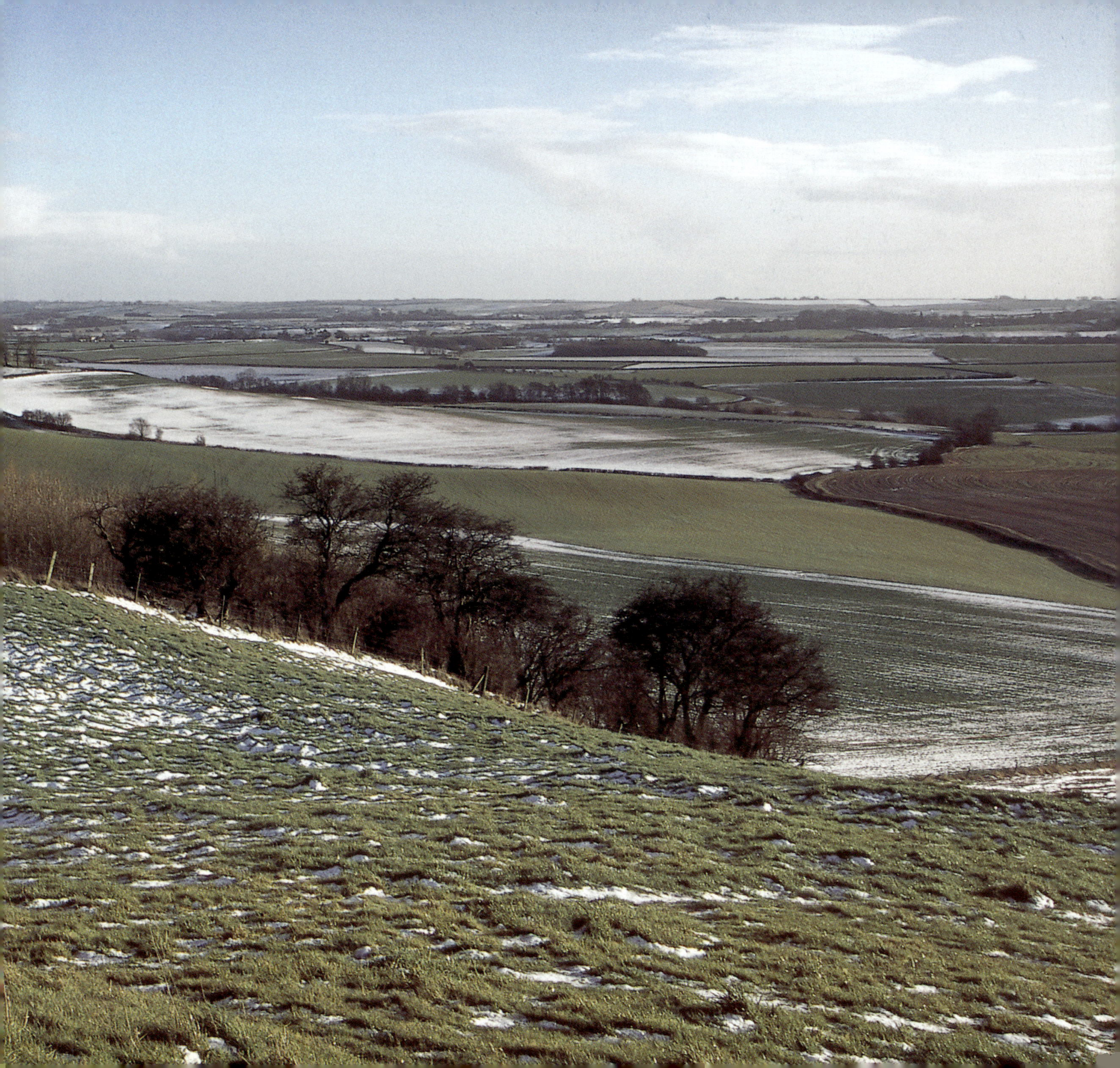

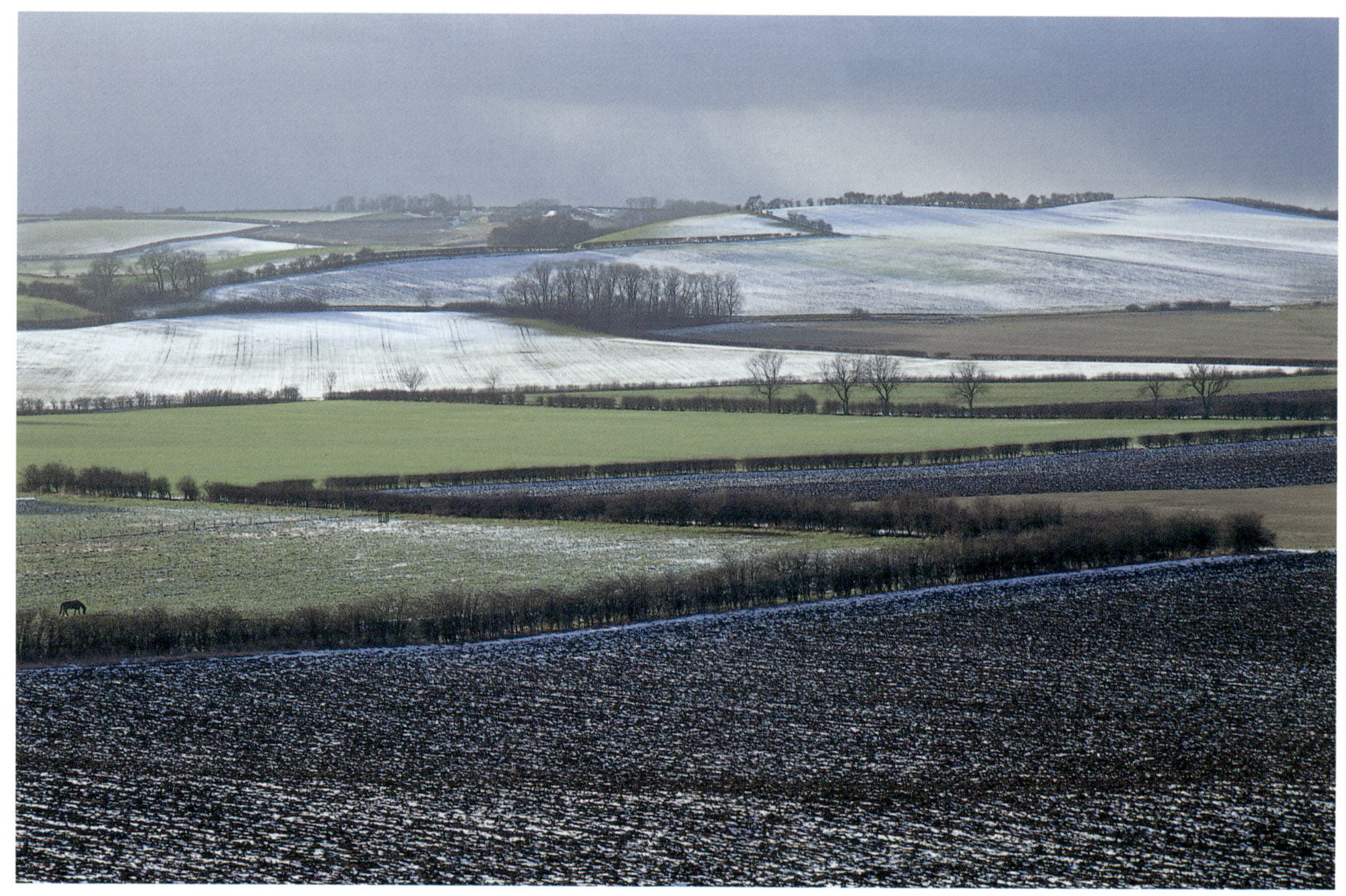

Park Hill near Belchford
The patterns of intersecting fields, hedges and woods are revealed under a light covering of snow.

Opposite: **Light and snow on Rowgate Hill**
The combination of late afternoon light and snow highlights the gently-undulating chalk wolds.

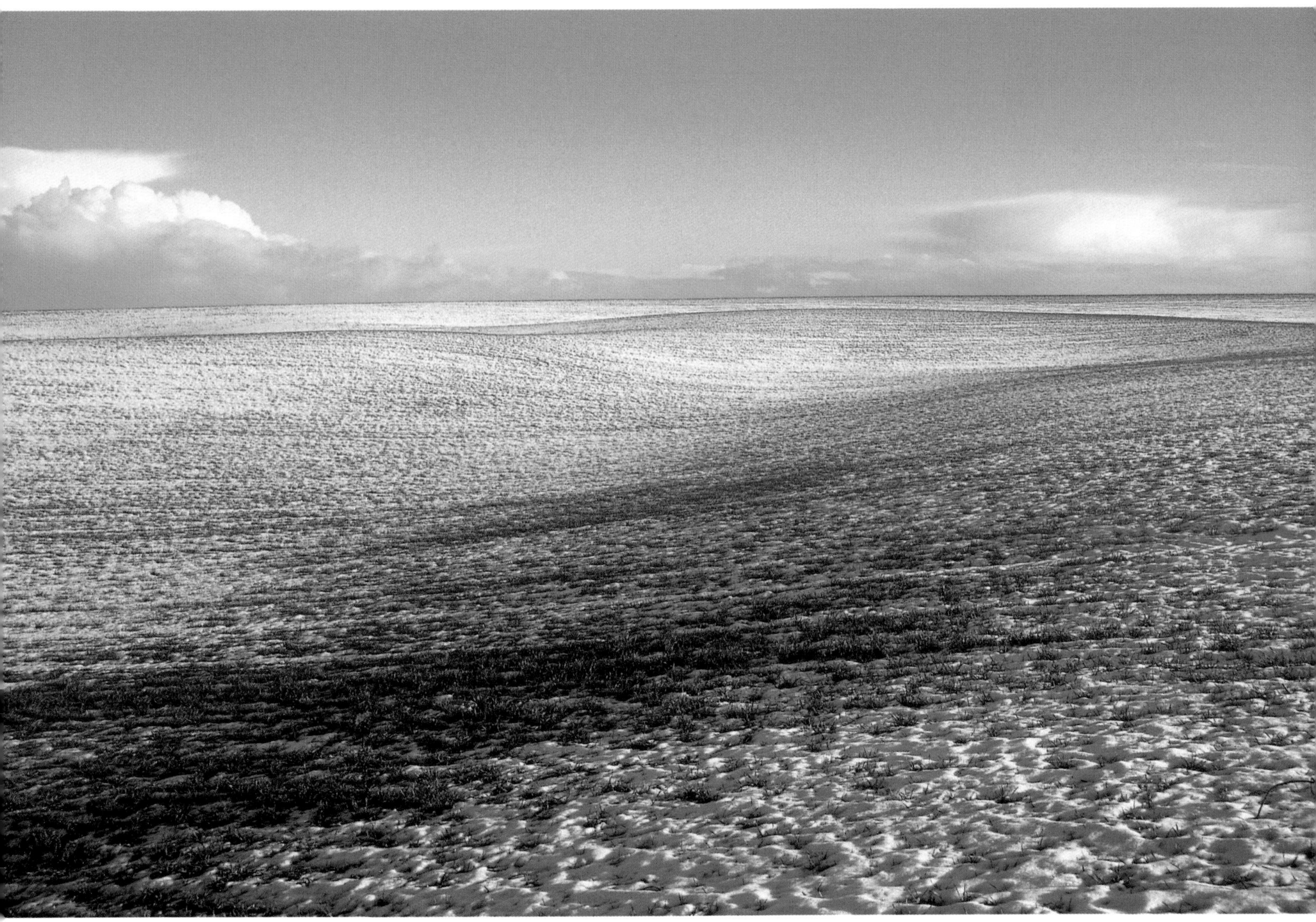

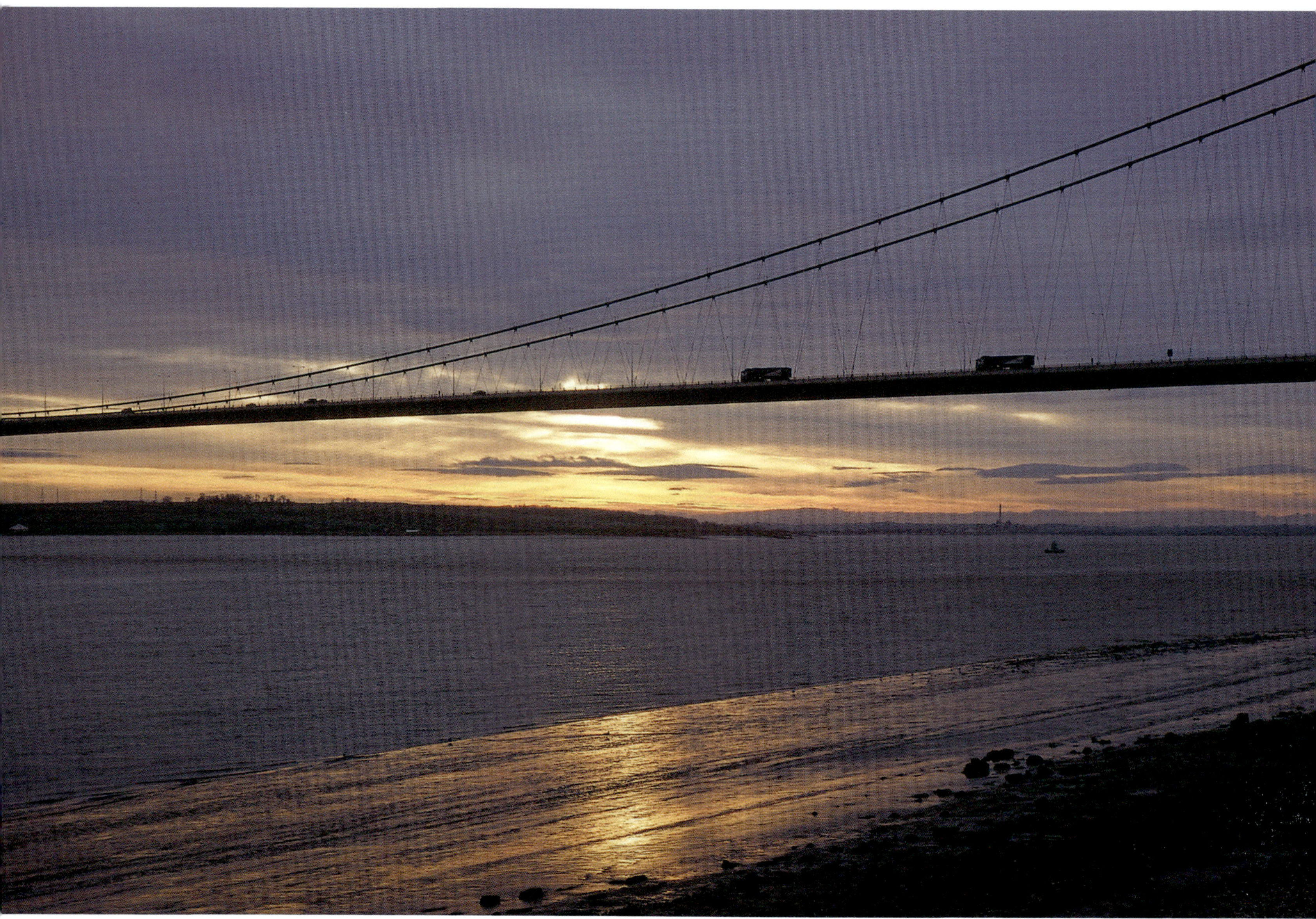

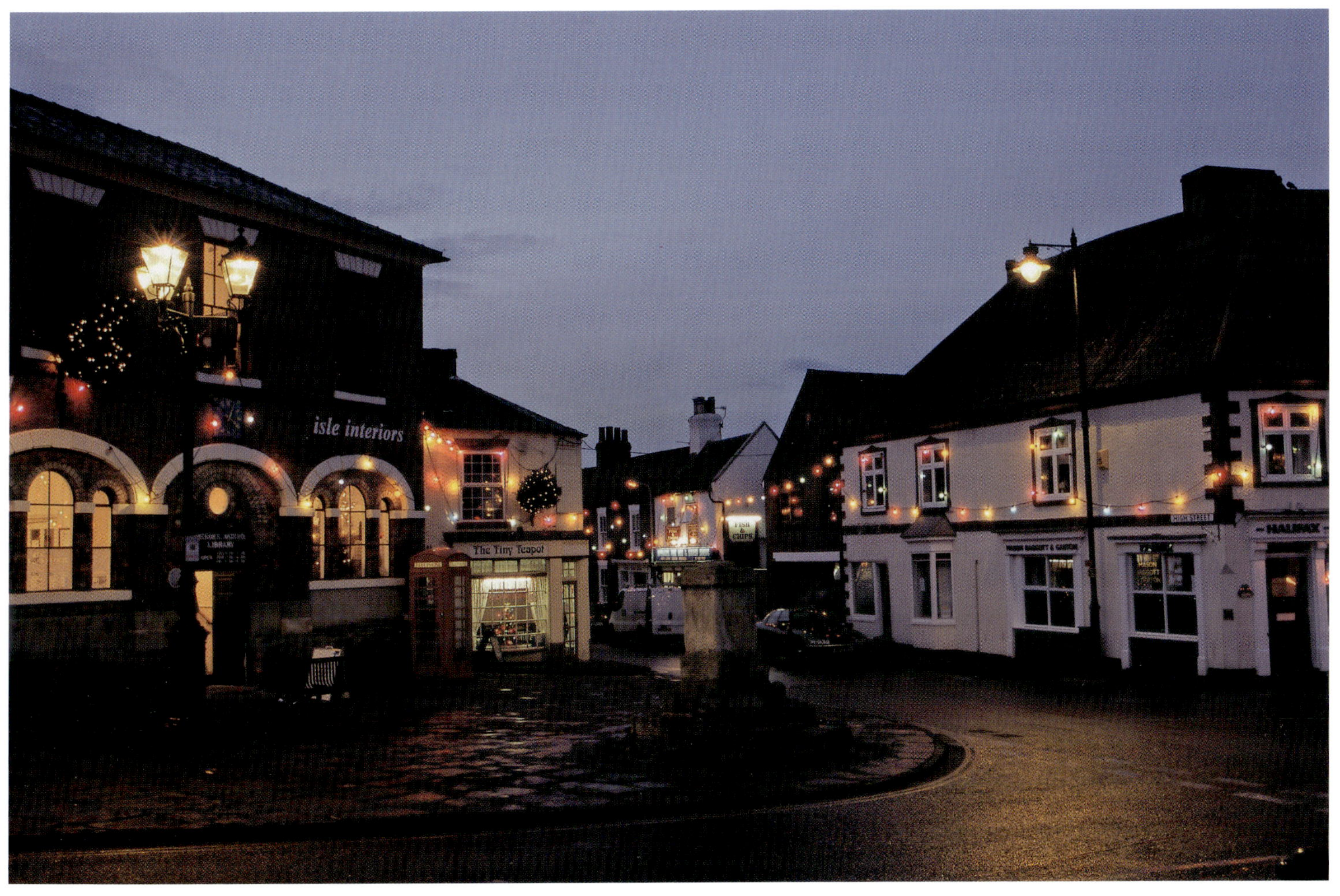

Christmas lights at Epworth
In the dark days of December the towns of Lincolnshire celebrate Christmas by decorating
their streets and shop fronts with pretty coloured lights.

Opposite: **Sunset over the Humber estuary**
The sun sets beyond the Humber Bridge, highlighting the mud on the foreshore
and revealing the outline of the tall chimney at Ferriby Sluice.

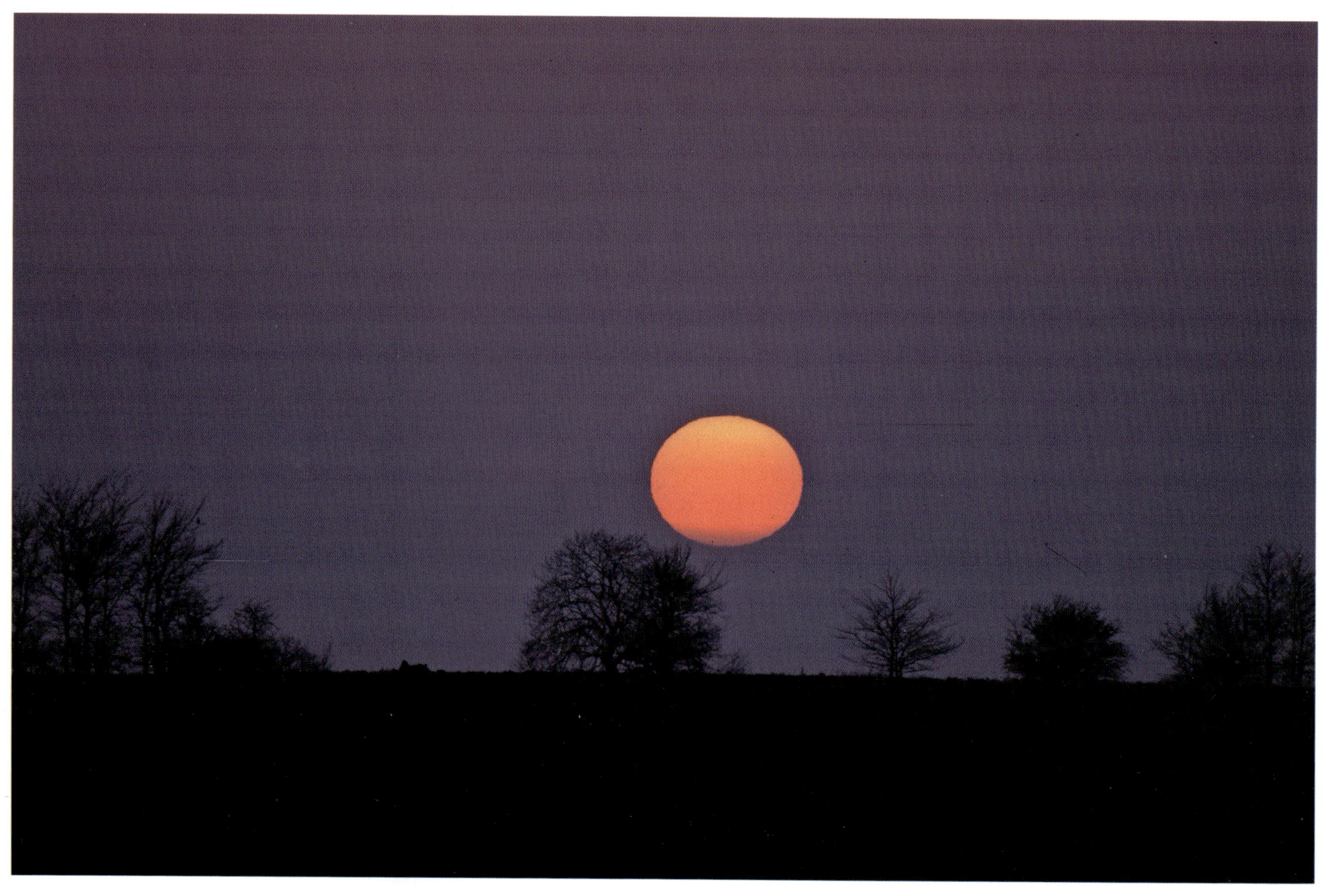

Setting sun
The orange orb of the setting sun descends at mid winter behind scattered trees and shrubs near Glentworth.